THE DIARY OF AN IRISH WATER BAILIFF

dressing for THE JUDGE

Hook	Partridge CS10/3 size 2/0
Eye	Twisted silkworm gut
Tag	Fine oval silver tinsel and light orange floss
Tail	Golden Pheasant topping
Butt	Bronze Peacock herl
Body	Flat silver tinsel
Rib	Small oval gold tinsel
Body hackle	Golden yellow
Throat hackle	Hot orange and dyed Guinea fowl (Blue Jay would have been used in smaller sizes)
Under-wing	Golden Pheasant tippets in strands
Wing	Speckled Bustard and Argus Pheasant dyed golden yellow with two Golden Pheasant toppings over
Horns	Blue and yellow Macaw
Head	Bronze Peacock herl

THE JUDGE

The Judge is an old Bann pattern (*circa 1850*) which was
devised by William Doherty of Bushmills, in his time a well-
known tier for the river Bann and its tributaries.
The fly was first recorded by Francis Francis in his *A Book on
Angling* (1867) as a fly for the river Bush.

THE DIARY OF AN
IRISH WATER BAILIFF
1791 – 1809

JOHN MACKY
Inspector of Keepers on the river Bann

Edited by E J Malone
with additional information on
the Honourable The Irish Society

Introduction by John Killen
Deputy Librarian, Linen Hall Library

First published in 2008 by
Ken Smith Publishing Limited

UK Smith Settle, Gateway Drive, Yeadon, West Yorkshire LS19 7XY
FRANCE Chavagnac, 16260 Cellefrouin, Charente

I S B N   978 1 906159 04 7 *standard edition*
978 1 906159 05 4 *leather edition*

British Library Cataloguing-in-Publication Data
A catalogue record is available for this book
from the British Library

Printed and bound by
Smith Settle Printing and Bookbinding Ltd

CONTENTS

LIST OF ILLUSTRATIONS

ACKNOWLEDGEMENTS

My sincere thanks for help and assistance given in the preparation of this publication are offered to the following people and institutions :

The Deputy Keeper of the Public Records Office, for permission to publish the transcription of John Macky's diary, which I accidentally discovered whilst undertaking research on another project; the original diary of John Macky came into the possession of the Moore family and I am grateful to Dr Moore-Colyer for the loan of the original diary for reproduction of pages to use in publication (Mr R L Moore was managing director of the Foyle and Bann Fishery Company in the 1890s, whose energy and ability enabled preservation work on the Bann to continue. In 1894, when the Board of Conservators were in financial difficulties Mr Moore gave his personal guarantee to pay the bailiffs their salaries, enabling the Bann to continue making returns); John Killen, Deputy Librarian of the Linen Hall Library in Belfast kindly agreed to write an introduction; Arthur Davidson, antiquarian book dealer with a specialist knowledge of Irish history, readily supplied material; Kevin McKenna, Dublin, for his encyclopaedic knowledge of Irish angling and its history and his encouragement; the Honourable The Irish Society allowed me to use the opening chapter of their publication *The Honourable Irish Society (1613-1963)* by Raymond Smith, helping to put the period covered by the diary into its historical perspective; Mr Edward Montgomery, the Society's representative in Ireland, readily gave responses to my requests for advice, and provided invaluable help in tracing the whereabouts of the original diary; finally my publisher, Ken Smith, cast an expert eye over the editorial, design and production process to ensure publication to his usual high standards.

The Bann Falls at Coleraine.

PREFACE

The lower river Bann flows from Lough Neagh to the sea, a distance of approximately 30 miles, dividing the counties of Derry and Antrim. It is the longest and most important salmon river in the north of Ireland, and its quiet deep-flowing waters carry great runs of salmon to all the Lough Neagh rivers; but like most of the great Irish rivers, it suffered badly from poaching for centuries. In 1903 Augustus Grimble, in his book *The Salmon Rivers of Ireland* stated:

'The poaching in the Bann district is of a far more lawless and ferocious nature than usual. Round Lough Neagh there are a desperate bad lot of men, and here, some years ago, an Inspector and two men were fired on, and the head-man, being wounded, nearly lost his life by being brutally knocked about after he had been disabled by a shot. Here too, on a previous occasion, the poachers attempted to burn down a house at Toome Bridge into which they had marked down a party of police'

Shane's Castle, Lough Neagh

Whilst lawlessness and poaching cannot be condoned, it has to be remembered that this situation had existed for centuries and most of it stemmed from the need to survive in a very harsh environment. There was little employment other than as servants in the houses of the gentry, and to raise a family on a half-acre of land, mainly potatoes, caused hardship and misery. The rivers had been in the hands of local chieftains, and then by the newly established gentry, many of whom turned a blind eye to tenants who took fish to feed their families; but others, many of whom were absent landlords, employed land agents to collect rents and manage the properties.

Land agents, in the main, were men who ruled with an iron hand, and woe betide the tenant who could not meet the due rent or was caught poaching. They ran the grave risk of their family being evicted from their miserable holding or, in extreme cases, being transported as a felon to Van Diemen's land, the name originally used by Europeans for what is now Tasmania, which up to 1853 was the primary penal colony in Australia.

Eviction has been a recurring theme throughout Irish history and I quote from Morrisey's *On the Verge of Want*, the writing of Francis S Sheridan, barrister-at-law:

> 'During the period from Philip and Mary to Cromwell, particularly in the time of the last mentioned, confiscated lands were given as rewards to the adventurers in various campaigns, and the eviction of the native Irish carried out. Under the Settlement Act of Cromwell's Parliament in September 1653, the owners of land who had not maintained 'a constant good affection to the Parliament', were ordered under penalty of death to leave their homes and remove their cattle and belongings to infertile land in the west.
>
> Those proscribed people included the best blood in the country – Irish nobility and gentry, along with descendants of the old English Norman settlers who had stood by the king in his war with Parliament.'

The Honourable Irish Society had been established by the various Livery Companies in London who believed that the lands around Derry and Coleraine could yield handsome profits if they were put under their control and taken over by settlers from England, Scotland and Wales.

Scottish incomers had, in the main, been driven from their homes by the Highland clearances whereby landowners had decreed that sheep rather than humans gave greater profit. The offer of their own land in Ireland gave them the chance of a fresh start. They proved to be most industrious and, even today, retain traces of their Scottish ancestry. The native Irish, many dispossessed and homeless, roved the countryside seeking food and shelter; it was a time of great lawlessness.

Another running sore which caused great pain and distress to the native population, who were Catholic, and the new settlers, who were mainly Presbyterian, was the law forcing them to pay tithes to the established Anglican Church. This played a great part in bringing together both religions and the forming of the United Irishmen; ultimately leading to the rebellion of 1798 when an attempt to overthrow the government was made. This attempt failed miserably, and the leaders, many of whom were Presbyterian, were sentenced to death by public hanging.

John Macky's diary shows that he played no part in any subversive acts or ideas, and indeed his writing portrays a faithful employee who was passed over for those who were less scrupulous.

The Irish Society is still composed of 'six and twenty honest and discreet citizens of London' and its current members, officers and representatives are acutely conscious of that heritage. But a body of people such as this is an organic entity, evolving and changing with the passage of time; succeeding generations applying values and judgments that the wisdom of their age dictates. What began centuries ago, nudged into reluctant action through instincts of survival and profit, and serving a sectional interest, has matured into a body whose paramount interest is to serve the community as a whole.

The Society's income is derived from the residue of its estate, investments, fisheries and, more recently, its sporting rights. Virtually all of that income is disbursed on charitable grants and maintenance of properties and administration, in line with the Society's aim of promoting the welfare of the county and in particular its two principal centres, the City of Londonderry and the Town of Coleraine.

One of the Society's main sources of income continues to be the lower Bann fisheries. In 1985, it was decided to operate these under the direct control of the Society and a subsidiary company. Bann System Limited was formed for this purpose, and is run by a board of directors drawn from both Northern Ireland and the City of London. This company now looks after some 250 miles of game and coarse angling waters. The best known of the angling stations is at Carnroe, near Kilrea, often referred to locally as 'the holy water'. As the company's angling operations have built up, the number of people employed as ghillies and water bailiffs has steadily increased.

The following extract from The Irish Society *by Raymond Smith (1966) is here reprinted by kind permission of the Honourable The Irish Society.*

'.... *in every of the said counties there shall be a convenient number of market-towns and corporations erected, for the habitation and settling of tradesmen and artificers; and that there shall be one free-school at least appointed in every county, for the education of youth in learning and religion. And that there shall be a convenient number of parishes and parish churches, with sufficient incumbents in every county; and that the parishioners shall pay all their tithes in kind to the incumbents of the said Parish churches.'*

THE CITY OF LONDON AND THE PLANTATION OF ULSTER, 1608–10

On 30 January 1610 the Court of Common Council of the City of London decreed that a Company should be constituted within the City to direct the affairs of the new plantation in Ulster; a Company which later became 'The Society of the Governor and Assistants, London, of the New Plantation in Ulster, within the realm of Ireland'.

What was the origin of this Society[1] and what were its objects?

From 1534 to 1603 Tudor rulers were engaged in struggles to bring Ireland completely under English law and English rule. The most prolonged resistance to the Tudor conquest came from Ulster. Hugh O'Neill's rebellion in particular (1595–1603), which was linked with the cause of the counter-reformation and the struggle between England and Spain, was the most dangerous the English government ever had to face. In the end the conquest of Ulster was achieved by enmeshing the forces of O'Neill and O'Donnell, the leaders of the rebellion, in a network of forts; the establishment of one of these forts at Derry by Sir Henry Docwra marked a turning-point in the war. The rebellion was finally broken in 1603, and ended with the submission and pardon of Hugh O'Neill, then created Earl of Tyrone, and Rory O'Donnell, then created Earl of Tyrconnell. The next four years were a period of change: a county system planned in 1585 was put into effect, and English law and administration began to operate; the Irish system of land tenure was superseded by English feudal tenure; the colonial element in Antrim and Down was strengthened; and in 1605 a royal proclamation announced the government's determination to enforce conformity with the Protestant established church. In this changing world the restored Earls appear to have found life very difficult. Whatever their grievances, motives, or apprehensions were, the historical fact is that on September 3, 1607 Tyrone and Tyrconnell embarked secretly on board ship and fled from Ireland.

By this flight, followed in 1608 by a futile revolt during which the town of Derry was burned, a new situation was created. Lands in six counties in Ulster – Donegal, Coleraine, Tyrone, Armagh, Fermanagh, and Cavan – were declared escheated to the Crown; and the government in London decided on the resettlement of Ulster on an entirely new basis.

This was the deliberate plantation of Ulster by English and Scottish colonists, with the object of making the new settlements strong enough to resist the native Irish, and of transforming Ulster into an Anglicised and law-abiding province. An effective plantation, it was thought, would 'establish the true religion of Christ among men . . . almost lost in superstition'. Land could be cultivated and planted with honest citizens, and those who by their services in the late rebellion had

---

[1] After the Restoration known as the Irish Society.

established claims on the Crown's generosity could be recompensed. Grantees or undertakers would be attracted by the advantages offered – low rents, fertility of soil, natural resources, and so on; at the same time most grantees should be men of standing, who could invest large sums in the business of planting.

In January 1609 a comprehensive plan was drawn up for the plantation and division of the escheated lands. This was embodied in two documents: 'A collection of such Orders and Conditions as are to be observed by the undertakers upon the distribution and plantation of the escheated lands in Ulster'; and 'A project for the division and plantation of the escheated lands in. . . Ulster'.

These documents defined three types of grants of land (great, middle, and small), three classes of grantees, and the terms on which grantees of each class were to plant. Briefly, these terms were that English and Scottish undertakers were: to pay rent to the Crown; to be empowered to erect manors and create tenancies; to have export rights for seven years, and free import rights for five years; and an allowance of timber from the King's woods in Ulster. Every undertaker of a great proportion was, within two years of the date of his grant, to build a castle with a strong court or bawn about it[2]; of a middle proportion, a stone or brick house with a bawn; of a small proportion, a bawn at least. All undertakers were within two years to plant a competent number of English and Scottish tenants upon their proportions, and cause them to build houses for themselves near the castles or bawns for their mutual defence and strength. Undertakers were also to keep in readiness arms to equip a competent number of men for defence; and to take the oath of supremacy and also 'conform themselves' in religion according to his Majesty's laws. Every proportion of land was to be made a parish, a parish church erected on it, and glebe lands assigned to each incumbent. Land was reserved for the maintenance of free schools to be erected in specified areas, and for Trinity College, Dublin.

In 1609–10 a fresh survey of the escheated lands was made and fresh arrangements worked out for the furtherance of the plantation. In April 1610 a new set of 'Conditions' was published which, sometimes described as the 'Printed Book' and sometimes as the 'Articles of Plantation', thereafter constituted the standard by which the conduct of the British undertakers was measured. This document corresponded closely to the 'Orders and Conditions', though certain provisions of the original scheme were modified or made more specific.

COLERAINE AND DERRY

During the time these plans were being made for the general settlement of Ulster, King James and his advisers began to negotiate with the City of London in

---

[2] A bawn was a fortified enclosure.

order to induce it to undertake a large block of the escheated land, namely the County of Coleraine and adjacent areas.

The City had at all times played a major role in the political and financial history of England, and under the Tudors the City became more and more the financial agent of the Crown. During Tyrone's rebellion of 1594–9 for example, when Elizabeth called on the City for men and money and ships, loans of £20,000 and £60,000 were raised in successive years. What more natural then that James I and his advisers should turn to the centre of wealth and power and endeavour to secure the support of its merchants and traders. Not only had the City the resources necessary, but the adherence of the City to the scheme would, it was thought, encourage private men to become planters and raise the whole undertaking in public estimation at home and abroad. Moreover there was much interest in the City in colonial enterprises at this time, and the Crown considered that merchants and traders might be induced to regard the projected colonisation of Ulster as a profitable undertaking.

The official prospectus drawn up for submission to the City, dated May 25, 1609, was entitled '*Motives and reasons to induce the City of London to undertake the plantation in the North of Ireland*'. It suggested that the most suitable areas for the Londoners to plant were the ruined city of Derry and the town of Coleraine. The King would be willing to create corporations in both towns and grant the Londoners the whole territory bounded by the Foyle, the sea, and the Bann (no southern limit being mentioned), together with the benefit of the customs on all imports and exports for twenty-one years, admiralty rights on the coasts of Donegal and Coleraine for the same period, and the fisheries of the Bann and the Foyle. They were also to have licence to export all commodities produced by their lands whose exportation was forbidden or restricted by statute. The citizens were assured that the land was well watered and suitable for breeding cattle; that it grew hemp and flax better than elsewhere, and was well stocked with game. The natural resources of the region, it was said, could be the basis of a flourishing trade with England, Scotland, Spain, the Straits of Gibraltar, and even Newfoundland; they would give employment to many of London's inhabitants, relieve overcrowding, and reduce the danger of infectious diseases. London merchants would obtain a new outlet for their goods throughout the North of Ireland and the Scottish Isles. Finally the precedent of Bristol was cited, Bristol which in the reign of Henry II had successfully undertaken the re-population of Dublin; and it was suggested that the profits to Londoners were likely to be far greater than those reaped by Bristol.

The territories referred to in this prospectus were within the area later known as the County of Londonderry. In 1609 they constituted four distinct parts: the County of Coleraine (or O'Cahan's country), lying north of the Sperrin mountains between the rivers Foyle and Bann; the barony of Loughinsholin, to the south-east, forming part of the county of Tyrone; the settlement of Derry and its vicinity, at the mouth of the Foyle, in the county of Donegal; the settlement of Coleraine and its vicinity, at the mouth of the Bann, in the county of Antrim.

O'Cahan's country was good grazing land, and cattle were numerous. The vicinity of Coleraine was considered to be as good corn-land as any in Europe. Game was plentiful, and wild-fowl abounded. The salmon fishing of the Bann and the Foyle, particularly of the former, was far-famed, and the eel fishery in the Bann was reputed to be unequalled in Europe. Off the coast there were rich fishing-grounds which attracted numbers of fishermen from Scotland and elsewhere. In Loughinsholin the woods were the most notable feature, and timber from them was suitable for all classes of building.

The two principal towns in the territory were Derry and Coleraine. The hill of Derry – a word meaning oak-wood stood on the west bank of the Foyle, about five miles from the junction of the Foyle with the loch. The hill, about 200 feet high, was half-encircled by the river, which here afforded safe anchorage in all weathers to fairly large vessels. Derry was a meeting-place of many land routes, and the soil about the mouths of the Foyle and the Faughan – a river draining the uplands to the south and east of Derry – was fertile. Coleraine – 'ferny corner' – lay some four miles from the sea on the east bank of the Bann, and about 37 miles from Derry along the coast. It too was a meeting-place of many land routes. The channel of the river below the town however was narrow and shallow; navigation was further impeded by a dangerous bar at its mouth, while above the town a great rock, called the Salmon Leap, extended right across the river and produced a drop of twelve feet.

The country between the Foyle and the Bann was bisected by the valley of the Roe, a river which ran between the basaltic highlands on the east and the northern projection of the Sperrins on the west. A great part of the boundary between Coleraine and Tyrone was formed by the central massif of the Sperrins; the upper tracts of the massif were bleak and bare, and lower down the surface was largely covered with peat bogs. Much of the eastern strip of the country consisted of lowlands containing fertile districts interspersed among extensive bogs and wastes.

As for the people, the native Irish, they were mainly a pastoral folk whose principal wealth was in their cattle. Their methods of cultivation were extremely primitive. Their food was chiefly milk, butter, oatmeal and wild vegetables; their principal meat was pork, but many ate no flesh at all. There were no towns in O'Cahan's country. The chiefs lived in castles, built after the English style, and apart from the cabins clustered round the castles the people lived in scattered hamlets. The native cabins were one-roomed, oval-shaped, with walls of wattle and clay and a roof of thatch or turf, usually without window or chimney. The staple article of clothing was a long home-made woollen mantle.

The Irish were stubbornly conservative and proud of their ancestry. Fighting was a more or less permanent occupation of the dominant class – the chief and his warriors – but learning was held in respect: and they were lovers of music and poetry. The substratum of Irish society was formed by a population of small peasants, some of them land-owners, but many were landless labourers, or churls. Finally, in matters of religion the Irish were staunch Catholics. Derry and Coleraine were essentially ecclesiastical settlements. Derry had been founded as a monastery in the sixth century and the town grew up in dependence on it. The population consisted almost entirely of monks and clergy and its buildings were devoted to their use.

Similarly in Coleraine a settlement had arisen round the sixth century abbey. As in other parts of Ulster, Henry VIII's Act of Dissolution was long inoperative both at Derry and Coleraine: monks and friars continued to inhabit the former certainly up to 1566, and the latter till after the turn of the century.

This, in very brief summary, was the sort of country the Londoners were being asked to remodel, stabilize, and (by contemporary English standards) civilize. It must have been apparent from the outset that the plantation would be a complex, difficult, costly and even dangerous undertaking. But, from the point of view of the Crown, it was essential that the danger of foreign invasion through the Swilly or the Foyle should be guarded against and that the settlement of Derry achieved by Elizabeth should be restored. On all counts the colonization and settlement of Ulster was a major issue of government policy.

THE FORMATION OF THE IRISH SOCIETY, 1609–10

Between May 25 and July 1 1609 the 'Motives and reasons' of May 25 were sent to the Lord Mayor (Sir Humphrey Weld), the Lord Mayor discussed them with Sir Thomas Phillips, and afterwards with Sir John Jolles and William Cokayne. Phillips was a soldier of fortune who had served against Tyrone in Ulster, and had acquired large estates there. Jolles and Cokayne were both Aldermen, wealthy and outstanding citizens, with some experience of Irish affairs. On July 1 the Lord Mayor called a special Court of Aldermen, when certain selected commoners were present, and laid before it the royal proposals as contained in 'Motives and reasons'. These were then said to have been recommended to the City by the Privy Council at the instance of the King, who had made the citizens the first offer of a project likely to be pleasing to God, honourable to the City, and profitable to the undertakers. Thereupon the Court ordered a precept to be sent to all the City Livery Companies, requesting them to consider the project, to consult together, and to report back. A copy of 'Motives and reasons' and a copy of the printed 'Orders and conditions' were sent to each Company.

Each Company was to appoint a suitable committee of four, to consult with similar committees of other Companies. But on 8 July the Lord Mayor addressed a further precept to the twelve great Companies and some others, to the effect that the Companies had not given the 'Motives' such proper and serious consideration as they warranted. The precept required the representatives of all the Companies to meet at Guildhall to consult and to report formally to the Court of Aldermen.

In the general committee of liverymen called under these precepts can be seen the first step in the evolution of the Irish Society.

On 14 July this general committee delivered their formal answer to the Court of Aldermen, to the effect that the Companies were not willing or not able to co-operate. Thereupon the Court of Aldermen appointed a deputation of Aldermen and Commoners to deliver this answer to the Council for Ireland and to confer with that Council.[3]

The appointment of this deputation marks the second stage in the evolution of the Irish Society.

From the minute of a Court of Aldermen of 18 July, four days later, it transpires that by that date the answer of the Companies had been made known to the Privy Council – but not with the 'allowance' of the Lord Mayor and Aldermen – before any conference had been held with the Council for Ireland. The Privy Council had not been pleased, and had intimated their displeasure to the Recorder and certain Aldermen and Commoners at a meeting of the Council. On hearing this, the Court of Aldermen forthwith instructed the Recorder to inform their Lordships that a mistake had been made, but with no undutiful intent or purpose; and they had therefore nominated certain Aldermen and Commoners to confer with the Council of Ireland and to report back.

It is impossible to determine from this carefully-worded and guarded minute, how the Privy Council had learned of the Companies' attitude to the proposals. But there is no doubt about their Lordships' displeasure. The Aldermen's dutiful and submissive reply is revealing: a mistake had been made, a conference should have been held and would be held with the Council for Ireland.

Such a conference in fact took place shortly after this rebuff, and as a result the Aldermen decided to fall in with the wishes of the Privy Council. A precept to the Companies of 24 July reports that the City deputation to the conference was satisfied in regard to the honour of the undertaking, the good that might result to

---

[3] The Mercers had said, quite bluntly, that they were for the most part men that lived by merchandise, and were therefore inexperienced in managing a business of that nature, nor had they the means to accomplish it; and they were not willing to have a hand in it.

the Kingdom and the City, and the profit that might accrue to the adventurers. Moreover the deputation had been told that representatives could be sent to view the lands; if they reported adversely, and that the project would not be profitable for the undertakers, 'we' would be free to leave it. The sting of the precept was in its tail: each Company was required to make a list of all its members, showing what each member would contribute, and the amount, and to take the names of those who refused.

These proceedings have been given in some detail for two reasons. First, they show the beginnings of the Irish Society. Second, they show that the livery companies had little stomach for the project; left to themselves without pressure from the Court of Aldermen and the heavy threat of the royal displeasure, they would have dismissed the project out of hand.

It was in fact on the 'motion and commandment' of the Privy Council that the Common Council decided (August 1) to send viewers to Ireland. The viewers were to survey the country and its resources at the City's charges, and to report their findings.

On August 3 1609 the Privy Council advised Chichester (the Lord Deputy of Ireland) formally that viewers had been appointed and directed him to afford them all possible assistance. A private note to the Lord Deputy from the Council emphasized the importance of securing the support of the City and ordered him to see that the viewers received only favourable impressions of their visit. Their conductors were to be discreet and plausible, to lead by the most attractive ways, to have the guests lodged comfortably, if possible in English houses, to show to the best advantage the resources of the country, and to conceal matters of distaste.

The viewers were, in effect, hood-winked and beguiled into making a favourable report, and this was presented to the Court of Aldermen on November 28 and to the Court of Common Council on December 2. On this latter date a Committee was appointed of the Recorder and leading Aldermen and Commoners – the latter mostly liverymen of the principal Companies – to draw up conditions on which the City would undertake the plantation. This Committee, appointed by Common Council to consider matters relating to the plantation, is the direct fore-runner of the Irish Society. The final shape of the Society is adumbrated in the Committee's report to Common Council of 15 December. This includes (inter alia) a recommendation that a company should be constituted in London for the management and ruling of the plantation; that corporations should be established in Derry and Coleraine; but that everything to be done in Ireland should be by advice and direction from the company in London.

Common Council approved the report and it was presented to the Privy Council. Discussions and negotiations continued until January 1610. During this period the sole concession made by the City was on the point of the total sum to be expended, viz. £15,000. This sum was deemed by the Privy Council to be insufficient; Common Council agreed to increase it to £20,000 and on 8 January ordered that one-quarter of that amount should be at once levied on the City Companies.

On 28 January 1610 Articles of Agreement relating to the Plantation were drawn up as between the Privy Council and the Committee of Common Council. These Articles constitute in the main a statement of what the City was to obtain from the Crown. There was no mention in the Agreement of any relation between it and the *'Orders and conditions'*. But, says Professor Moody, it was well understood that except in so far as the *'Orders'* were modified by the Agreement, they were to obtain for the Londoners as for all other undertakers. In other words, the Agreement did not purport to be a final and complete statement of the City's rights and duties in respect of the plantations, but a general outline of the special terms of its compact with the Crown.

The Articles of Agreement came before the Court of Common Council on January 30 1610 and were ratified. At the same time the Court of Common Council enacted that for directing the affairs of the plantation a Company should be constituted, consisting of a Governor, a Deputy Governor, and twenty-four Assistants. The Governor and five Assistants were to be Aldermen of the City; the Deputy Governor and the rest of the Assistants were to be Commoners ('of the Commonalty'); and the Recorder was always to be one of the Assistants. The Company was to be elected each year at the first Common Council to be held after February 2, when the Deputy and half the Assistants were to retire, and their places filled by the election of a new Deputy Governor and twelve new Assistants. Each Deputy therefore was to hold office for one year and each Assistant for two years. The persons so elected were authorized to hold courts, and in the courts to determine all matters concerning the plantation, to direct operations in Ireland, to administer all money raised for the purpose of the plantation, and generally to exercise control 'for and on the part of' the Corporation over the whole undertaking. Nine members, including the Governor or the Deputy, were to form a quorum. The decisions of the courts were to be 'firm and stable' by the Common Council. The court was given power to appoint its own officers. The City Chamberlain was appointed to receive all the money raised by the City for the plantation and to disburse it according to warrants signed by the Governor or his Deputy and three of the Assistants. The Wardrobe in the Guildhall was designated as the place where courts should be held, the times of meetings being appointed by the Governor or his Deputy. The order also nominated the first Governor of the Company Mr. (later Sir) William Cokayne, Alderman and Sheriff – the Deputy Governor and twenty-four Assistants, to serve for the first year. The Aldermen and Commoners so nominated were all liverymen and most of them were members of the twelve great Companies. There is a strong presumption that members of Common Council at this time were liverymen of various City Companies, as indeed most of them are today. Therefore there would be a strong nexus of policy and interest between the Companies in general, the Common Council, and the Company.

Administratively, the Company was at this stage a standing committee of the Court of Common Council to which had been delegated full authority to manage the affairs of the plantation. The Common Council stood in the same relation to it as joint stock companies, like the East India Company, the Virginia Company, the Newfoundland Company and the Bermuda Company, stood to their respective committees of management.

At this time the Company had no legal reality outside the sphere of the City's authority. Nor did it possess any formal grant of the property for which the City had contracted with the Crown by the Articles of Agreement. For this it would have to wait until it was granted a formal charter under the Great Seal, and three years were to elapse before such a charter was forthcoming.

REVENUE: FISHERIES

The Charters of 1613 and 1662 granted to the Irish Society the salmon, eel, and other fishings of the river Bann from the sea to Lough Neagh and those of the Foyle from the sea to Lifford. The Bishop of Derry had certain fishing rights in the Foyle and the Bann which had given rise to controversy before 1635, when the Society's rents were sequestrated. Upon the restoration of its property in 1662 the Society sought to obtain possession of all the fishings in the Foyle and the Bann alleged to be usurped by the Bishop. In 1677 the Society secured from the then Bishop, Robert Mossom, a lease of all his fishings for twenty-one years at £200 a year, and the promise to help the Society to obtain an Act of State enabling him to grant the fishings to the Society in fee farm. Six years later however this arrangement broke down, and Mossom's successor Ezekiel Hopkins proceeded against the Society in the Irish Court of Chancery in 1683. The dispute was still unsettled in 1691, when William King succeeded Hopkins, and two years later the fishery case became linked with a controversy over the quarterlands, or the 1,500 acres.

These lands were part of the 4,000 acres adjoining the City of Derry granted to the Society in 1613, and were assigned by the Society in 1614 at a small rent to the use of the corporation of Derry. After the sequestration of 1635 the then Bishop of Derry, John Bramhall, claimed the quarterlands as church land which had been improperly included in the Society's grant. In August 1637 Bramhall obtained from the Crown a grant of them, subject to a perpetual rent charge of £90 10s. reserved to the corporation of Derry. They were then (1638) leased by the Bishop to the corporation for sixty years as from 1634 at an annual rent of £50. Before this lease was due to expire the corporation endeavoured to secure a renewal of it; but the Bishop would not grant it on the terms they wanted. The corporation thereupon approached the Society who decided in 1693 to assert its claim to the quarter-lands, and undertook to allow the corporation £90 10s a year should the claim be successful. From 1694 to 1699 the controversy raged. A suit of ejectment was brought against the Bishop; the Lord Chancellor of Ireland made an order in favour of the Society; the Bishop appealed to the House of Lords in Ireland and obtained a ruling re-establishing him (1697); the Sheriffs and other inhabitants of Derry resisted the order and were arrested and taken to Dublin. Finally the Society appealed to the English House of Lords (1698), and that Court ruled against the Bishop and decided that the lands should be restored to the Society But these decisions proved ineffectual. The Lord Chancellor issued an injunction to the Sheriffs of Derry to reinstate the Society, and in December 1699 the King commanded the Bishop of Derry to be brought to London in custody to answer for his contempt of court. The Bishop however pleaded ill-health, an excuse accepted by the English House of Lords. At long last a compromise was reached. In 1703 the Bishop agreed to surrender to the Society the quarterlands and all his fishings and fishing rights in the Foyle and the Bann. In return he was guaranteed a perpetual rent-charge of £250 a year and (upon the expiration of the existing lease) the freehold of his palace or Bishop's House. This settlement was embodied in an Act (3 & 4 Anne c.19, 1704) of the English Parliament.

The later eighteenth century witnessed a further great fishing suit or series of suits, commenced in 1769, in which the Society's salmon-fishing rights in the Bann, near Coleraine, were seriously threatened by the claims of the Earl of Donegal.[4] In the background of this long and complicated suit is the very curious story of the Bann fishings. The Society in its charter of 1613 had been granted these fishings from the sea to Lough Neagh – i.e. in both the tidal and non-tidal sections of the river. But in 1621 a grant was made by patent to Lord Chichester, ancestor of the Earl of Donegal, of *inter alia* – the eel fishings in the Bann from Lough Neagh to the Salmon Leap. In 1640 these particular rights were surrendered to the Crown; and in 1660 Charles II confirmed *inter alia* a lease of these rights made by Oliver Cromwell to Sir Arthur Clotworthy (afterwards Viscount Massareene) for ninety-nine years. In 1661 Charles II granted and confirmed to the then Earl Donegal and his heirs all the fishings in Lough Neagh and the Bann from the Lough to the Salmon Leap, and the rents reserved upon any leases of them. In 1662 Charles II confirmed and regranted to the Society the previous grant of James I in 1613. Thus the part of the Bann lying between the

---

[4] For a detailed account by David Babington, the Society's law agent in 1804, see Appendix page 135.

Lough and the Salmon Leap had been granted at different times both to the Society and the Donegal family. That the Society in the eighteenth century acquiesced in or recognised the *de facto* if not the *de jure* rights of the Earls of Donegal is apparent from a statement of 1739, that their Bann fishings extended from the sea to the Leap a mile above Coleraine, being about five miles.[5] The consequence was that the Bann fishings fell into two parts: the salmon fishery held by the Society and the eel fishery held by the Earls of Donegal.

In 1771 the then Earl contested the right of Sir Henry Hamilton, the Society's lessee, to employ traps on the rock forming the Salmon Leap. Suits were prosecuted through various courts for more than thirty years, and not until 1801 did the plaintiff abandon his claims. While the case was being argued in the Irish Court of Exchequer in 1792 and the House of Lords in 1795, the point was raised that the Society's grants might be defective since they were made under the great seal of England only. To remedy this, an Act was passed by the Irish Parliament whereby all grants of land in Ireland under the great seal of England were given equal validity with those under the great seal of Ireland.

Though the fisheries of the Foyle and the Bann were potentially rich and a source of considerable revenue, there was a period in the eighteenth century when the Society could not find a suitable tenant and either took over the selling of the salmon or authorised its agent to sell for it. Nor is it easy to determine the net yield from year to year. Rents paid for fishhouses and rights amounted to £30 a year in 1739, and in addition to these a part of the Bishop of Derry's rent-charge, would have to be set off against profits. Irrespective of these there must have been expenses for labour and equipment, and for preservation of the salmon spawn and fry in the breeding rivers; expenses normally defrayed by the tenant but presumably borne by the Society when it ran the fisheries itself. In 1722 the charges attending the Lough Foyle fishery exceeded the value of the fish taken. Yet taking one year with another the fisheries must have accounted for a large proportion of the Society's income.[6] From before 1676 to March 1696 they were let at £1,265 a year. After the siege of Derry there was a heavy fall in value; the Society advertised the fishings to let from 25 March 1690 but apparently could do no better than continue with Viscount Massareene, the previous tenant, at rents totalling £1,340 for two years. Thereafter Massareene agreed to pay £1,050 a year and continued to hold them at this rate until 1700.

[5] The Society bought up sundry rights in the Bann fishings in 1869. Its own rights in the Bann from Lough Neagh to the sea were vindicated in a judgement of 1873.
[6] The salmon of the Foyle were inferior both in size and quality to those of the Bann, and the fisheries less valuable. In 1802 the Foyle fisheries were let by Sir George Hill, the Society's tenant, to an undertenant for £300 per year; but the undertenant was anxious to surrender his lease as it had proved unprofitable.

According to the *Concise View*, in 1720 the fishings were again advertised; and though certain lessees agreed to pay a rent of £2,000 a year for forty-one years, they would not complete a contract. The Society in fact was unable to find satisfactory tenants, and authorised its agent in 1721 to dispose of the fish according to his discretion and render an account. But the best price he could get then was £12 a ton Irish currency, though the following year the Society was able to get £14 11s. a ton in London. In 1723 the quantity of salmon produced was 97½ tons, which the Society sold at £15 a ton, representing a gross profit of £1,462 10s. The following year the fishings were let by auction at £16 5s a ton; the produce was over 137 tons. But immediately afterwards, 'having taken into their serious consideration the great charges attending the fishings while they continued in their hands, the uncertainty of their produce and their remoteness from the Society', it was decided to let them to Mr. William Richardson at £1,200 a year for twenty-one years. Mr. Richardson however subsequently thought better of his engagement and refused to complete it.

In 1729 Alderman Richard Jackson contracted to pay £1,200 a year for twenty-one years. The lease may have allowed for a break at the end of seven years, as in 1735 the Society

> appeared at this time to be greatly embarrassed in what manner to dispose of their salmon, not being able to obtain any satisfactory proposals; propositions were made to the Society for exporting the same to Venice and Leghorn, which were acceded to. The Society accordingly became merchants of their fish, and the casks containing the salmon were ordered to be marked with the City dagger, and in the name of the Irish Society.

The Society's first venture was not very successful, the cargo fetching about £1,023. A later voyage was attended with disaster. In 1739 the ship with the salmon on board was wrecked off shore at Venice, all the crew with the exception of the captain being lost. Three hundred and thirty-five barrels were recovered, but the fish was bad. Fortunately the cargo had been insured for £1,000. From a statement drawn up at this time the average number of tons of fish taken on the Bann and the Foyle together was estimated at 120-130 tons. The Foyle fishings extended from the sea about twenty-five miles up the river.

In 1749 the fishings were let to Mr. Richardson at £620 a year for twenty-one years, determinable at the end of seven or fourteen years. Seven years later the Society secured better terms from Henry (afterwards Sir Henry) Hamilton, its General Agent – £910 a year English currency, payable in London, for twenty-one years. This lease was renewed in 1762 and 1769, at the latter date for thirty-four years. In 1778 Sir Henry obtained a new lease, for the life of his wife Marianne and twenty-four years. He died in 1782 and under his will his lease was bequeathed to his wife. In 1797 Lady Hamilton agreed to assign her interest in the lease to Sir

George F. Hill and Mr. J. C. Beresford, and in 1799 the Society granted a new lease to these gentlemen for twenty-one years at £1,048 a year. Subsequently Sir George Hill took over the lease completely, and by 1811 had spent £5,423 on the mill on the Bann and the fisheries. In 1812 he was granted a new lease to expire in 1847 at the rent of £1,250 a year. It is of interest to note that the gross annual income from the fisheries at the end of our period was in actual monetary terms £15 less than it was at the beginning of it. This was possibly due in part to the increased expenses involved. In the words of the Secretary in 1802

> Independent of clerks, fishermen, boats and boatmen ... there must be a number of persons employed as guards and watchmen in the neighbourhood of all the little rivers communicating with the Bann, and into which the motherfish resort in the breeding season; ... the increased cultivation of flax and the establishment of additional bleaching grounds which tend to enhance the value of the Society's property in one respect, contribute on the other hand to injure the fishery, by poisoning the waters and producing additional stoppages in their course; to say nothing of the workmen themselves, who, if not properly managed by douceurs and indulgencies, become poachers, capable of doing much mischief.

In 1827 a Bill was introduced into the House of Commons to regulate salmon fisheries. Its provisions were in the opinion of the Society detrimental to the best interests of the industry and likely to affect adversely the Society's own holdings. It was decided therefore to oppose the bill and a petition in that sense, to which the Society's seal was affixed, was presented to the House. After a long and arduous fight the Bill was abandoned, at least for the time being; and in June 1827, apprehensive that it might be brought up again at a later date, the Society resolved that a special Deputation consisting of the Deputy Governor and one of the Secretaries should go to Ireland expressly to survey the fisheries and prepare evidence which could be adduced if necessary before the Committee of the House of Commons.

The special Deputation made a detailed examination of the Society's two great fisheries on the Bann and the Foyle, and talked to a number of people with first-hand knowledge of the habits of salmon and salmon-fishers and poachers. They amassed a body of evidence, some of which was included in their report, but not all. Some of it, they thought, it might be prudent not to make public at that stage, as it might be very valuable in opposing any future Bill liable to injure the Society's interests. In the event the caution of the Deputation and the Society was justified. A Salmon Fishery Bill was again introduced into Parliament, in 1828, and eventually defeated. And the Society had the additional gratification of receiving letters of thanks from various owners of fisheries for their services to the industry.

INTRODUCTION

On 3 September 1607, Hugh O'Neill and Rory O'Donnell, chiefs of Ulster and recently pardoned for their rebellion against Elizabeth I of England, stepped on board ship for an uncertain future on the continent. Their fears and apprehensions in a dangerous political, civil and military world drove them from their native shore. With them went a way of life that would never return. The clan system, with its Brehon laws, was doomed: to be increasingly and relentlessly supplanted by English law, where the crown took to itself for disposal the lands of the departed chiefs.

In January 1609, the rules and regulations underpinning the plantation of the escheated lands of Ulster were embodied in two documents – *A collection of such Orders and Conditions as are to be observed by the undertakers upon distribution and plantation of the escheated lands in Ulster*; and *A project for the division and plantation of the escheated lands..... in Ulster*.

Loyal and adventurous Englishmen, Welshmen and Scotsmen were encouraged to take land tracts in Ulster; to pay rent to the crown; to erect manors and strong houses and create tenancies; to enjoy export and import rights for varying periods of time; and to enjoy the benefit of the king's woods. The king and his council entered into negotiations with the merchants of the City of London to encourage them to speculate in the forced change of land ownership in Ulster. The area that interested the London merchants was around the towns of Derry and Coleraine in the newly created County of Derry. In addition to land the bounty of the salmon rivers was an incentive and an attraction.

The salmon fishing on the Bann and Foyle rivers, and their tributaries, was far famed and believed to be unequalled in Europe. The Charters of 1613 and 1662 granted to the London merchants, through the newly formed Irish Society, the salmon, eel and other fishing of the river Bann from the sea to Lough Neagh, and those of the Foyle from the sea to Lifford in County Donegal.

In 1769, the Earl of Donegal challenged the right of the Irish Society to the fishing rights on the river Bann. After prolonged legal representations, it was decided that the salmon fishing rights belonged to the Society; and that the eel fishing rights belonged to the earl. The leasing of the salmon fishing rights in the eighteenth century represented the not inconsiderable income of over £1462 per annum to the Irish Society. In 1756 the Society leased the rights to its former General Agent, Sir Henry Hamilton, for a period of twenty-one years at a rent of £910 per annum payable in London. This lease was renewed in 1769 for thirty-one years; and in 1778 was again renewed, this time for the life of Sir Henry's wife, Marianne. On Hamilton's death in 1782, Lady Hamilton came into possession of the potentially lucrative fishing rights on the river Bann. For some fifteen years she held this lease, improving the management of the fisheries until she sold her interest in the lease to Sir George Hill in 1798. Hill held the lease until 1847. It is interesting to note that the annual income at the end of this lease was actually £15 less than at the beginning. The secretary of the Irish Society explained the situation thus:

> 'By 1811, Sir George Hill has spent £5423 on the mill on the Bann and the fisheries ..... Clerks, boats and boatmen [were deployed] ..... There must be a number of persons employed as guards and watchmen in the neighbourhood of all the little rivers communicating with the Bann, and into which the motherfish resort in the breeding season....the workmen...if not properly managed...becoming poachers, capable of doing much mischief....'

The diary of John Macky, active on the river Bann from 1791 until 1809, gives us a fascinating insight into the economic and management difficulties of a little known employee of the landed gentry, the water bailiff, in the latter part of the eighteenth century and the first decade of the nineteenth.

Akin to the more familiar land or estate manager, the water bailiff was employed to manage, in the best interest of his employer, the rivers under his charge. Very little has been written about the estate manager; much less about the water bailiff. In England, the loss of Thomas Sisson in 1736, estate manager to the Cotesworths :

> 'were a very great loss, as he was trained up in the family and understood all the several transactions and engagements Mr Cotesworth had been concerned in, and to many good qualifications had the addition of an unbiased integrity, his information was always of great use to us and to be had immediately upon any emergency......'

John Macky tells us, by his own pen, that he was employed by Lady Hamilton in 1785, and he proved to be the epitome of the honest, diligent servant who always sought the best return for his employer. He records the difficulties he encountered, the hardships he endured and the personal dangers he overcame; and, later, he tells of his experiences under a change of ownership of the fishing rights on the river Bann.

At the outset of his employment Macky set out to recruit reliable water-keepers to police the rivers, but found good men difficult to find:

> '22 August 1791
> We can find no keeper at Portglenown.....
>
> 29 August 1791
> Went to Coagh and agreed with Mr Mallon and indeed I don't like him.

30 August 1791
Went to Benburb...agreed with Mr Trotter of Blackwater Town as Head Keeper at 5 guineas, and with him 4 others....

5 November 1791
Went to Kells and restored old Mathews into office and from thence to Ballymena where I cannot find a man for my purpose but Owen Trainor....and am this night very tired....'

To travel the many miles of river Macky bought from a curate at Ballintoy ' a horse....of good sound Protestant principles...' which beast carried him for many years. He rode to Kilrea on 14 August 1793, then on to Portna, Ballymoney, and the Cranagh where:

'... we went with the Constable and six soldiers and seized boats and broke them.....'

As the last decade of the eighteenth century progressed, political unrest in Ireland grew. In pursuing poachers, mainly at night, Macky was aware of groups of armed men, either Defenders or United Irishmen, gathered in secret:

'4 October 1796
Went to McCasky and down all the river....can get no man in charge and I plainly perceive they are all in combination...they say they are threatened but will not say by whom they are threatened....

Met McWilkin who tells me he can get no person willing to assist him in any shape. What is the meaning of this?

October 31st
Went to Benburb... and passing the chapel at Killyman I see 3000 persons assembled there and am told that these people are Defenders...'

A year later, in 1797, Macky finds the country further unsettled and the activities of the United Irishmen more open:

'27 October 1797
Went to McCasky river but no person will take it in charge, they laugh at me and ask me if you are up...'

[in United Irishmen terms – Are you up? meant are you a United Irishman and prepared for armed insurrection against English rule in Ireland]

Despite all these difficulties Macky acquitted his duties rigorously and faithfully, and the profits of Lady Hamilton rose year on year.

On 9 April 1798 Lady Hamilton sold her interest in the salmon fisheries to Sir George Hill. Macky was kept on by Hill, but as is often the case in such a new regime his position was no longer as it had been. What followed is a classic example of the new broom wielded by inexperienced hands.

A new water bailiff, Charles McFillin, was taken on and after a year superseded Macky, who was retained in a lesser position, but at the same salary. There began a slow but steady decline in the maintenance and performance of the fisheries. Macky's fears for the profits of his employer are progressively realised. Now, in almost every aspect of the working of the fisheries, Sir George Hill is plundered and imposed upon:

> 'I observe 2 great oak creels brought here from Bellaghy for repairing the Cutt walls, they are too large… and cost 8 shillings and a penny halfpenny… and their carriage will be two shillings and eight pence ha'penny per piece and in that case each creel costs ten shillings and ten pence. Now I really think they will not answer and in Coleraine they might have got 7 crates at the same money and our boat bring them from town and we would then have 14 crates in place of 2 creels….I already see he [McFillin] will render the New Cutt conspicuous in Botchwork….'

More serious than incompetence and bad workmanship was the systematic fleecing of their employer by the new bailiff and his family:

> '27 July 1801
> This morning before day John Heyland the younger came to this office and requested me to go to his father's house….[where] he told me that last night peeping through the hole in [the] Cutt gate he saw McFillin… and another man…stooping and taking up some salmon they had killed…
> Perdition to the man who first plans this infernal design in drafting all the old loopers from this place and in their stead has left us a wolf to guard the folds…'

Macky increasingly found himself isolated from his overseers and held in suspicion. His realistic fears for his own position kept him from speaking out:

> '22 May 1804
> I sincerely wish Sir George Hill would come here were it but for one day, or even a few hours. I dare not write to him. No, it is dangerous and therefore to my inward vexation I must be silent….'

And so, in this unhappy state John Macky, honest servant, saw out his working life. The diary he has left to posterity gives us a fascinating insight into a world now long past, but whose challenges, loyalties, gullibility and deceit are echoed in our own.

JOHN KILLEN
Linen Hall Library

The Cranagh Fishery, Coleraine

COPY MEMORANDA AND DIARY OF JOHN MACKY
Inspector of Waterkeepers on the Bann from 1791 to 1809

EXPLANATION OF TERMS USED IN THE DIARY

Abbreviations	*agt.*	:	against
	clk.	:	clerk
	rect.	:	receipt
	wart.	:	warrant

Are you up?
In United Irishmen terms, this asked if the subject was a United Irishman and if he was prepared for armed insurrection against English rule in Ireland.

Cott
A small flat bottomed boat locally made, operated by one or two men and carrying a short net for poaching salmon. A cott 'at trade' denotes a cott caught in the act of poaching. When not in use and during daylight hours, cotts were often hidden from sight by sinking them in deep water.

Coghill net
A long purse net used as a fish trap.

Keelog
A kelt or 'spent' salmon out of season and unfit for human consumption.

Grawls
Large grilse.

Lammaas
Is the festival of the ripening corn and first fruits, usually at the beginning of August in England and at the end of August in Ireland

Loopers
So called because of their use of long-handled nets, or 'loops' to remove salmon from holding pools.

Seneschal
A person appointed to represent the landowner, with sometimes additional responsibilities such as dispensing of justice and military command.

The Cutts
The commercial fishery, dwelling house and stores, 1½ miles upstream from the town of Coleraine, better known as 'the Salmon Leap'

The Cranagh
The commercial netting grounds with dwelling house and stores, midway between Coleraine and the sea (Bann mouth)

Thrave
24 (or in some places 12) sheaves of wheat or straw

Publisher's note: The transcription has followed John Macky's spelling throughout his diary, and the reader may therefore find instances of apparent misspelling. No attempt has been made to correct these, preferring instead to follow John Macky's hand in the manner he wrote his entries.

1791 Augt. 13 this evening went up the river Bann.
I observe the Loughan Cotts, one of them drawn up
the other on the Water ____ I have agreed with
D. McGonagle, from the Loughan to Gills Boat ____
Calld on Ben. Mitchel & has fix'd him to watch at
the Roochan shott ____ Met Pat McKeaG of AGivy
& engaged him for the Bann and foot of the two rivers
Crossed the Bann at the ferry and found Andw. Boyds
Cott in a Barn, McKeaG will certainly do for him ____
        Passed by the Eden in the Night and observed 2 Cotts
on the Bann ____ By the Moon light I see Drumale
Cotts and Will Ros puts me over to Bryan Dempseys
where I have agreed with Bryan and stayd all night ____
Augt. 14 Crossed the Bann and called on Willm. Kaine &
the 2 Crawfords who tell me the Eden men will certainly
be up the river this Night ____ Calld at Kibrea and
agreed with J. Dempsy for Portneill & and slept all
night in McCays ____ 15 at Portna agreed with Dan.
McKinny as head Keeper & with Ned McCann to assist
him ____ Calld at Dan. Elders at Portneill & helped
him home with his Cotts, but I think he will soon get
them down again ____ At Moorlodge met Kane &
Crawford looking for me, they last night saw the Eden Cotts
with Jn Kane the older Jn Kane the younger Jn Murphy & Dan.
McLain fishing the Bann below Drumale ____ Took them to
Ballimony, wrote their information & Warrt. Signd by McLeods
and put into the hands of Jn Higgins Constable who promises
to levy the fines this very week ____ Can find no Keeper for
Ballimony river, old Boyd is become uncapable ____
returnd the Cotts by 11 this night & slept in L. Hamiltons

1791. Augt. 13.	This evening went up the river Bann I observe the Loughan Cotts, one of them drawn up the other on the water. I have agreed with D. McGonagle from the Loughan to Gills Boat. Calld on Ben. Mitchel and has fixed him to watch at the Roochan shott – Met Pat McKeag of Agivy and engaged him for the Bann and foot of the two rivers. Crossed the Bann at the ferry and found Andw. Boyd's Cott in a barn, McKeag will certainly do for him.
	Passed by the Eden in the night and observed 2 Cotts on the Bann. – By the moonlight I see Drumale Cotts and Will Ross puts me over to Bryan Dempsey's where I have agreed with Bryan and stays all night.
Aug. 14	Crossed the Bann and called on Willm. Kane and the 2 Crawfords who tell me the Eden men will certainly be up the river this night. – Calld at Kilrea and agreed with J. Dempsey for Portneill &c. and slept all night in McCays. –
15	at Portna agreed with Dan McKinney as head-keeper and with Ned McCann to assist him. – Calld at Dan Elders at Portneill and helped him home with his Cotts, but I think he will soon get them down again. – At Moorlodge met Kane and Crawford looking for me, they last night saw the Eden Cotts with Jno. Kane the older, Jno Kane the younger, Jno. Murphy and Dan McLain fishing the Bann below Drumale. – Took them to Ballimony, wrote their information and Warrants signed by Mr. Leslie and put into the hands of Jno. Higgins Constable, who promises to levy the fines this very week. – Can find no Keeper for Ballimony river, old Boyd is become incapable – returned to the Cutts by 11 this night and slept in L. Hamilton's.
1791 Aug. 19th	This day the Constable of Ballymoney has got Jno. Kane's horse which we auctioned at £5 to old Galt of the Eden, who pd. me the fine and also £2.10.0 for D. McLain who has this day sworn before Mr. McNaghten never to be concerned in fishing during L.H.'s. incumbency. – I have paid the Const. £1. 2. 9 and the remn of the fines to Kane and Crawford, sum is £6. 7. 3.
Augt. 22	Rode up Antrim side of the Bann and am told there are a pair of Cotts now at Trade on Portglenown ford. – Calld on D. McKinny at Portna who goes with me. We can find no keeper at Portglenown who dare venture. I have at last agreed with Pat. McTeer or as they call him Paddy the Buffer, who engages to seize and bring me these 2 Cotts and for which I have promised him a Guinea. – Calld at Ballinagarvy and has agreed with J. McG. he is a Bailiff on these lands. I have given him £5.5.0 for his information and he engages to

find out P. McAlisters Cott which is sunk – returned by Claudy and there agreed with 2 Keepers as in the following list. Slept in Kilrea 23rd went back to Portna and there seized Harry Parkinson's Cott which lay conceald since Novr. last – paid Jas. Gillespie 2s 0½d. for drawing it from the Vow to Colerain. Called at Agivy and found Jno. McLeeses Nett set across the foot of the river, it is new and I have brought it home.

2nd Sept	Paddy the Buffer this day brought me the 2 Cotts belonging the Dalis's at Portglenown and this eveng I paid him at the Cutts £1.2.0 agreed. from Lady Hamilton and 3 Guins. to myself.
13th	Heavy rains, the 14th rode up to Aughadowy and Boveagh rivers and agreed with 2 Keepers we can see no fish in these rivers, the flood is too little and dirty.
20th	went to Mr. Casky and from thence walked downwards in search of Keepers, I can find none but Andrew McAlister of Knockadoo and I have agreed with him and got him attested. Called at the Cutts. Jack Heyland says he has seen nothing near that place.
1791 Septr. 27th.	Went up the Bann in the night and at Gills Boat ferry found a Cott which I have sent to the Cutts by D. McGonagle – Walked on to Agivy and wakened McKeag and in going up found 3 large netts near Mr. Lecky's gardens, sent a line to L. Hamilton along with these Netts – On calling at Glenkeen McGraw tells me he and the other Keepers have 4 fine netts taken off the foot of Aughadowey river and one very large nett from the Bann. – Went on to Vow ferry nothing here –
28th	returng. homeward met Larky of the Wood at Ballaghanea and gave him 5/5d. engages to bring me the Mulloy Cott this night by 12 o'clock. – Glenkeen men go with me to the Cutts and produce their 8 netts for which L.Hm. has paid them 8/-. and sent them home very hearty.
Octr. 8th	Bovagh and Aughadow Keepers have brought me 4 fine new netts and I have sent them with a note to L.Hamilton for their money. She paid and made them happy.
Octr. 17	Went to Mr. Forrester's Green and agreed with Wm. M'Faul, on my return stoppd. at Clare Hill for a dram and on going into a back house found 2 large Gaffs and a new nett about half made, these I have brought to the Cutts.
Octr. 27th	Set out for Mettigan river I agreed with Mr. Allen who can find no partner. In Garvagh I have agreed with 5 men and this eveng. in Glenullar agreed with the 2 Mullans and returned to Garvagh.

Octr. 28	at Swatragh met and agreed with 4 men of that neighbourhood and this day I have wrote all their appointments and their several Oaths and ordered them to Garvagh to-morrow and Harry Mullin will get them all sworn into office. –
29th.	went to Coagh and agreed with H. Mullon and indeed I don't like him.
Octr. 30th	went to Benburb. –
31st	Agreed with Mr. Trotter of Blackwater Town as Head Keeper at 5 Guins. and with him 4 others at and near Benburb.
Novr. 1st	Got these all sworn into office by Mr. Cawfield at Moy and returned this evening to Coagh.
Novr. 2nd	At Ballinderry found 3 men which I have appointed on Coagh river to serve along with H. Mullon and this eveng. I lodge at Manola Waterfoot and have agreed with my Landlord Pat. McLornan.
Novr. 3rd.	at Toom agreed with 3 men and have got them attested by Mr. Jones of Moneglass. –
Novr. 4th	in Randlestown met with our Head Keeper Mr. T. Black and have engaged 3 others to assist him and have got them attested by Mr. Lang at Shanes Castle.
Novr. 5th	Went to Kells and restored old Matthews into office and from thence to Ballymena where I cannot find a man for my purpose but Owen Turner and have got him attested at Broughshane and am this night very tired.
Novr. 6	To Gillgorm where I have got my two old Keepers appointed and have ordered them to Broughshane to be attested and by 7 this eveng. have got into Rasharken wet and hungry.
Novr. 7	Came to Kilrea and called on J. Dempsy who has three fine salmon rods and lines and a large nett which he says he took at Bovanagher and he brings them with me to the Cutts where L.Hamilton paid him 4/4d. with his dinner and a long drink. Before parting she has presented me with £2. 5. 6. to buy a new great coat. My list comes £7.19.3 short of last season's amount and if this winter's floods are favourable I make no doubt of our continued increase of fish.
Novr. 12	Went to Bovagh and in the night with Hugh McKeeman lifted 5 netts between Cornamucklagh and the river foot.
Novr. 13th	This morng. at 6 o'clock met Jas. Kane and Fred McGraw with 4 fine netts lifted last night off the Roe and foot of Aughadowy river; on

our way to the Cutts found McAlister on the road with a great Cochill nett off Mr. Casky river at Merns's Flaxmill, Ballinrea. Lady Hamilton has paid them 11/4½ and some glasses of rum.

Decr. 7   Wm. Kane and Craford have brought a large cott to the Cutts and have got half-a-guinea from L.Hamilton.

Waterkeepers for Winter 1791 and Spring 1792.

On the River Bann.

No.1 John Heyland	Castleroe	pd.	£2.	5.	6
2 Dan. McGonagle	the Loughin	pd.	2.	5.	6
3 Pat McKeag	Agivy	pd.	2.	5.	6
4 Ben Mitchell	Glascort	pd.	2.	5.	6
5 Bryan Dempsy	Drumale	pd.	2.	5.	6
6 James Craford	Vowferry	pd.	2.	5.	6
7 Will Kane	at Newbuildings	pd.	2.	5.	6
8 Hu. Crawford	Lignafern	pd.	2.	5.	6
9 John Dempsy	Portneill	pd.	2.	5.	6
10 Ned McCann	Portna	pd.	2.	5.	6
11 Dan. McKinny head-keeper,	Monigran	pd.	5.	13.	9
			£28.	8.	9

1791. On Bovagh River.

12. Hu. McKeeman	Cullycapple	pd.	£1.	14.	1½
13. Edwd. Mullan	the new Green,	pd.	1.	14.	1½
14. Jack McFetrish	Innishdochill	pd.	1.	14.	1½
15. Hu. McClern	at Bovagh Gardens,.	pd.		11.	4½
			£5.	13.	9

1791. On Aughadowy River.

16. James Kane	Keely Green	pd.	£1.	14.	1½
17. John McGraw	Clare Hill	pd.	1.	14.	1½
18. Fred McGraw	Glenkeen	pd.	1.	14.	1½
19. Will McFawl	at Mr. Forresters Green,	pd.	1.	14.	1½
			£6.	16.	6

1791 On McCasky River.

20. Andw. McAlister,	Knockadoo,	pd.	£2.	5.	6
	Carried over		£43.	4.	6½

Waterkeepers for Winter 1791 and Spring
1792 ————

On the River Bann ————

No.	Name	Place		£	s	d
1	John Heyland	Castleroe	p.d	2	5	6
2	Dan. McGonagle	the Loughin	p.d	2	5	6
3	Pat. McKeag	Agivy	p.d	2	5	6
4	Ben. Mitchell	Glascort	p.d	2	5	6
5	Bryan Dempsy	Drumale	p.d	2	5	6
6	James Craford	Newferry	p.d	2	5	6
7	Will. Kane	at Newbuildings	p.d	2	5	6
8	Hu. Crawford	Lignafern	p.d	2	5	6
9	John Dempsy	Portneill	p.d	2	5	6
10	Ned McCann	Portna	p.d	2	5	6
11	Dan. McKinny head keeper	Monigran	p.d	5	13	9
			£	28	8	9

1791 On Bovagh River

No.	Name	Place		£	s	d
12	Hu. McKeeman	Cullycapher	p.d	1	14	1½
13	Edw. Mullan	the new Green	p.d	1	14	1½
14	Jack McTetrish	Innishdoehill	p.d	1	14	1½
15	Hu. McClern	at Bovagh Gardens	p.d		11	4½
			£	5	13	9

1791 On Aghadowy River

No.	Name	Place		£	s	d
16	James Kane	Keely Green	p.d	1	14	1½
17	John McGraw	Clare Hill	p.d	1	14	1½
18	Fred. McGraw	Glenkeen	p.d	1	14	1½
19	Will McFawl	at Mr. Forresters Green	p.d	1	14	1½
			£	6	16	6

1791 On McCasky River

No.	Name	Place		£	s	d
20	Andw. McAlister	Nockadoo	p.d	2	5	6
		Carried over	£	43	4	6½

		Brought forward		£43.	4.	6½
1791. On Mettigan River						
21.	John McAllen	Mettigan	pd.	£1.	14.	1½

1791. On Garvagh River.						
22.	Harry Mullan	Head Keeper,	pd.	£2.	5.	6
23	Hu. Hill,	near James Orr's Green,	pd.	2.	0.	0
24	Neill McWilkin	near Wm. Orr's Green,	pd.	1.	14.	1½
25	Matthew Wilson	at Ballinameen	pd.	1.	14.	1½
26	John Wilson	For Garvagh Carry	pd.	1.	14.	1½
				£9.	7.	10½

This day I see 3 fish below H. Mullan's House.

1791. On Glenullar river.						
27.	Paddy the Man Mullan	Brockagh	pd.	£1.	14.	1½
28.	Bryan the Man Mullan		pd.	1.	14.	1½
				£3.	8.	3

1791. On Claudy River.						
29	Barny McLain	Claudy.	Pd.	£2.	5.	6
30	James McLain	do.	Pd.	2.	5.	6
31	Art. McCann	Swatragh	Pd.	2.	5.	6
32	John Doorish	Near do.	Pd.	1.	10.	0
33	Dan. Doorish	Tirgarvill	Pd.	1.	10.	0
34	Frank McShane,	Upperland flaxmill.	Pd.	1.	10.	0
				£11.	6.	6

1791. On Coagh & Ballinderry River.						
35.	Hu. Mullon, Headkeeper,	Coagh	Pd.	4.	11.	0
36	John Donnelly,	at Ballinderry.	Pd.	2.	5.	6
37	William Buck	at do.	Pd.	2.	5.	6
38	Ambrose Taylor	Salterstown	Pd.	2.	5.	6
				£11.	7.	6

39	On Black Water, Mr. J. Trotter,	Headkeeper	Pd.	5.	13.	9
40	William Clark,	Benburb,	Pd.	1.	14.	1½
41	Arth. Hobson,	do.	Pd.	1.	14.	1½
42	James Hughes,	Maydown,	Pd.	1.	14.	1½
43	Mr. Jacksons Watchman,	Tullydowy,	Pd.	1.	14.	1½
				£12.	10.	3

			£	s	d
1791 —	Brought forward — £		43	4	6½
	On McHigan River —				
21	John McAllen	McHigan . . — p?	1	14	1½
	1791, On Garvagh River				
22	Harry Mullan . . . . head Keeper	p?	2	5	6
23	Hu. Hill . . . . near James Orrs Green . . .	p?	2	—	—
24	Neill McWilkin near Wm Orrs Green	p?	1	14	1½
25	Mathew Wilson . . . at Ballinameen . . .	p?	1	14	1½
26	John Wilson . . . . for Garvagh Carry . .	p?	1	14	1½
	this Day I see 3 fish below H: Mullans House	a?	9	7	10½
	1791. On Glenullar river				
27	Paddy the Man Mullan . . . Brockagh . . —	p?	1	14	1½
28	Bryan the Man Mullan . . . . —	p?	1	14	1½
		£	3	8	3
	1791, On Claudy River				
29	Barny McLain . . . . Claudy . . .	p?	2	5	6
30	James McLain . . . . do . . .	p?	2	5	6
31	Art. McCann . . . . Swatragh . .	p?	2	5	6
32	John Doorish . . . . . near Do.	p?	1	10	—
33	Dan. Doorish . . . . . . Tirgarvill . . .	p?	1	10	—
34	Frank McShane . . . . Upperland flax mill	p?	1	10	—
		£	11	6	6
	1791 On Coagh & Ballinderry River				
35	Hu. Mallon head Keeper . . . . . Coagh . . .	p?	4	11	—
36	John Donnelly . . . . at Ballinderry	p?	2	5	6
37	William Buck . . . . at Do. . . .	p?	2	5	6
38	Ambrose Taylor . . . . Salterstown	p?	2	5	—
		£	11	7	6
39	On Black Water Mr J. Trotter head Keeper . . —	p?	5	13	9
40	William Clark . . . . Benburb . . . —	p?	1	14	1½
41	Arth. Hobson . . . . Do	p?	1	14	1½
42	James Hughes . . . . Maydown . . —	p?	1	14	1½
43	Mr Jacksons Watchman . . . Tullydowy . . —	p?	1	14	1½
		£	12	10	3

1791.		Brought forward		£92.	19.	0
	On Loughbeg.					
44	James Scullin,	Ballyscullin,	Pd.	1.	10.	0
45	Peter Scullin,	Near do.	Pd.	1.	10.	0
				£3.	0.	0

July 10th 1792. I find these men useless.

	1791. On Moyola River and Loughneagh.					
46	Pat McLornan,		Pd.	2.	5.	6
	1791. On Toom Wiers etc.					
47	Patroe Neeson	Creagh	Pd.	1.	14.	1½
48	Edward Magee	Toome	Pd.	1.	14.	1½
49	Owin Neeson,	Mullagh,	Pd.	1.	14.	1½

I don't like this last man.   £5.   2.   4½

	1791. On the River Main.					
50.	Mr. Thomas Black,	Headkeeper,	Pd.	6.	5.	1½
51	Tatty O'Neill,	at the Paper Mill,	Pd.	3.	8.	3
52	Hugh McCann,	at Randlestown Bridge,	Pd.	2.	5.	6
53	James Tork,	at Aughabuoy Carry,	Pd.	2.	5.	6

I see Mr. Black much faild.   £14.   4.   4½

	1791. On Kells River.					
54	Nathaniel Mathews,	at Kells	Pd.	1.	14.	1½
	1791. On Ballymena River.					
55	Oliver Turner		Pd.	1.	14.	1½
	1791.On Gillgorm River.					
56	William Armstrong,		Pd.	1.	14.	1½
57	Thomas Mitchell,		Pd.	1.	14.	1½

£3.   8.   3

Novr. 6th. I see several fish near Ballykennedy.

1791. On Ballymoney River.

58	William Boyd,	nearly worn out.	Pd.	1.	14.	1½

	Amt. to Keepers this Season	£126.	1.	10½

1791		Brought forward	£	92	19	—
	On Loughbeg —					
44	James Scullin —	Ballyscullin	fo	1	10	—
45	Peter Scullin — near Do.		fo	1	10	—
	July 10th 1792 I find these men useless —		£	3	—	—
	1791 On Mayola River & Loughneagh					
46	Pat. McLolnan		fo	2	5	6
	1791. On Toom Wiers &c					
47	Patroe Neeson	Creagh	fo	1	14	1½
48	Edward Magee	Toome	fo	1	14	1½
49	Owin Neeson	Mullagh	fo	1	14	1½
	I don't like this last Man		£	5	2	4½
	1791. On the River Main					
50	Mr. Thomas Black head Keeper		fo	6	5	1½
51	Tatty O'Neill at the Paper Mill		fo	3	0	3
52	Hugh McCann at Randlestown Bridge		fo	2	5	6
53	James Sork at Aryhabuoy Carry		fo	2	5	6
	I see Mr. Black much faild		£	14	4	4½
	1791 On Kells River					
54	Nathaniel Mathews at Kells		fo	1	14	1½
	1791 On Ballymena River					
55	Oliver Turner		fo	1	14	1½
	1791 On Gillgorm River					
56	William Armstrong		fo	1	14	1½
57	Thomas Mitchell		fo	1	14	1½
	Novr 6th I see several fish near Ballykennedy		£	3	8	3
	1791 On Ballymony River					
58	William Boyd nearly worn out		fo	1	14	1½
	amt. to Keepers this season —		£	126	1	10½

Amount of the Rivers this Season as follows:

				£.	s.	d
1.	The River Bann,	11 Men		28.	8.	9
2.	Bovagh River	4 ,,		5.	13.	9
3.	Aughadowy River,	4 ,,		6.	16.	6
4.	McCasky River,	1 ,,		2.	5.	6
5.	McKiagan River,	1 ,,		1.	14.	1½
6.	Garvagh River	5 ,,		9.	7.	10½
7.	Glenullar,	2 ,,		3.	8.	3
8.	Claudy River,	6 ,,		11.	6.	6
9.	Coagh River,	4 ,,		11.	7.	6
10.	Blackwater,	5 ,,		12.	10.	3
	Loughbeg,	2 ,,		3.	0.	0
11.	Moyola River,	1 Men		2.	5.	6
12.	Toome &c.	3 ,,		5.	2.	2½
13.	Main River	4 ,,		14.	4.	4½
14.	Kells River,	1 ,,		1.	14.	1½
15.	Ballymena River,	1 ,,		1.	14.	1½
16.	Gillgorm River	2 ,,		3.	8.	3
17.	Ballymoney River	1 ,,		1.	14.	1½
	John Macky, Inspector.			22.	15.	0
	Amount exclusive of Powder & Shott.			£148.	16.	10½

1792. May 3rd. Mr. Thomson has paid me 13 Guins.   £13. 13. 0
May 17th. Recd. from do.   6. 7. –
25. Recd. from L.Hamilton 2½ Guins.   2. 16. 10½
                                                     _____
In full for last Winter's salary –   £22. 16. 10½
                                                     _____
Aug.20th 1792. Recd. of Mr. Thomson 17½ Guins.   £19. 18. 1½
Change recd. from do.   1. 10½
Septr.7th. Recd. from Lady Hamilton 2½ Guins.   2. 16. 10½
                                                     _____
As Clark's Salary at the Cutts —   22. 16. 10½

Septr. 9th. Orders me 3 Drafts of salt salmon
          3 Large Do. for Smoaking recd. this day.
Septr. 20th. Sent money by Bryan Deehan 4½ Guins.

1792.
Augt. 13th.
Sold out the remainder of last night's fish amounting to £13. 5. 8.
Dined with L.Hamilton and at 7 this evening walked up the Bann and
called at the Loughan where the Semples have promised to lodge
their Cotts with me in the Cutt house and they shall have them by the
1st Jany. next. – Crossed the river and replaced Daniel McGonagle and

walked on to Agivy but cannot find the Cotts, they are certainly
fishing or else sunk. Returnd to Gowds Mill and agreed with Jack
McCarter – then set out for Glenkeen – it is now daylight.

14th Augt. I here have engaged 3 men and near Bovagh have agreed with 3 others
as in the following List. – Went to Bovanagher and secured the
Jamisons Cotts. – In Kilrea, have replaced Jno Dempsy Senr. for
Portneil and Jno. Dempsy Junr. for Bovanagher and have got them
attested. Dined in Kilrea and then to Monigran and replaced Dan.
McKinney and slept there. McKinny says there are no Cotts at
Portglenown since the last were seized. –

15th. Crossd the Bann and fixed Ned McCann at Portna and returning
homeward on the Antrim side found Dan Elders Cotts drawn home
and locked and I have brought the key. – Called at the Killins but
cannot find McCools Cotts. – At the Vow have appointed Wm. Kane
for the ferry and James Craford for Carnroe and downwards, – Crossd
the river to Drumale and appd. Bryan Dempsy. – Crossd again and see
Willroes Cott at his house near the Bannshore – Called at cross ferry
and agreed with Jno. Boyd a sturdy fellow. – Below the Loughin I see
a man working a Cott up the Derry side, passd over at the Loughin
came to Castleroe by 8 o'clook. –

Aug. 21st. This day Larky has got and brought me the Cott from Ballinagarvy
which he engaged to bring on the 28th Septr last. – I will give him
nothing he broke his promise, and I suppose this Cott has been
fishing all the last winter, it is an excellent Cott and stands me 5/5d.
and therefore I take it home.

Sept 1st This evening set up the Bannshore and can find nothing a-doing, calld
on J. McCarter, he has made out nothing yet. At Agivy I have found a
fine new nett set in the Bann and suppose it is Gib. McAlisters – I have
left it with Fred McGraw, Glenkeen, to bring to the Cutts by next
Saty. – Called at Cullycappel nothing doing near this place yet. – Went
forward to Bovanagher and I see Hegarty's new Cott and it is now
clear day. –

Septr. 2 went on to Monigran and breakfasted with D.McKinny who came
with me to Bovanagher and by the help of Jno. Dempsy Junr. have
taken Hegarty's Cott. – On our way homeward I see old McKenna's
Cott, he looks suspicious – met Wm. Kane and a Wart. from Mr.
Leslie agt. Willroes Cott, I have at the foot of the Wart. appointed
him as a Special Constable and thereupon seized the Cott which I see
is daubed with blood and scales. – Murphy and young Kane met us at
Eden and there surrendered to me at discretion. I see Murphy is very

made out nothing yet —— At Agivy I have found a fine new Nett set in the Barn & suppose it is Gib. McAlisters — I have left it with Fred. McGraw Glenkeen to bring to the Cutts by next Satr —— Calld at Cullycappel nothing doing near this place yet — Went forward to Bovanagher and I see Hegartys new Cott & it is now clear day — Septr 2 went on to Monegran & breakfasted with D. McKinny who came with me to Bovanagher & by the help of Jno Dempsey Junr have taken Hegartys Cott —— on our way homeward I see old McKennas Cott she looks suspicious — met Wm Kane & a Warrt from McLeslie agt Will roes Cott, I have at the foot of the warrt appointed him as a Special Constable and thereupon seized the Cott which I see is daubed with Blood and Scales —— Murphy & young Kane met us at Eden and there surrendered to me at discretion. I see Murphy is very lean & sickly & Kane is very young and I have a Heart which tells me not to imprison them in their present state and therefore acquits them after swearing voluntarily on old Galts great Bible not to offend during Lady Hs incumbency at 3 oClock got to Castleroe where these Keepers got their dinner and drink from L: H. and 11:4½ to Will Kane and I have brought Hegartys cott to my House Septr 10th Rode to McCasky and down the river and no man will engage in the Keeping so that I find I must agree with McAlister again & yet I dont like him —— Rode on to Aughadowry & have there fixed with McJawl & Kane Crossed the Country to Mullinabrone & have engaged S. Gilmore and at Monycarry have placed H. Hill and McWilkin at McOrss ford — I find my Horse very ill I wish he may carry me Home Septr 18 Glenkeen men have brought me 5 choice netts off the foot of Bovagh & Aughadowry rivers and I have given them 5:5 and their Breakfast. Heavy rain this day —— Octr 1st my Horse is found dead in the Stable this morng and so I find I must set out on foot this day up the Bann for I perceive the flood

is

lean and sickly and Kane is very young and I have a heart which tells me not to imprison them in their present state and therefore acquits them after swearing voluntarily on old Galts great Bible not to offend during Lady H's. incumbency, at 3 o'clock got to Castleroe where these Keepers got their dinner and drink from Lady H. and 11/4½ to Will Kane, and I have brought Hegarty's Cott to my house.

Sept. 10th

Rode to McCasky and down the river and no man will engage in the Keeping so that I find I must agree with McAlister again and yet I don't like him. Rode on to Aughadowy and I have there fixed with McFawl and Kane. Crossed the country to Mullinabrone and have engaged S. Gilmore and at Monycarry have placed H. Hill and Mr. Wilkin at Mr. Orr's ford. – I find my horse very ill, I wish he may carry me home.

Septr. 18

Glenkeen men have brought me 5 choice netts off the foot of Bovagh and Aughadowy rivers and I have given them 5/5d. and their breakfast. Heavy rain this day. –

Octr. 1

My horse is found dead in the stable this morning and so I find I must set out on foot this day up the Bann for I perceive the flood is fallen. – Called at the Cutts and L.H. has given me 5 guineas to purchase a poney at first fair in Bushmills or Dervock. Called at Gowds Mill and find McCarter has got 2 netts last night on the foot of the Ree. Went on to Agivy and Glenkeen, no netts there. Crossed the waterfoot at Mr. Leeses and at Innishdochill have got a very large nett and one smaller; they were taken last night near the old church at Agivy by John McFetrish who says he will call on McCarter to accompany him to the cutts with these 4 Netts by Sat. next. – Went on to Bovagh and finding nothing there, returned homeward and on calling at the Cutts was asked by L. Hamilton to sleep there all night.On my way this day the Keepers tell me there are great plenty of fish taken into these rivers by this last flood so that by next flood they will run a head upward. – When I get a horse I must go to Garvagh and place the Keepers there in good time.

Octr. 12 & 13th

Very heavy rains.

15th

Walked to Garvagh and replaced the former Keepers and got them attested.

16th

went to Swatragh on a hireling and replaced the Keepers there and then down to Claudy where I see the fish are got forward and therefore have placed the McLains in charge at this place and returned by Kilrea and slept there. –

17th	sent the horse home to Garvagh and I went to Ballymoney and after searching all day I can find no person to take charge of it. Damnation to them, they are all Freemasons combined in favour of old Boyd, but I'm Dam'd if I give him a sixpence this year. Better let the river lie waste than lose her Ladyship's money and the fish along with it and this to Ballymoney I bid Goodnight.
Octr. 24	Seeing this weather fair and favourable I think of setting out immediately on my long tour. I have bought a horse from a Curate Minister at Ballintoy and he appears to be a horse of sound protestant principles.
Octr. 26	Rode to the Cutts and called with L. Hamilton who gave a glass and 2/5/6, and then to Garvagh; nothing new here, the fish are very few.
27th	went on to Swatragh, no fish there yet. – Pass by Grillagh a fine little river but very unfavourable to Brooding fish. The river being so small would require several men by day as well as night.
Octr. 28	At Coagh agreed with John Mallon for 4 Guineas and 2 others at 2 Guineas each.
29th.	At Blackwatertown sent for and replaced the former Keepers, some few fish have reached Benburb.
Octr. 30	Called at Moy and got these Keepers sworn into Office and by 8 o'clock got into Coagh. –
31st	From Coagh down the river to Salters town and obliged to stay all night in the house of a Mr. Adams a very hospitable weaver. –
Nov. 1st	Went on to Moyola river foot and there replaced Mr. Lornan and indeed I fear he is a dam'd villain. Stayd here all night being very stormy.
Novr. 2nd.	At Toom agreed with 2 men for this season and set forward to Randlestown and there replaced old Tom Black and 3 others.
Novr. 3rd.	Set out for Kells and there replaced Nath. Mathews a worthy old Veteran. I have given him a dram while my horse is eating his oats. At 3 o'clock got into Ballymena and put Turner in charge of the river in which I find there are some fresh run fish. After night went to Gillgorm and there appointed the former keepers.
Novr. 4th.	Homeward by Rasharken, the Vow and the Cross ferry and have found nothing new in my way.
Novr. 6th	Rode to Drumcroon and have agreed with Mr. John Wilson's watchman Hunter at ½ a guinea a year and Mr. Wilson has engaged

as security for his good behaviour, and by the way and manner of this season I have every reason to conclude we shall have a grand fishery next summer. Called at the Cutts where L.H. askd me to dinner and shewd me 4 netts by Bovagh and Aughadowy last Saturday. They are all new.

Decr. 4.

McGraw and McKeeman have brought me 3 large netts from the Brick Hills and I have given them 3/3d. and their breakfast.

Janry. 25th
1793:

Went to Portna, nothing new there, came in the night to Glenkeen and with McGraw and James Kane lifted 3 new netts off the waterfoot in which were 3 large Keelogs all alive. Paid them 3/3d. and half a pint of spirits.

1792. Keepers on the River Bann.

		£.	s.	d
I.	John Heyland, from the Cutts to the Loughin.	Pd.	2.	5.	6
2.	Dan McGonagle, from the Loughin to Gills Boat &c.	Pd.	2.	5.	6
3.	John McCarter for the Ree and foot of McCasky river.	Pd.	2.	5.	6
4.	John Boyd from Cross ferry up to the Roochan.	Pd.	2.	5.	6
5.	Bryan Dempsy at Drumale and Ballinagarvy.	Pd.	2.	5.	6
6.	James Crawford at New Buildings &c.	Pd.	2.	5.	6
7.	Willm. Kane from New Ferry to Bovanagher	Pd.	2.	5.	6
8.	Jno. Dempsey Junr. from Bovanagher to Portneill	Pd.	2.	5.	6
9.	Jno. Dempsey Senr. from Portneill to Portna.	Pd.	2.	5.	6
10.	Ned McCann from Portna up to Gortreaghy.	Pd.	2.	5.	6
11.	Dan. McKinney at Monigran head keeper.	Pd.	5.	13.	9
			£28.	8.	9

1792. On Aughadowy River.

			£.	s.	d
12.	Wm. McFawl at Mr. Forrester's Green	Pd.	1.	14.	1½
13.	James Kane at Mr. James Orr's Green,	Pd.	1.	14.	1½
14.	John McGraw at Glenkeen,	Pd.	1.	14.	1½
15.	Fred McGraw, at ,, a good Keeper	Pd.	1.	14.	1½
			£6.	16.	6

1792. On Bovagh River.

			£.	s.	d
16.	Hu. McKeeman near Mr. Alex. Orr's new Green,	Pd.	1.	14.	1½
17.	John McFetrish at Innish Dochill	Pd.	1.	14.	1½
18.	Pat. Quinn, near Ballydavitt	Pd.	1.	14.	1½
			£5.	2.	4½

1792. On McCasky River.

19.	Andw. McAlister at Knockadoo,	Pd.	2.	5.	6

1792. On Garvagh River.

20.	Neill McWilkin at James Orr's ford,	Pd.	1.	14.	1½
21.	Hugh Hill at Monecarry	Pd.	2.	0.	0
22.	Sam. Gilmore at Mullanabrone,	Pd.	1.	14.	1½
23.	Jno. Wilson at Garvagh Mull in lair,	Pd.	1.	14.	1½
24.	Mathew Wilson at Ballinameen;	Pd.	1.	14.	1½
25.	Henry Mullan, headkeeper Garvagh Bridge,	Pd.	2.	5.	6
			£11.	2.	0
	Carried Forward		£53.	15.	1½

Winter 1792.	Brought Forward		£53.	15.	1½
On Mettigan River.					
26. John McAllen			1.	14.	1½
Charles McAllen .. would not be attested.			–	–	–
			£1.	14.	1½

1792. On Glenullar River.

27.	Paddy the man Mullan,	Brockagh.	Pd.	1.	14.	1½
28.	Bryan the man do.	do.	pd.	1.	14.	1½
				£3.	8.	3

1792. On Claudy River.

29.	James McLain,	near Claudy,	Pd.	2.	5.	6
30.	Barny McLain	do.	Pd.	2.	5.	6
31.	Pa. McLain	near Innishrush,	Pd.	2.	5.	6
32.	John Doorish,	near Swatragh,	Pd.	1.	10.	0
33.	Dan. Doorish,	Tirgarvile,	Pd.	1.	10.	0
34.	Frank McShane,	at Upperland flaxmill	Pd.	1.	10.	0
35.	Art. McCann,	at Swatragh Mill.	Pd.	2.	5.	6
				£13.	12.	0

1792. On Coagh River.

36.	John Mallon	Coagh sworn.	Pd.	4.	11.	0
37.	Alex. McKinny,	Ballygoney	Pd.	2.	5.	6
38.	Ambrose Taylor,	gone to Scotland.		–	–	–
				£6.	16.	6

1792. On the Black Water.

39.	Wm. James Trotter,	Headkeeper.	Pd.	5. 13.	9
40.	Willm. Clark,	Benburb, sworn in	Pd.	1. 14.	1½
41.	Arthur Hobson,	do.	Pd.	1. 14.	1½
42.	James Hughes.		Pd.	1. 14.	1½
43	James Neill,	at the Island.	Pd.	1. 14.	1½
				£12. 10.	3

1792. On the Moyola and the Lough.

44.	Pat. McLounan,	Sworn in.	Pd.	2. 5.	6
		Carried Fordw.		£94. 1.	9

Winter 1792.   Brought Forward   £94. 1. 9

On Toom Wiers &c.

45.	Ned McGee,	sworn	Pd.	1. 14.	1½
46.	Barny Toal	sworn in	Pd.	1. 14.	1½
	Nov.2. Seized a long nett set on the Barr.			£3. 8.	3

1792. On the River Main.

47.	Thomas Black of Randlestown, first keeper.		Pd.	6. 5.	1½
48.	Clotworthy O'Neill, at the Paper Mill.		Pd.	3. 8.	3
49.	Hu McCann, at Randlestown Bridge		Pd.	2. 5.	6
50	James Tork. at Aughabuoy Dam.		Pd.	2. 5.	6
				£14. 4.	4½

	I see Tatty O'Neill has got 7 netts in his house.				
51.	On Kells river – Nath. Mathews,		Pd.	1. 14.	1½
52.	On Ballymena River — Oliver Turner		Pd.	1. 14.	1½

On Gillgorm River.

53.	Thomas Mitchell,	sworn.	Pd.	1. 14.	1½
54.	William Armstrong,	do.	Pd.	1. 14.	1½
				£3. 8.	3
	Ballymoney River,	Waste.		– –	–

On Drumcroon Rivulet.

		Pd.		
55.	Wm. Wilson's Watchman – Hunter,	Pd.	11.	4½

To Keepers this Season		119.	2.	3
To my Salary as Inspector	Pd.	22.	15.	–

Amount exclusive the cost of Ammunition.   £141. 17. 3

1793. Aug. 16. Recd. from Mr. Thomson, 10 Guin.   11. 7. 6
22. Recd. from do.   8. 12. 6
Septr, 1 Recd. from L. Hamilton 2½ Guins.   2. 16. 10½

To Jno. Macky as Clk. at the Cutts-   22. 6. 10½

5th. Sent me 1½ Hund. W. Galt, Salmon and two large
ditto for smoaking.
Septr. 16. Sent Jamy Gray for me and after Dinner gave me
5 Guineas.

<table>
<tr><td>1793. Augt.
13th.</td><td>We have this day sold of the remr. of yesterday's fish and I find my Abstract tells well and better than last season. 4 o'clock this evening walked up the Bann, the Loughan Cotts are drawn up, called on and agreed with D. McGonagle and forward to Agivy – I cannot see the cotts and suppose they are sunk and go on to Drumale and replaced Bryan Dempsey and stayed all night.</td></tr>
<tr><td>Aug 14</td><td>Went upward on Derry side the river and called at the Jamisons, who say they have had no share of the river this season. Went on to Kilrea and replaced J. Dempsey and from thence to Portna and replaced D. McKinny and McCann and slept there. –</td></tr>
<tr><td>Aug. 15</td><td>returned on the Antrim shore but cannot make out the McCools cotts – called at Moorlodge and agreed with P. McClern from the Killins to Bovanagher. Called at the Vow and replaced Wm. Kane and J. Crawford, who came with me down shore and say they saw Cotts on the river last night – called at Eden and see Galts Cotts and then returned to the Vow and stayd there till 10 o'clock at night – We set out again and lurking down the shore at length see Galts cotts with 4 men fishing. We there waited their landing and see old and young Galt and don't know the 2 others who run off on our approach. We here got the cotts the nett and 10 good salmon. I sent the salmon by Crawford home to his house and Kane with me bring the cotts to the cutts where L.H. paid him £1. 2. 9. with drink.</td></tr>
<tr><td>Aug. 21</td><td>In Ballymoney put Warts. into the hands of Higgins the Constable, who instantly saw old and young Galt on the street and seized them</td></tr>
</table>

18   THE DIARY OF AN IRISH WATER BAILIFF

and on taking them to his house old Galt paid down 8 Guineas and I gave him a rect. and acquittance. I there gave Higgins a Guinea for his job and 7 Guineas to Kane for him and Crawford.

Aug. 30   Fine dry weather all the last week.

Aug. 31   With the 4 Loopers went down the Bann and there saw Leslies and Matthew Henry's boats fishing near Bann brook and on next eveng. we went with the Constable and 6 soldiers and seized the boats and broke them at the Cranagh.

Septr. 12   I see vast numbers of fish under the Leap. Went up the Bann to Drumale and stayd. all night and have agreed with Jimmy Loobagh Dempsy to watch the Roochan in place of J. Boyd.

Septr. 13.   Went to McKinneys who says there are cotts now fishing at Portglenown – at 4 o'clock McKinny and McCann set out with me to the foot of Claudy river and lurking there discovered the cotts fishing and several persons along the Antrim side of the river all in waiting for fish. By 2 o'clock the cotts are landed below the Bridge and the people all dispersed upon which we crossed Claudy river foot and proceeded on to the Bridge and passed unperceived. We then made for the cotts and found one of them fast locked by a chain to a great post and other unlocked – having no instrument wherewith to break the lock we were obliged to make off with the loose cott which carried us to Portna as hastily as we could.

Octr. 3.   I see very few fish appearing below the Cranagh, the river at present very low. – Rode up the Derry side of the Bann to Kilrea and dined there. 3 o'clock passed at Portneill Bridge and homeward on the Antrim side, called with all the Keepers and find nothing new.

Octr. 27th.   Heavy rains there 2 nights past which must have raised the rivers.

28th.   Rode to Aughadowy and Bovagh rivers and placed the Keepers. McKeeman and McGraw have 5 fine new netts lifted last night. Called at Dowds Mill and replaced McCarter, then up the river to Knock also and replaced McAlister and stopped at L. Hamiltons who gave me a hearty glass of Port and 34/1½ to help me on my journey up the rivers which I intend for as soon as I have got my poney prepared by Andy McAteer.

1795. Octr. 30.   Went to Garvagh and appointed 7 men to sundry placed, and got them attested.

31st.   Went to the Glen and replaced the Keepers there and after dinner at Garvagh set on to Swatragh and replaced the Keepers as formerly.

Novr. 1.	At Claudy fixed with the old keepers and got them attested in Portglenown and then to Bellaghy and stay all night.
Novr. 2nd.	To Coagh and there agree with Mr. Robt. Dunbar as head keeper who promises to have 2 keepers provided by the time I return.
Novr. 3	Went on to Black water town and at Mr. Trotters sent for Benburb men etc. whom I have appointed to meet me tomorrow morng. at Moy to be attested.
Novr. 4	Met these Keepers and had them attested by Mr. Caufield and then returned to Coagh.
Novr. 5	went down the river to Salterstown and from thence by the Lough side to Moyola river and there stayd all night.
Novr. 6th	To Toom and there appointed 3 men for the different Eelfisherys and got them attested by Mr. Jones at Moneyglass and returned to Toom.
Novr. 7th	To Randlestown and there replaced old Mr. Black and 3 others. –
Novr. 8th.	To Kells river where I see some fish and have replaced Old Mathews in charge of them and proceed on to Ballymena and there replaced Oliver Turner and got forward to Gillgorm and restored the late Keepers. –
Novr. 9th.	Set homeward by Rashackin and Ballymoney but can find no man to take charge of the river. –
Novr. 10th.	Waited on L. Hamilton and produced her my list and she produced to me 5 excellent Netts brought her from Aughadowy and the Bann. The great number of fish seen on my passage induced me to employ more men than what I had at the first intended but my confident our Fishery will shew that I am not wrong.
Novr. 11th.	I have this day a Keeper for Ballymony river.
Decr. 27th.	In Kilrea met D. McKinney and with him seized McCool's cott and another the owners fled, took 4 great spent keelogs which I have given to Kane and Crawford; at Cullycappel McKeeman has given me 2 choice netts, pd. him 2/2d. and a dram.

1793. Keepers on the River Bann.

1.	John Heyland from Sumerseat to the Loughin.	Pd.	2. 5. 6	
2.	Dan McConagle from the Loughan to Gills Boab	Pd.	2. 5. 6	
3.	John McCarter from the Mill down the Ree.	Pd.	2. 5. 6	
4.	James Dempsey for the Roochan and downwards.	Pd.	2. — —	
5.	Bryan Dempsey at Drumale and upwards.	Pd.	2. 5. 6	
6.	James Craford for Carncoe &c.	Pd.	2. 5. 6	
7.	Wm. Kane from Vow ferry to Moorlodge.	Pd.	2. 5. 6	
8.	Pat. McClern from Moorlodge to the Killens &c.	Pd.	2. 5. 6	
9.	John Dempsey for the Rod fishers about Portneill &c.	Pd.	2. 5. 6	
10.	Ned McCann at Portna ford &c. and to Gortreaghy,	Pd.	2. 5. 6	
11.	Dan McKinny at Monegran, Head Keeper.	Pd.	5. 13. 9	
			£28 3. 3	

1793. On Aughadowy River

12.	John McGraw, near Keely Green.	Pd.	1. 14. 1½	
13.	Fred McGraw for this and foot of Bovagh river.	Pd.	1. 14. 1½	
14.	Neill McAllen, (to be discharged)	Pd.	1. 14. 1½	
15.	Pat. Quinn, at Ballydavitt Green,	Pd.	1. 14. 1½	
16.	Wm. McFawl, at Mrs. Forrester's Green.	Pd.	1. 14. 1½	
17.	Alex. Thompson above the 2 Bridges at Ballinakelly	Pd.	1. 14. 1½	
18.	Dan. Garvin, at Shanlargy ford.	Pd.	1. 14. 1½	
19.	John Henry near Orr's Green (A Deceiver).		— — —	
			11. 18. 10½	

1793. On Bovagh River.

20.	Hugh McKeeman, at Cullycappel.	Pd.	1. 14. 1½	
21.	Ned Mullan, at Mr. A. Orr's new Green.	Pd.	1. 14. 1½	
22.	John McFetrish, at Innishdochill.	Pd.	1. 14. 1½	
			£5. 2. 4½	

1793. On McCasky River.

23.	Andrew McAlister, at Knockadoo.	Pd.	2. 5. 6	
24.	Ballymoney River, Henry Mullaghan.	Pd.	1. 14. 1½	
25.	Drumcroon Rivulet, Mr. Wilson's watchman.	Pd.	— 11. 4½	
	Carried forward		50. 1. 0	

Winter 1793.	Brought over		£50.	1.	0
On Garvagh River.					
26. Harry Mullan, Head Keeper,		Pd.	2.	5.	6
27. Mathew Wilson, at Ballinameen,		Pd.	1.	14.	1½
28. Robert Craig, for the Mill Carry.		Pd.	1.	14.	1½
29. Mark Moony,		Pd.	1.	14.	1½
30. Sam. Gilmore, at Mullinabrin.		Pd.	1.	14.	1½
31. Hugh Hill, above Wm. Orr's Green.		Pd.	2.	0.	0
32. Neil McWilkin, near Jas. Orr's Green & Ford.		Pd.	1.	14.	1½
			£12.	16.	1½
1793. On Glenullan.					
33. Paddy the Man,		Pd.	1.	14.	1½
34. and Bryan the man Mullan,		Pd.	1.	14.	1½
			£3.	8.	3
35. On Mettigan River, John McAllen.		Pd.	1.	14.	1½
1793. On Claudy River.					
36. Art. McCann at Swatragh Mill		Pd.	2.	5.	6
37. John Doorish,		Pd.	1.	10.	0
38. Dan Doorish, at Tirgarvill,		Pd.	1.	10.	0
39. Frank McShane at Upperlands Plaxmill.		Pd.	1.	10.	0
40. Pt. McLain, near Innishrush, off		—	—	—	—
41. James McLain, near Claudy .		Pd.	2.	5.	6
42. Barny McLain		Pd.	2.	5.	6
43. Neil Mulholland at Drumnacannon ford.		Pd.		11.	4½
			£11.	17.	10½
Nov. 1st. I observe 4 good fish on this ford.					
1793. On Coagh River.					
44. Mr. Robert Dunbar at Coagh		Pd.	6.	16.	6
45. Johnny Collum, near Ballinderry		Pd.	2.	5.	6
46. Ambrose Taylor, Salterstown.		Pd.	2.	5.	6
			£11.	7.	6
47. On Blackwater – Mr. Trotter.		Pd.	5.	13.	9
48. William Clarke		Pd.	1.	14.	1½
49. Arthur Hobson,	Benburb.	Pd.	1.	14.	1½
50. James Hughes,	do.	Pd.	1.	14.	1½
51. James Neill,	the Island.	Pd.	1.	14.	1½
			£12.	10.	3

Winter 1793.	Brought Fowd,		£103. 15. 1½

52.	On Moyola River, Pat. McLounan.	Pd.	2.	5.	6

1793. On Toome Wiers &c.

53.	Pat Neeson Junr.	Pd.	1.	14.	1½
54.	Barny Toal.	Pd.	1.	14.	1½
55.	Henry Gribbin – all sworn in.	Pd.	1.	14.	1½
			5.	2.	4½

1793. On River Main.

56.	Thomas Black of Randlestown.	Pd.	6.	5.	1½
57.	Tatty O'Neill, at the paper Hill	Pd.	3.	8.	3
58.	Hu. McCann, refuses to be attested.		—	—	—
59.	James Tork, at Ballindrade,	Pd.	2.	5.	6

I see T. Black has got 10 Bag Netts.   11. 18. 10½

60.	Kells River, Nathaniel Mathews.	Pd.	1.	14.	1½

61.	Ballymena River, Oliver Turner.	Pd.	1.	14.	1½

1793. On Gillgorm River.

62.	Thomas Mitchell	Pd.	1.	14.	1½
63.	William Anderson.	Pd.	1.	14.	1½

These men have 5 fine rods and one nett.   £3. 8. 3

To Keepers for this Season.   129. 18. 4½
    John Macky Inspector   Pd.   22. 15. 0

Whole amount besides powder and shott due Mr. Rice   £152 13. 4½

1794. May 13th. Got from Mr. Thomson   13. 13. 0
    17th May. Recd. from do.   6. 7. —
    20th May. Recd from L. Hamilton 2½ Guin.   2. 16. 10½

Recd. in full for my last winter's salary   22. 16. 10½

Aug. 20th. Mr. Thomson paid me   20. 0. 0
Septr. 2nd. L. Hamilton by Betty Holmes,   2. 16. 10½

My Salary as Clk. at the Cutts   £22. 16. 10½
Sent me 1 hund. salt salmon by my boy and
4 nice Do, for Smoaking and cash in paper 5 guins.

1794. Aug. 13th	This morng. we have cleard. off the remn. of last night's fish and on closing my abstract finds we have a profitable fishery this season, but at same time our Keepers List is very high altho' less by £74. than that of the year 1785, when L. Hamilton sent for me. I still think of reducing the wages of some of the Bann Keepers and to employ less men elsewhere.
Aug. 14th	At 2 o'clock walked up the Bann to Gowds Mill and replaced McCarter and went on to Drumale.
Aug. 15th	At Bovanagher agreed with J, McDaid and at Moorelodge fixed McClern and got them sworn in Kilrea, where I have replaced J. Dempsey for Portneill and went on to Monegran and replaced McKinny and Ned McCann at Portna. –
Aug. 16	on the Antrim, side calld. at the Vow and met W. Kane and Crawford who tell me they saw Drumale men fishing last night. Here I have wrote their information and Warts. and have sent them to prove their informations before Justice Graham. Coming homewd. I see the McCarrels have got a large new Cott above the Loughan which I must inquire into. – Jack Semple of the Loughan tells me quietly that McCarrells have got a new Nett. –
Aug. 24th	Rode to Kilrea and to Mr. Kings who tells me there is a large nett set across the Bann at Claudy river foot – At 6 o'clock he and McCann set out with me to Claudy river foot where we found a small cott by which we lifted the nett and in doing so we are seen by a fellow on the Antrim side who alarmed some houses whose inhabitants turned out and coming round by the Bridge at Portglenown we gaind. just time to get off the cott and nett and keeping at a proper distance from shore got happily escaping home to Portna.
1794. Sept. 13th.	Aprehended T (?) Dempsey on the street in Coleraine and taken by the Constable to Bovagh to be taken from thence to Derry by Richd. Millikin the Barony Constable, who being a blockhead took Dempsey to Mr. Heyland who being unacquainted in the Statutes set him at liberty on bail.
	At Glenkeen I have fixed with the Keepers for this winter.
Sept. 17	Met the Aughadow men and have got them all sworn into office.
Sept. 27	Went down McCasky river from the town of McCasky to the Collins Mill and see no fish, calld. on A. McAlister at Knockadoo and agreed with him and McCarter is to watch the foot of this river from his mill to the Bann.

Septr. 29	With my son watched at the Sandy Hills and saw the Doogans of Dunboe fishing the Bann.
Septr. 30th	With the Constable and the Loopers took a boat from the Cranagh down the river and seized this and Keightley and brought them to the Cranagh and broke them.
Octr. 13	Went up the Bann on foot and at Gowd's mill found McCarter sitting by the fireside muffled and says he got a severe beating last night. I do not believe him as I can see no marks of violence upon him. Calld. at Glenkeen and find there are fish in plenty all about Agivy river foot and in Bovagh river. Went forward to Bovagh and returned with H. McKeeman and in the night with Glenkeen men lifted 4 netts, in one we got 3 small fish alive but none in the others.
Octr. 14th	Returnd to the Cutts when L.H. paid these men 4/4 and a hearty glass.
Octr. 17th	Rode to Kilrea and from thence to Claudy Where I find there are some fish and agreed with the McLains and have appointed a third McLain for Claudy river foot. Returned to Kilrea.
Octr. 18th	Called at L. Hamiltons and dined there and recd. half a Guinea from her Ladyship and desired me to call at her house as I go up the country.
Octr. 27th	Called at L. Hamilton's and received a letter for Lord Wells at Thorn Hill and 5 Guineas in paper. Went to Garvagh and got the Keepers all attested, then to Glenullan and appointed the men Mullans to attend in Garvagh along with Jack McAllen of Mettigan to be attested.
Octr. 28th	At Swatragh appointed the Keepers and travelled down the river and at Drumnacannon assisted Mulholland and the Constable to levy a fine off the McLaughlins &c. Canted a horse for £5 paid me by a Trav. Henry. Paid the Constable 5/5d. and the remn. to Mulholland. Rode into Bellaughey.
	Went to Coagh and replaced the Keepers.
Octr. 30th	To Blackwater and got the old Keepers all sworn into office.
Octr. 31st	Returnd. to Coagh very unwell.
Novr. 1st	Rode down Coagh river to Ballinderry where Jno. Donnelly shewd. me 3 new netts he had lifted last night. – Went down to Salterstown I see no netts on the Bann – proceed to Manola and there agreed with Pat Walls in place of McLounan – stay all night in town and replacd. the old Keepers.

Novr. 3rd.	At Randlestown sent for old Black and 2 new Keepers and agreed with them.
Novr. 4th	Went to Kells and restored old Mathews – a great many fish in the river. Went to Ballymena and agreed with 2 new Keepers and got them attested, Mr. Adair being in town.
Novr. 5th	Came to Gillgorm and there fixed with the former Keepers, rode on to Rasharkin and slept there.
Novr. 6th.	Came home to Kilrea and dined there and from thence to Castleroe where I produced my List, and think if the Season suits as well forward we shall enjoy a good season's fishg.
Decr. 24th.	With McFetrish and McGraw lifted 3 netts near Agivy. Paid them 3/3d and half a pint at Ferry House, – a desperate cold night.

Waterkeepers for Winter 1794 and Spring 1795.
1794. On the River Bann.

1.	Jack Heyland, to the Loughin.		Pd.	2. 5. 6	
2.	Jack McCarter, I think cowardly.			– – –	
3.	Hugh Craford, At the Roouchan ford.		Pd.	1. 14. 1½	
4.	Bryan Dempsy, at Drumale,		Pd.	2. 5. 6	
5.	James Craford – a Gun.		Pd.	2. 5. 6	
6.	Wm. Kane – a gun.		Pd.	2. 5. 6	
7.	Jno. McDaid, a gun at Banagher;		Pd.	2. 5. 6	
8.	Pat. McClern, – a gun at Moorlodge,		Pd.	2. 5. 6	
9.	Jno. Dempsy, for Portneill,		Pd.	2. 5. 6	
10.	Ned McCann, Portna – all sworn.		Pd.	2. 5. 6	
11.	Dan McKinny, Monegran, Head Keeper		Pd.	5. 13. 9	

25. 11. 10½

1794. On Bovagh River.

12.	Hugh McKeeman,	Sworn in –	Pd.	1. 14. 1½
13.	Ned Mullan, – has misbehavd.	I stop 11/4½d	Pd.	1. 14. 1½
14.	John McFetrish,	Sworn in	Pd.	1. 14. 1½

£4. 11. 0

1794. On Aughadowry River.

15.	Alex. Thomson	Sworn in	Pd.	1. 14. 1½
16.	Manus Kane,	Sworn in McFawls Place	Pd.	1. 14. 1½
17.	Robt. Thompson,	Sworn	Pd.	1. 14. 1½
18.	Fred McGraw	Sworn in.	Pd.	1. 14. 1½
19.	Pat. Quinn.	at Ballydavit Green.	Pd.	1. 14. 1½

£8. 10. 7

20.	On McCasky River – Andrew McAlister, sworn.	Pd.	2. 5. 6
21	On Mettigan River – John McAllen.	Pd.	1. 14. 1½
22	On Ballymoney River – Henry Mulloughan.	Pd.	1. 14. 1½

Carried forward   £44. 7. 3

Winter 1794.   Brought over   £44. 7. 3

On Garvagh River.
23. Harry Mullan a Gun by L. Hamilton, Sworn.   pd.   2. 5. 6
24. Barny Mullin,   for the Mill carry   ,,   pd.   I. 14. I½
25. Mark Moony,   Sworn in.   pd.   I. 14. I½
26. Robert Craig, a gun.   Sworn in.   pd.   I. 14. I½
27. Hugh Hill at Monycarry,   sworn.   pd.   2. 0. 0
28. Neill McWilkin, at Gortonford, sworn.   pd.   I. 14. I½
                                                       _____
                                                       £II. 2. 0

1794. On Glenullar.
29. Paddy the man,   sworn.   pd.   I. 14. I½
30. and Bryan the man Mullan.   do.   pd.   I. 14. I½
                                                       _____
                                                       £3. 8. 3

1794. On Claudy River.
31. James McLain   sworn in.   pd.   2. 5. 6
32. Barny McLain   sworn in.   pd.   2. 5. 6
33. Frank McLain, on the river foot. sworn in.   pd.   I. 14. I½
34. Neill Mulholland Drumnacannon ford. sworn.   pd.   I. 2. 9
35. An. McCann, at Swatragh.   sworn in.   pd.   2. 5. 6
36. John Doorish, near do.   sworn in.   pd.   I. 10. 0
37. Dan Doorish, Tirgarvill,   sworn in.   pd.   I. 10. 0
38. Frank McShane, I see fish here   – sworn   pd.   I. 10. 0
                                                       _____
                                                       £14. 3. 4½

1794. On Coagh River.
39. Mr. Robert Dunbar,   Coagh   pd.   6. 16. 6
40. Hugh McAuly,   sworn in.   pd.   2. 5. 6
41. John Donnolly, Ballinderry,   sworn in.   pd.   2. 5. 6
                                                       _____
                                                       £II. 7. 6

1794. On the Blackwater.
42. Mr. James Trotter, Blackwater, Sworn   pd.   5. 13. 9
43. Arthur Hobson   Benburb.   sworn   pd.   I. 14. I½
44. James Hughes,   sworn in.   pd.   I. 14. I½
45. William Clarke,   sworn in.   pd.   I. 14. I½
46. James Neill, The Island.   sworn.   pd.   I. 14. I½
                                                       _____
                                                       £12. 10. 3

Winter 1794.		Brought Forwd.		£96.	18.	7
47.	On Moyola River, Pat Walls	Sworn in.	pd.	2.	5.	6

1794. On Toon Weirs etc.

48.	Pat Neeson Junr. Creagh,	sworn in	pd.	1.	14.	1½
49.	Barny Toal, Toom	sworn.	Pd.	1.	14.	1½
50.	Harry Gribbin, Upper Creagh,	Sworn in.	pd.	1.	14.	1½
				£5.	2.	4½

1794. On the river Main.

51.	Mr. Thomas Black, Randlestown		pd.	6.	5.	1½
52.	Clottworthy O'Neill, at the paper mill		pd.	3.	8.	3
53.	Thomas Moffet, near Aughabuoy.		pd.	2.	5.	6
54.	John Bates, of Ballygrooby all sworn.		pd.	2.	5.	6
	Fish in plenty here,			£14.	4.	4½
55.	Kells River Nath. Mathews,	sworn.	pd.	1.	14.	1½

1794. On Ballymena river.

56.	John McMullan, Paper Mill entry.	sworn.	pd.	1.	14.	1½
57.	Barny Gorman, near Do.	sworn in.	pd.	1.	14.	1½
				£3.	8.	3

1794. On Gillgorm River.

58.	Thomas Mitchell,	sworn in.	pd.	1.	14.	1½
59.	William Armstrong,	sworn.	pd.	1.	14.	1½
				£3.	8.	3
60.	Drumcroon Bleachgreen the Watchman.		pd.		11.	4½
61.	Bovagh Gardens Mayochill river Hu. McClern.		pd.		11.	4½
	John Macky, Inspector.		pd.	22.	15.	–
	Amount of the rivers this year			£150.	19.	3

1795. Aug 27. Mrs. Thomson has pd. me 15 gns.		£17.	1.	3
Aug. 30. Recd. from Mrs. Thomson more		2.	18.	9
On Sunday from Lady Hamilton, 2½ gns.		2.	16.	10½
For my last summer's salary		£22.	16.	10½

Her line to Mrs. Thomson for my allowance of salt fish on hand and bids me
come see her tomorrow for her own present.

1795. August 13th	I have this morng. got clear of all our last night fish and I find my Abstract counts agreeable to my expectations and I see we are yearly and every year getting better since I came to this place, and as my present Benefactress behaves so friendly I think it is my duty to reward her by my best endeavours, and will therefore march up the river by 12 o'clock this night.
	By 12. walked up the Bann and can spy nothing – by daylight have got to Portneill where I have met with the first pair of Cotts – Went on to McKinnys and finds he is dead. I breakfast with his widow. Crossed the river to Portna and agreed with McCann who came with me to Moor Lodge where I see all the Cotts which he had let to the fishers for the season. I asked Mr. Warren what he intended to do with them and he told me he would let them to the first persons who should apply for them. With all my heart Sir, said I and damn the first who rues such ungentlemanlike treatment, and so left him and on my way to the Vow met Pat. McCoy gone of Mr. Moors old Loopers whom I engaged in place of McKinny, and think he may do as well and perhaps better. Slept at the Vow –
August 15th	Crossed the Bann to Bovanagher and with Kane and Craford found the Jamisons Cotts in suspicious manner daubed with fresh scales and blood, whereupon we seized them and took them to the Vow till in the evening old Jamison came to me and begged I would go with him and his son to Kilrea where we instantly went and there were sworn by Mr. Grames never to offend during L.H's. incumbency.
Aug. 16	This day I have got all appointed for the Bann and this night to Ballymoney and appointed Hu. Mullaghan.
17th	Came to the Cross ferry and passed over to Glenkeen where meeting with F. McGraw returned to the foot of Agivy river and there took up Mr. Leeses nett, which we brought to the Cutts and there pd. McGraw 2/8½d.
1795. Aug. 31	Very heavy rains and I see we shall have a flood in the small rivers. –
Sept. 3	Went up the Bann to Kilrea and in the eveng. returned to Cullycappel and with McKeenan stopped at Glenkeen and at 12 in the night with McKeeman, McGraw and Thompson seized 3 netts set in the river between Brick Hills and the old Church Agivy.
Septr. 4th	This day I have made out all appointments for this river of Agivy, Aughadowy and McCasky and now I go home.
Septr. 9th	Rode up Antrim side of the Bann to Cross ferry and then pass over to Agivy where I see a nett set –went to Fred McGraw and Jas. Kane

who I find have got 5 netts, and with these 2 men lifted this fine nett which we have brought with the others to L. Hamilton who paid them 6/6d. and a hearty dinner and drink.

Sept. 17th   This night being lying at the Sandy Hills I see a Boat fishing at the black Point and 6 men on Dunboe shore, they have taken some fish and I see them now carry their boat away into the country; this is damned hard.

Septr. 18th   Went to L. Hamilton and told her and requests her to give me cash to employ men to assist me in searching for and seizing this boat, but she refuses the money bidding me go get the Constable and Loopers so that I plainly see she must suffer this and much more.

Septr. 22   Heavy rains all day –

23rd   At Aughadowy with James Kane and McGraw this night have taken 2 netts off the river foot.

24th   At Orr's ford I have got a nett drying at Mr. Henry's house.

Octr. 7th   I see some fish in Purgatory near John Carrs the water very high.

18th   These continued rains must certainly carry our fish far up the rivers and therefore I go to Garvagh tomorrow.

Octr. 20th   Called with L.H. who bids me wait for a few days till Mr. Thomson comes to her that she may consult him upon the Dunboe fishers and I have told her she is too late and that the boatfishing is over for this season. She bids me go home and call to-morrow.

1795. Oct. 21   Called with L.H. who gave me 43/4d. and a glass of wine. She orders me to make all the haste I can on my way and to call at her house on my return. 12 o'c. Set out for Garvagh which I reached in good time and met all the Keepers at Market and have got them all appointed and Harry Mullan got them all sworn into office to-morrow, at 8 o'clock for Swatragh with John Doorish.

Octr. 22nd   Fixed all men for this place and by 1 o'clock at Claudy have appointed all here and rode into Bellaghy.

23rd   At Coagh I have made out the appointments and Mr. Dunbar will have his men sworn into office before my return.

Octr. 24   Went to Blackwater Town and from thence to Benburb, met the Keepers and this eveng. have got them all sworn in Moy where I slept this night and am told there are vast numbers of fish in Blackwater already.

Octr. 25	I returnd. to Coagh and slept at Mr. Dunbars.
26th	To Ballinderry, Salterstown and Moyola river foot where I have fixed P. Walls, rode on to Toom and appointed 2 men for this year.
Octr. 27th	At Randlestown have agreed with 4 men and discharged old Mr. Black as unserviceable, got these all sworn into office and rode on to Kells Town where I stay all night and sent for old Mathews to whom I have given a hearty draught of whiskey while he relates all his exploits in the late German Wars.
Octr. 28th	To Ballymena and got the Keepers appointed and Sworn into office by Mr. Adair the Seneschal, and then forward to Gillgorm where I have fixed a new keeper with Mitchell.
	Came to Rasharkin and the Vow where I find Kane and Craford with a Cott seized at John Coulters and with them crossed the Bann and set homeward and they follow with the Cott on the river.
	In 2½ hours they have reached the Cutts and L. Hamilton has paid them 11/4½d. and some strong Rum punch and to me 45/6d.
Novr. 27	Went to Bovagh and in the night with the Keepers took 3 fine new netts, they came home with me and got 3/3d. from L.H.

Waterkeepers for winter 1795 and Spring '96.

On the River Bann:

1.	John Heyland Castleroe.	Sworn.	pd.	2.	5.	6
2.	Robert McCarrell, Carnes –	Sworn	pd.	2.	5.	6
3.	Pat Dempsy, Drumale,	Sworn	pd.	2.	5.	6
4.	James Craford, a gun, Newbuildings, Sn.		pd.	2.	5.	6
5.	William – a gun, at Vowferry,	Swn.	pd.	2.	5.	6
6.	John McDaid, a Gun, at Bovanagher, Swn.		pd.	2.	5.	6
7.	John Dempsy, Portneill,	sworn.	pd.	2.	5.	6
8.	Ned McCann, Portna,	sworn.	pd.	2.	5.	6
9.	Daniel McKinney, Monegran –	dead,		~~5.~~	~~13.~~	~~9~~
10.	Pat McCoy, near Portna –	sworn.	pd.	2.	5.	6

£20.	9.	6

1795. On Aughadowy River.

11.	Fred McGraw a Gun,	sworn in.	pd.	2.	5	6
12.	James Kane	sworn in.	pd.	2.	5.	6
13.	Robt. Thomson a gun Sworn	these keep the Ban also.	pd.	2.	5.	6
14.	Joseph Wright	sworn in	pd.	2.	5	6
15.	Alex. Thompson,	sworn in	pd.	1.	14.	1½
16.	John McFetrish,	sworn in	pd.	1.	14.	1½

Fish in great numbers here 13 Novr.   £12. 10. 3

1795. On Bovagh & Mayochill.

17.	Neill McWilkin, near Jas. Orr's ford. Swn.	pd.	1.	14.	1½
18.	Hugh McKeeman, at New Green, sworn.	pd.	1.	14.	1½
19.	Hugh McClern, at Bovagh Gardens do.			11.	4½

£3.	19	7½

A number of fish here Novr. 17th.

Carried forward   £36. 19. 4½

Winter 1795.	Brought forward		£36. 19. 4½	

McCasky River.   Burnd over and over.

20. Andrw. McAlister – found him twice off duty, x   ~~2. 5. 6~~

21. Drumcroon Rivulet – Hunter,   pd.   11. 4½

22. Ballymoney river – Henry Mullaghan, sworn   pd.   1. 14. 1½

23. Mettigan River – John McAllin,   sworn.   pd.   1. 14. 1½

1795. On Garvagh River.
24. Harry Mullan, first keeper, sworn   pd.   2. 5. 6
25. Mark Moony,   sworn   pd.   1. 14. 1½
26. Robert Craig,   do.   pd.   1. 14. 1½
27. Barny Mullan,   do.   pd.   1. 14. 1½
28. Hugh Hill, at Monycarry,   pd.   2. 0. 0

     Oct. 21. I see 2 fish at the Carry.   £ 9. 7. 10½

1795. On Glenullar.
29. Paddy the man,   Sworn   pd.   1. 14. 1½
30. And Bryan the man Mullan, sworn.   pd.   1. 14. 1½

                                                           £3. 8. 3

1795. On Claudy River.
31. James McLaine,   sworn into office   pd.   2. 5. 6
32. Barny McLain,   do.   pd.   2. 5. 6
35. Frank McLain,   do.   pd.   1. 14. 1½
34. An. McCarn,   do.   pd.   2. 5. 6
35. John Doorish,   do.   pd.   1. 10. 0
36   Dan. Doorish   do .   pd.   1. 10. –
37. Frank McShane,   do.   pd.   1. 10. –
38. Neill Molholland   Drumnacannon ford.   pd.   1. 2. 9

                                                           £14. 3. 4½

                      Carried forwd.   £67. 18. 6

Winter 1795.

		Brought forward		£67.	18.	6

On Coagh River.

39.	Mr. Dunbar,	first Keeper	pd.	6.	16.	6
40.	Hugh Mallon,	Sworn.	pd.	2.	5.	6
41.	Ambrose Taylor,	Sworn.	pd.	2.	5.	6
				£11.	7.	6

1795. On the Black Water.

42.	Mr. Trotter, left the Country.		x	~~5.~~	~~13.~~	~~9~~
43.	Arthur Hobson, first Keeper,	sworn	pd.	5.	13.	9
44.	John Hobson,	sworn	pd.	1.	14.	1½
45.	James Hughes, a steady Keeper,	sworn	pd.	1.	14.	1½
46.	Eneas Quinn,	sworn in.	pd.	1.	14.	1½
				£10.	16.	1½

47.	On Moyola and the Lough Pat Walls.		pd.	2.	5.	6

1795. On Toom Wiers etc.

48.	Ned McGee, at Toom,	Sworn.	pd.	1.	14.	1½
49.	John Campbell, at Brackare,	do.	pd.	1.	14.	1½
				£3.	8.	3

1795. On the River Main.

50.	Mr. Thomas Black,	Superseded,	x	~~6.~~	~~5.~~	~~1½~~
51.	Tatty O'Neill Junr –	his father dead.	pd.	2.	5.	6
52.	Frank O'Neill,	sworn.	pd.	1.	14.	1½
53.	John Bates,	sworn.	pd.	2.	5.	6
54.	Pat Coshnaghan – don't look well,	sworn.	pd.	2.	5.	6
				£8.	10.	7½

55.	On Kells river – Nath. Mathews,		pd.	1.	14.	1½

1795. On Ballymena River.

56.	John McMullan,	sworn in	pd.	1.	14.	1½
57.	Barny Gorman,	do.	pd.	1.	14.	1½
				3.	8.	3

		Carried forward,		£109.	8.	10½

Winter 1795.	Brought forward			£109.	8.	10½

On Gillgorm River.

58.	Thomas Mitchell,	sworn	pd.	£1.	14.	1½
59.	John McElmon,	sworn	pd.	£1.	14.	1½

				3.	8.	3
John Macky Inspector		pd.	£22.	15.	–

Amount of this season.			£135.	12.	1½

1796. April 10th. Recd. from Mr. Thomson,	8.	10.	7½
May 13th, Recd. from do. 10 Guin & change,	11.	9.	4½
May 22nd. By Lady Hamilton, 2½ Guin.	2.	16.	10½

In full for last Winter's Salary –	22.	16.	10½

2nd July, Mr. Thomson gave me 6 Guins.	6.	16.	6
August 20th. Recd. from do.	13.	3.	6
22. Lady Hamilton by Jamy. Gray,	2.	16.	10½

My Salary at the Cutts – –	£22.	16.	10½

Recd. her note by Gray to Mr. Thomson for my salt fish and 3 larger for smoking.

Augt. 27. Mr. Thomson has paid me Turff	£1.	16.	6
For Paper on the rivers,			10½

Sept. 1st. Waited on L. Hamilton who presented to me
5 Guins. which she says will mend my wages.

| 1796. Aug. 13th | I have this day made out my Abstract of Sales at the Cutt Fishery which keeps increasing – I have left all my acts. with L. Hamilton, who orders me to go up the river tomorrow morning. |

1796. Aug. 13th   I have this day made out my Abstract of Sales at the Cutt Fishery which keeps increasing – I have left all my acts. with L. Hamilton, who orders me to go up the river tomorrow morning.

This night went down the river with Harry Mullan and others and seized Wm. Knox's boats which we brought and broke at the Cranagh –

Aug 14   Went up the Bann on Derry side the river and appointed 5 Keepers on my way and slept in Kilrea,

15   Went to Portna and got all the Eel Cotts secured by Ned McCann, went up to Portglenown and see nothing there, agreed with 2 of the McLains at Claudy and return to Portna.

16th   In my way to the Vow met McGarril the Bailiff and took his name in my List as a Good Spy who takes me with Kane and Craford to the Pattons Gardens and there seized a new Nett. McGarril says the Cotts are sunk. He then took me to Glenstall where we seized the Millers Cochell and a rare good one. I have appointed 4 men on the Antrim side and think it will do. On my way homeward I see nothing amiss.

Septr. 2nd   Wm. Kane came to my house and tells me he last night saw a pair of Cotts fishing and saw them landing into Jno. Coulters at Vow ferry, and that he knows 2 of the fishers. I then set out with him to Colerain where he proved his information before the Mayor who appointed me special Constable and by daylight the 3rd Sept. we seized the cott at Coulters door and the other being sunk we returned with one cott to L.H. who paid Kane 11 / 4½. and a stout drink of rum.

Septr. 5th.   This night I see a boat fishing under Barnbrook and it may fish there till Christmas as L.H. will allow me no assistance.

Octr. 4th.   Very heavy rains. Went to McCasky and down all the river can get no man in charge and I plainly perceive they are all in combination and a sett of damnd Villians – returned home – wet to the skin – .

1796. Octr. 8.   Went to Garvagh and appointed all the men for this river and for Mettigan and Glenullar I can't get a nab to engage upon either they say they are threatened but will not say by whom they are threatened, and so I see our fish are to be destroyed this season, Good Heaven what shall my employer do – marched down the river all the way to Bovagh and met McWilkin who tells me he can get no person willing to assist him in any shape. What is the meaning of this – Slept at Millekins in Bovagh.

Octr. 9th	Calld. on Hu. McKeeman and McGraw who have 5 new netts lifted off their river last night. I gave them 5/5d. and a 6½ to drink and carryd. the netts on my horse to the Cutts.
Octr. 12th	All night at the Sandy Hills and see 2 boats fishing by day light they have landed them at Finlays and taken them by Cars up into the country. I also see 3 men with guns on their shoulders What can I do – I find no assistance I am sick, wet and wearied for nothing. –

At the Cutts waited on L. Hamilton who presented me with a dram and 26/3, rode on to Garvagh and find fish in plenty there – rode on to Swatragh and slept there and the Keepers tell me there are some fish at Upperland. |
Octr. 30th	Went to Coagh and in the night went with Mr. Dunbar to Mulholands beyond Tamlaght Church and seized 2 Loops.
31	Went to Benburb and fixed all our Keepers as usual, and passing the Chappel at Killyman on Sunday I see 3,000 persons assembled there and am told by my Landlord Burrows of Killyman that these people are Defenders; I have passed by different crowds of them who take no notice of me.
Nov. 1st	Returned to Coagh and appointed those people.
Nov. 2nd	Down the river I see nothing, rode on to the waterfoot of Moyola and replaced Walls and went on to Toom and there met McGee and Campbell and
Nov. 3rd	Got a Constable and went with these men to Drumremond where we got a cow belonging to Harry McLain which the neighbours endeavoured to rescue. Mr. Jones appearing in view our quarrel ceased and the McLains agree to follow me with what ready money they can raise among their partners, at 3 o'clock brought me £2.16.10½ and swear against setting a nett for L. Hamilton's incumbency, gave the Constable 2/8½ and £2. 14. 2 to McGee and Campbell.
Nov. 4th	Went to Randlestown and have mended Bates wages. He has 13 bag netts taken off the river already – got him and 2 others attested.
Novr. 5th	To Kells and agreed with Mathews and R. Shaw who go with me to Ballymena and on meeting the Magistrate Shaw refuses to be sworn – at 6 o'clock met with Jno. McMullan and Gorman both drunk from Brughshane market. Took horse and rode to Gillgorm.
Novr. 6	McMullan and partner came early and I have given them appointments, but I fear they are not for my purpose, at 5 o'clock I have got home to my house very sick.

Novr. 20th	Went to Aughadowy and in the night with McKeeman McGraw and Thomson seized 4 netts near the old Church and the waterfoot got a very large new nett worth a guinea. Paid them 6/6 and a bottle of whisky in Mr. Leeses, where I have wrung and dried my shirt and cloaths. –
Decr. 30th	This night on Bovagh &c. with 2 Keepers have got 2 charming new netts and a dead Keelog which I give to McKeeman's wife, pd. them 2/2 and ½ a pint of whisky.
1797. Jany. 22nd.	Went up the Antrim side of the Bann to Kilrea, a great run of Keelogs and fine weather, came home by Aughadowy and I have got 2 fine netts from McFetrish, paid him 2/2d. he says the Keelogs are mostly left his river.

Waterkeepers for Winter 1796 and Spring '97.

1796. On the River Bann,

1.	John Heyland,	Castleroe.	pd.	2.	5.	6
2.	Robert McCarrie,	at Cames,	pd.	2.	5.	6
3.	John Cashidy	a gun at Tully.	pd.	2.	5.	6
4.	John McDaid	a gun at Bovanagher.	pd.	2.	5.	6
5.	John Dempsy	at Portneill.	pd.	2.	5.	6
6.	Edward McCann	at Portna	pd.	2.	5.	6
7.	Wm. Kane	a gun at the Vow.	pd.	2.	5.	6
8.	James Craford,	a gun N. buildings.	pd.	2.	5.	6
9.	John McGarrel	at the Roochin.	pd.	2.	5.	6

£20. 9. 6

a great shew of fish.

1796. On Aughadowy River.

10.	Fred McGraw	Glenkeen. sworn	pd.	2.	5.	6
11.	Hugh McKeeman	this river & the Bann.	pd.	2.	5.	6
12.	Robt. Thompson	sworn.	pd.	2.	5.	6
13.	John McFetrish,	Innishdochill.	pd.	1.	14.	1½

8. 10. 7½

1796. On Bovagh River.

14.	Neill McWilkin,	sworn in	pd.	1.	14.	1½

No person hereabout but disaffected.

1796. McCasky River, none here will take it in charge.

15.   1796. On Drumcroon rivulet Hunter the watchman.   11. 4½

1796. Mettigan River, no person to accept of this place.

Carried forward   £31. 5. 7½

Winter 1796.		Brought forward		£31.	5.	7½

On Garvagh River.

16.	Harry Mullan – Headkeeper,	sworn.	pd.	2.	5.	6
17.	Robert Craig most active on this river,		pd.	2.	0.	0
18.	Hu Hill, dead –	his son sworn in.	pd.	2.	5.	–
19.	Mark Moony,	sworn in	pd.	1.	14.	1½
20.	Barny Mullan,	the Mill .	pd.	1.	14.	1½

			£9.	13.	9

Fish plenty here.

Glenullar river, no man here will venture in charge.

1796. On Claudy River.

21.	James McLain,	sworn in	Pd.	2.	5.	6
22.	Barny McLain,	sworn	pd.	2.	5.	6
23.	Au. McCann,	sworn	pd.	2.	5.	6
24.	Daniel Doorish,	sworn	pd.	1.	10.	0
25.	John Doorish,	sworn	pd.	1.	10.	0
26.	Frank McShane,	sworn	pd.	1.	10.	0
27.	Neill Mulholland,	sworn	pd.	1.	2.	9

Store of fish here.   £12. 9. 3

1796. On Coagh River

28.	Mr. Dunbar.	first keeper	pd.	6.	16.	6
29.	James Wilkison,	sworn in	pd.	2.	5.	6
30.	Ambrose Taylor	sworn in	pd.	2.	5.	6

Vast number of fish at the Carry.   £11. 7. 6

1796. On the Black Water:

31.	Arthur Hobson,	first Keeper sworn	pd.	5.	13.	9
32.	John Hobson	sworn in	pd.	1.	14.	1½
35.	James Hughes,	sworn.	pd.	1.	14.	1½
34.	Mr. Jacksons Watchman Tullydowy	sworn	pd.	1.	14.	1½

A number of fish already here.   £10. 16. 1½

          Carried forward   £75. 12. 3

Winter 1796.   Brought forwd.   £75. 12. 3

35.   Moyola river and the Lough Pat Walls.   pd.   2. 5. 6

36.   On Toom Wiers &c. Jno Campbell,   pd.   1. 14. 1½
37.   Ned Magee, both sworn in.   pd.   1. 14. 1½

                                                                       ─────────────
                                                                       £3. 8. 3

1796. On the Main River.
38.   John Bates, worthy of advancement. sworn.   pd.   £2. 16. 10½
39.   William McCormick,   sworn.   pd.   2. 5. 6
40.   James Shales   sworn.   pd.   2. 5. 6

                                                                       ─────────────
                                                                       £7. 7. 10½

41.   On Kells river, Nath. Mathews, Shaw off.   pd.   1. 14. 1½

1796. On Ballymena river.
42.   John McMullan – I don't like him.   Swn.   pd.   1. 14. 1½
43.   Barny Gorman,   the best of them – sworn.   pd.   1. 14. 1½

                                                                       ─────────────
                                                                       £3. 8. 3

1796. On Gillgorm River.
44.   Thomas Mitchell,   sworn.   pd.   1. 14. 1½
45.   Jack McElmon.   sworn.   pd.   1. 14. 1½

                                                                       ─────────────
                                                                       £3. 8. 3

46.   On Ballymony River, Henry Mullaghan.   pd.   1. 14. 1½

                                                                       ─────────────

      Amount to Keepers besides Powder & Shott.   98. 18. 7½
      John Macky, Inspectr.   22. 15.   –

                                                                       ─────────────
      Amt. for Winter 1796.   £121. 13. 7½

1797. May 15th. Mrs. Thompson has paid me   £20. 0. 0
        16th. L.H. By Betty Holmes,   1. 2. 9
      June 1st. Lady Hamilton this morng.   2. 16. 10½

                                                  ─────────────
      In full of last Winter's salt,   £23. 19. 7½
      She has paid me last winter's paper … 8 pence.
      Sent me 2 Guins. to buy a new great coat.

1797. Aug. 18. Mr. Thomson has brought to me from			
Lady Hamilton 2.Guins. and change 9/6d.	2.	15.	0
Presents me with a Guinea from her L'ship.	1.	2.	9
He pays me now 15 Guins. in part —	17.	1.	3
Bids me call on Mondy first for my fish & remn,	2.	18.	9
My Summer's salary —	£23.	17.	9
Aug. 22. Settled the above and paid me turf bill —	£1.	16.	6

Aug. 24th.
1797.

On looking thro my papers this day I cound 23 Warrts. obtained at sundry times against Dunboe men since summer 1794 and find I am to get no manner of assistance to levy their fines or in any manner to suppress such daring ruffians – The Civil power in Colerain are getting very shy in action and I cannot I don't well understand whether they are piqued at L. Hamilton or lazie to interfere with these Shakers at Dunboe. I have got sundry threatnings by anonimous letters dated from Dunboe and left at my door in the night. – Upon an order from the War Office address'd to Col. Warburton – Went with the Mayor of Colerain to Col. Warburton and applied for his assistance to detect this armed and rebelly crew assembled every night on the Bann shores and robbing a lonely widow of her property in particular and to the general and public loss; he says he is not impowered to meddle with them until they first shoot and kill some of us – In His kitchen I see fresh salmon roasting this moment on the Brander and more lying on the table. Perdition surely awaits this old lowlif'd Traitor.

1797.
Aug. 13th.

On making up my acts. this day I see we have a grant Abstract notwithstanding the great defficiency of Keepers last winter.

Aug. 14

went up the Derry side of the Bann and appointed 5 Keepers, slept at Kilrea.

Aug. 15

Crossd to the Antrim side and there agreed with 5 Keepers and have got them all sworn into office. Moony of Gortreaghy to be chief about Portna &c. and Jno McDaid of Dreen is to get the 2d load of salmon, Jack Shannon the first Load and 2 Guins. Returning homeward I crossed the Bann and have appointed Keepers for Aughadowy river and the Bann but can get none for Bovagh river but McWilkin who is a man not to my mind.

Aug. 16.

The Loughan men have brought their cotts and lodged them with me in the Cutt House.

Aug. 25 & 26

up the Bann in search of fishing cotts but found none.

Sept. 10	Went to Kilray and got Jno. Dempsy's information proven and Mr. Heylands Warrt against the Elder Cott at Portneill.
Sept 11th	Seizd this cott and brought it to the Cutts and paid Dempsy 11/4½.
Octr. 7th	With an Officers Guard, went up the Bann as far as Carnroe and in our passage seized 4 pair of Cotts which we brought to the Cutts and I have given two of them to Col. Foster to make a doghouse. Paid his 2 Sergts. 6/6. Corporals 4/4 and to 20 privates I have paid 21/- together some bread and beer. Col. Forster is very civil but will give us no assistance to levy the fines off these robbers in Dunboe.
Octr. 15th	heavy rain
Octr. 16	Went to Aughadowy and from thence to Bovagh and met McKeeman and at Bed time set out and on our way to the Waterfoot lifted 3 excellent netts, Met McGraw and Thomson and have given them all a quart of spirits in McLeeses – and 3/3d. for the netts which I have sent to the Cutts. –
Octr. 27	Went to McCasky river but no person will take it in charge, they laugh at me and ask me are you up –
1797. Nov. 2	Calld. at L.Hamiltons, she gave me a glass of rum and one guinea. Went to Garvagh and appointed Keepers but can get no keeper for Glenullar or Mettigan Rivers – Mr. Allen swears he dare not venture out of doors at nights.
Nov. 3	At Swatragh appointed as in the following list – Went down the river to Claudy, fixed the keepers and get to Bellaghy –
Nov. 4	Went to Coagh, wrote appointments and Mr. Dunbar will have his men attested by my return here.
Novr. 5	Went to Blackwater Town and to Benburb.
Novr. 6th	Returned to the Moy and got them attested and reached Coagh by sunset.
Novr. 7	Went down the river and the Lough to Manda and appointed Walls who goes with me to Toom and on to Monyglass where I have got him sworn into office with Toom Keepers.
Novr. 8	Went to Randlestown and replaced the 3 former keepers and have got them attested by Mr. Lang –
Novr. 9	Rode to Kells town and met old Mathews who swears he fears no man whether up or down – went to Ballymena and from thence to Gillgorm, where these men appointed to follow me –

This night I have made out all their appointments for Broughshane to be there sworn into office by Mr. Lang who returns home tonight.

Novr. 10th   This morng. I have walked to Cullybacky and see a number of fish but no man here will take them in charge. I really imagine the people of this country are all disaffected, they are at present very rude and uncivil.

Decr. 18th   McGraw, McKeeman &c. have brought me 6 netts, paid them 6/6d. and their breakfast at my house.

27th   Kane and Craford have this day found a hidden cott and brought to the Cutts for which they have got 11/4½ with their dinner and some stout spirits.

Decr. 30th   Aughadowy men brought me 13 new netts, paid them 14/1d.

Waterkeepers for Winter 1797 and Spring '98.

On the River Bann

1.	John Heyland,	at Castleroe.	pd.	2. 5. 6
2.	Jno. Shannon 1st load of Salmon and		pd.	2. 5. 6
3.	John McAlister, at Mullan,	sworn.	pd.	2. 5. 6
4.	John Bradley, a Gun, near Bovanagher do.		pd.	2. 5. 6
5.	John Dempsy, for Portneill,	sworn.	pd.	2. 5. 6
6.	On Antrim side John Boyd a gun near Crossferry do.		pd.	2. 5. 6
7.	do. Willm. Kane, a Gun, at the Vow		pd.	2. 5. 6
8.	On do. Jas. Craford, a Gun, n. Buildings.		pd.	2. 5. 6
9.	On do. side, Jno. McDaid, a Gun, 2nd load of fish – sworn.		–	– – –
10.	On do. side. Pat. Mooney, as Superientd. on the Bann,		pd.	5. 13. 9

£23. 17. 9

1797. On Aughadowy River and the Bann.

11.	Fred. McGraw Decr. 11th. got McDaid's Gun Swn.		pd.	2. 5. 6
12.	Hu. McKeeman,	do.		2. 5. 6
13.	Robt. Thompson,	do.		2. 5. 6
14.	John McFetrish,	sworn.		1. 14. 1½

£8. 10. 7½

Decr. 9th. I see fine store of fish here this day.

1797. Bovagh River.

15.	Neill McWilkin near Jas. Orr's ford. Swn.		pd.	1. 14. 1½

Decr. 9th. I see some fish roods near this place.

McCasky River Waste (Combined crew all up this river).

16.	On Drumcroon river – Mr. Wilsons watchman,		pd.	– 11. 4½

1797. Mettigan river waste, all Villains in League here.

1797. Glenullar, no Keepers – Damnation to them altogether.

Carried forward   £34. 13. 10½

Brought Forward £34. 13. 10½

On Garvagh River.

17.	Harry Mullan, – first keeper,	sworn.	pd.	2.	5.	6
18.	Robert Craig 2nd Keeper,	sworn.	pd.	2.	0.	0
19.	Mark Moony,	sworn.	pd.	1.	14.	1½
20.	Barny Mullan,	sworn.	pd.	1.	14.	1½
21.	Arthur Henry, in H. Hill's place,	sworn.	pd.	1.	14.	1½

£9. 7. 10½

Decr. 18th. I see several roods on this river finished.

1797. On Claudy River.

22.	James McLain.	Sworn in.	pd.	2.	5.	6
23.	Barny McLain.	Sworn.	pd.	2.	5.	6
24.	An. McCann.	sworn.	pd.	2.	5.	6
25.	Jack Doorish.	sworn.	pd.	1.	10.	–
26.	Dan. Doorish.	sworn.	pd.	1.	10.	–
27.	Frank McShane.	sworn.	pd.	1.	10.	–
28.	Neill Mulholland, Drumnacannon ford, Swn		pd.	1.	2.	9

12. 9. 3

Decr. 19th. See some roods finished near Innisrush

1797. On Coagh River.

29.	Wm. Dunbar,	at Coagh.	pd.	6.	16.	6
30.	James Wilkison,	near Ballinderry.	pd.	2.	5.	6
31.	Amby. Taylor, Waterfoot,	both sworn.	pd.	2.	5.	6

£11. 7. 6

Novr. 4th. I see some fish at the Mill Carry.

Carried over, £67. 18. 6

1797.	Brought forward.		£67.	18.	6

On the Blackwater

32.	Arthur Hobson, talks disaffectedly,	sworn.	pd.	5.	13.	9
33.	John Hobson, do.	sworn.	pd.	1.	14.	1½
34.	James Hughes, appears honest,	sworn.	pd.	1.	14.	1½
35.	Wm. Jacksons Watchman, Quinn, a queer fellow.		pd.	1.	14.	1½

			£10.	16.	1½

Novr. 5th. I see some fish near Tully Doway Green.

36.	On Moyola river, Pat Walls,	sworn.	pd.	2.	5.	6

1797. On Toom Wiers &c.

37.	Ned Magee at Toom,	sworn.	pd.	1.	14.	1½
38.	John Campbell, at Brackare,	sworn.	pd.	1.	14.	1½

			£3.	8.	3

Novr. 7th. Seized 2 fine netts on Toom Barr.

1797. On the River Main.

39.	John Bates, has taken 8 netts already this year.		pd.	3.	0.	0
40.	James McCormick, 5 do.	sworn.	pd.	2.	5.	6
41.	James Shales, 2 long netts.	sworn.	pd.	2.	5.	6

			£7.	11.	0

Novr. 9th. Refus'd admittance to view Lord Neills Pound.

1797. On Kells river.

42.	Nathaniel Matthews –	sworn.	pd.	1.	14.	1½

Novr. 9th. Matthews shews me a number of fish here.

	Carried forward		£93.	13.	6

Winter 1797.	Brought Fowd.	£93.	13.	6
43. Ballymena, John McMullan,	sworn.	I.	I4.	1½
44. do. Barny Gorman,	sworn.	I.	I4.	1½
		£3.	8.	3

Say they have seen but 5 salmon yet.

1797. On Gillgorm river.				
45. Thomas Mitchel,	sworn.	I.	I4.	1½
46. John McElmon,	sworn.	I.	I4.	1½
		£3.	8.	3

Novr. 10. I see a number of fish at Cullybacky.

47. Ballymoney river, Henry Mullaghan, sworn.		I.	I4.	1½
Jno. Macky, Inspector in the rivers,	sallary	22.	15.	0
Amt. to Keepers this season, Amunition &c.		124.	19.	1½

1798. April 9th.

This day Lady Hamilton did by her Agent Mr. John Thomson deliver up unto Sir George Fitzgerald Hill Bart. and John Claudius Beresford Esqr. all and whole the possession of the Salmon Leap and Cutts Fishery, and all the Cutts and Cribbs thereon together with all the ground and commonage appertaining thereto with the cabbins or office houses thereon. And the said Jno. Thompson did at same time deliver into the hands of Rowley Heyland Esq. as Atty. for the above Gentleman, the keys of the Cutts, Gate and Fish House and everything therein and the whole was accepted by said Mr. Heyland for the sole use and behoof of the above named gentlemen in as ample manr. as the same was held and enjoyd. hitherto and as the whole lies enclosed by the present Stone and Lime walls compassing the same. Witness present on the occasion. Jno. Macky.

1798. Cutts Fishery.

On taking an Inventory of L. Hamilton's furniture &c. she presented me with 10 Guineas, saying she hoped Sir George Hill would take care to become acquainted with me and that she was certain he would find me a person still worthy of his notice on the fishery.

May 15. Mr. Thompson has pd. me in part	20.	9.	6
Aug.16. Recd. from Do. 18 Guins. more	20.	9.	6
bids me call next Monday for	4.	11.	0
My salary	£45.	10.	0

Aug. 20. Recd. my allowance of salt salmon 2 Cwt.
      Paid me my Turff bill   2. 4. 0
      Candles 4 lb.   2. 8
      Gave me the 10th inst. 3 large salmon
        for kippering and smoaking.

      Aug. 30.Mr. Thompson has pd. me by L. Hamilton's order
        5 Guins. for part services and may
        my God reward her.

Memoranda. On the 16th inst. Sir George Hill sent for me to the Custom House, Colerain, and he then and there in a friendly manner reinstate me in my employments on the fishery and says he will allow me as much and more than I ever had from L. Hamilton, and at same time he has for himself and Mr. Beresford perfected a new power of Atty. to me as inspector of the rivers as formerly and my said new power he has signed sealed and delivered to me in presence of Mr. John Thorn our late and worthy manager of the fishery.

Aug. 17   Went up the Bann and employd. 6 of the Keepers as mentioned in the following list, and I have taken Bryan Spallen upon trial, there are no cotts or boats this day on or near the river in my walk or view.

Augt. 18   Returnd homeward and on my way has appointed other Keepers for Bovagh and Aughadowy river, 3 of them I have engaged to watch the Bann also and on that acct. I have added 11/4½ to each of their wages.

Augt. 23   This day Sir G. Hill orders me to employ James Rowan as Keeper at the Loughan and upon my soul the man is not worth a sixpence as a Keeper and I have told this to Sir George but he insists that he shall be employed and therefore I shall engage him tho' against my will, and I shall give his name a place in my list but his wages is lost.

Recd. a note from Sir G. Hill ordering me to employ Tom Dempsy and Dickfeet Dempsy as Keepers on the Bann. I know them well. Notorious fishers and if their wages do not exceed their yearly sales of salmon, they will I think deceive him.

Recd. another note from Sir G. Hill ordering me to employ John Stephens of Clagan as a Keeper on the Ban, indeed I know Stephens as an honest man but he is a mere stranger to waterkeeping and to fishing. I know his sons are notorious villians on the river these several years past.

Sir George bids me tell the Keepers they shall get 5/5 for every nett they bring off the rivers and I have told him that for 14 years past Lady Hamilton gave no more than 13 pence for every nett brought to her off the rivers and numbers of them I helped to lift myself and her recd. of the netts she paid her people and gave each man a hearty bumper and sent them home as happy as Princes.

For Winter 1798 on the River Bann.

No.

1.	John Heyland at the Cutts, a gun, sworn.	2. 5. 6
2.	John Shannon 1st load salmon pr. order of Sir. G.	2. 5. 6
3.	Jno. McAlister near Bovanagher, sworn.	2. 5. 6
4.	Jno. Bradley near do. sworn.	2. 5. 6
5.	Jno. Dempsey, Portneal. sworn.	2. 5. 6
6.	Jno. Stephens, Gun. Clagom, lost money, sworn.	2. 5. 6
7.	Thos. Dempsey, Drumale, his wages send.	– – –
8.	Dickfeet ,, – a bad prt at 2 Guins.	2. 5. 6
9.	James Rowan a sorry bargain at	2. 5. 6
10.	Pat. Mooney at Gortreaghy, 3 load salmon or	3. 13. 9
11.	Jno. McDaid omitted in place 2nd load salmon	– – –
11.	Jas. Crawford on Antrim side near Vow, a gun.	2. 5. 6
12.	Wm. Kane new building near do. a gun.	2. 5. 6

On Aughadowy River and Bovagh.

1.	Fred McGraw this and the Bann, a gun, sworn.	2. 5. 6
2.	Hu. McKeeman do. a gun, sworn.	2. 5. 6
3.	Robt. Thomson do. a gun, sworn.	2. 5. 6
4.	Neill McWilkin near Gorton Greens – sworn.	1. 14. 1½

£8. 10. 7½

Octr. 12. I see a number of salmon here.

McCasky River, no Keeper, all in combination here.

5.	Drumcroon, Mr. Wilson's watchman at	11. 4½

Glenullar and Mettigan rivers will I fear lie waste this season and J. McAllen honestly tells me he dare not go out on the river but he will steal all the netts he can come at and bring them to me, and that last winter the Keepers had brought in from 40 to 50 netts and that I myself saw and assisted on sundry nights in taking up some of them. That the sum he now proposes will induce them to hunt for and collect all they can gather, and if his Manager is not skilled in the matter, he will pay them for netts that have not touched water for 7 years past. – He further orders me upon going to Coagh there to appoint a Mr. James Kane in the room and place of Robert Dunbar the late Superintendt. there.

I see we are happily secure on the Bann this season by Lord H. Murray's general order that no boats or cotts. are to be used on the river. Lord Henry has this day given guns to Hu. McKeeman, Fred McGraw and Robt. Thomson as being Waterkeepers this season under Sir George Hill, Bart.

There may be some Blazes seen on the river this winter but I am certain they will not be many.

Sir George this day has mentioned his intentions of sending a person along with me this season on the rivers in the Countys of Derry, Antrim, Tyrone and Armagh. I suppose this intended person is no other than a Mr. Charles McFillin who (as I am told) has renderd. some services to Government by his various and ingenious modes of practice and conduct through the late unhappy Rebellion.

Octr. 15th

Went this day with Mr. McFillin in search of a Keeper or two for McCasky river and can find none for our purpose. Stoppd. at Gowds Mill and at length agreed with one Thomas Millikin of Killeroa and really I don't like him. I observe some faint looking roods below the Bridge but have reason to suspect the fish are killd off these too early roods at such a public place on any river.

1798. Octr. 20th

This day Hu. McKeeman tells me some fish are got into the foot of Aughadowy and Bovagh rivers but it is too early for rooding on that ground and they will fall back into the Bann by the falling of the flood, this I know by long experience and I don't like to see a fish rood in these rivers until Christmas when the waters may better suit and secure rooding fish than at present.

Mr. McFillin says, Mr. Brown has appointd. Pat Dougherty on the Bann from the Cranagh to the Barr and that he himself has appointed Ned Thorp at Artecliff – They are indeed both old offenders and perhaps know where netts are still in keeping thro' their neighbourhood which they don't wish to discover without some wages which I look upon as no more than a bribe, for at present there are no fish in that part of the river nor any boats now in Dunboe, it being Novr.

Sir George will be pestered with recommendations from gentlemen who will furnish him with Waterkeepers and yet have nothing else in view than that of securing from him a yearly support to the Creatures in their own employment.

Octr. 25.

Rode to the Cutts where Mr. McFillin promises to follow me. Got to Garvagh and made appointments for the keepers whom I got attested by Justice Purvience and really he is never very friendly to the Fishery nor myself altho' my early and intimate acquaintance.

26th

Went up to Glenullar and not finding the old Keepers, stay'd all night in Johnny Kanes ill with rheumatism in my back.

27

Returnd to Garvagh and orderd H. Mullan to get the Glen Keepers sworn, and he says Mr. McFillin has passed thro' Garvagh. Rode on to Swatragh and appointed the Keepers to be sworn to-morrow at Garvagh.

Went forward to Mr. Bob. Patterson's at Grillagh and slept there, very ill with my back.

28th

Calld. at the Loop and find Mr. McFillin gone on before me. By 2 o'c. met him in Coagh at Mr. Kane's who asked us to dinner and used very civilly. I perceive they are well acquainted with each other and appear very happy at this interview and each in his turn recounts the grand intrigues and the dark and horrid designs of a number of their acquaintances late high in office thro' that country the curious methods invented and ingeniously improved and practis'd in the more easy and effectual methods of Swearing Up and of Swearing Down and of Swearing Forward and last of all by Swearing fairly Backward as being the then only and safe line of conduct for every wellmeaning and honest hearted man to embrace and abide by. That some foolish fellows had indeed been rather scrupulous in matters of Conscience and had thereupon suffer'd the very just inflictions of the Law. They both seem very happy on their manner of conduct throughout the whole and appear duly sensible of their merit to the present fortunate places under the Honourable Sir G. Hill, Bart. and his Great and good Health in a Bumper, The Fishery of Coleraine; &c.&c. I am at sometime not altogether pleas'd with Mr. Kane, who seems rather to triumph too much over my friend McFillin by his too frequent mention and exulting in his present happy seat in the new

Orange Lodge now established in Coagh where none are accepted but men of known worth and verocity and strict advocated for the Protestant interests as deriving from the Glorious and Immortal King William and consequently no Papist can be admitted amongst men of such worthy principles.

1798. Octr. 29 This morng. walked out on Coagh river with Messrs Kane and McFillin up to the Carry and then down the river and see no salmon. Mr. Kane has found a Loop deserted by its last night's employer: After dinner, Mr. McFillin sets out for the Loop where a Free Mason Lodge assembles this night. I now am invited by sundry acquaintances to the Orange Lodge this night in Coagh where I am promised a hearty welcome to a set of most worthy men, loyal and steady to the present establishment. I could not avoid thanking those worthy Chieftains for their kind offer, but being already promised to spend the eveng. with Mr. Lawson I could not favor myself with their happy entertainments and therefore wishd. them a convivial good-night. – 6 o'c. Went to Mr. Lawson's and past the night cheerfully in company with Mr. Miller and others, there till 10 o'clock. Set out to my lodgings and after getting into bed, was suddenly alarmed by the confused and dreadful noise of men all in uproad and dreadful conflict – some had got to the street and others within doors and nothing but Pell Mell Rogue and Villain resounded thro' the whole. Being perfectly easy about these truly loving brothers and martyrs to the Glorious Memory I knocked for the Waiter who came to my room and on my inquiry of the matter he told me it was nothing but the Orangemen cordially beating each others brains out but could not tell for what reason except that of their great Loyalty to King William or King James or some of the Queen Marys, he could not tell which. Perhaps said I, it is all for the good of the Country: He said he could not venture to say much more on the subject and therefore bade me Good Night, and by 12 o'clock those Warriors finished.

1798. Octr. 30th. This morng. I see Mr. McFillin returnd from the Loop Lodge. I doubt his mare has not relished her last night's supper; she looks dam'd lank and coverd with dry dirt. I wish he had adjusted his neck handkerchief before he set out, his breast ruffle has changed its colour. 8 o'clock breakfasted and set out for Blackwater Town and got there in good time. Benburb men came to us in the night and are to meet us in Moy to-morrow.

31st Set out to Moy and there got Arthur Hobson and 3 others sworn into office by Justice Caulfield, and returning to Coagh my back faild me at Stewartstown and there stopped all night.

Novr. 1st	Rode into Coagh and from thence to Ballyconan and there met with Mr. Greves who is well acquainted with Mr. McFillin and wishes he may be careful of himself at Ballymena &c. That should some people there find who he was they would instantly butcher him. 3 o'clock – Set forward and on our way saw some pollin netts which Mr. McFilin and Kane seized and also the boat used in setting these netts, and left them in charge of the Keeper at Moyola river foot. My back much paind obliged me to stay in the house of Widw. Walls all night.
Novr. 2	Met Mr. McFillin and Kane at Breakfast in Toom, they have fixed on 2 Keepers as in the following List and I have appointed them with Mr. Kane to Mr. Jones to be attested. Mr. McFillin is detained in Toom on some private business where I have left him with Mr. Kane and proceed to Randlestown alone and there found the old Keepers whom I have replaced in charge of the River Main.
Novr. 3	Set out for Kells river and there appointed Nath. Mathews who swears he can find no person to join him on the river, that they are all old Rebels and Villains about him and that his son is all he depends on for assistance in the night. 11 o'clock got into Ballymena and replaced the old Keepers by Mr. Adair and leaving these men in charge I set on to Gillgorm and on sitting down to dinner Mr. McFillin just arrived after tracing me all day. Here we appointed the former Keepers ordering them to Broghshane to be there attested.
Novr. 4th	Mounted horse and by 4 in the afternoon reached the Crown Inn, Coleraine, where we alighted and there left our last sixpence.
Decr. 30th	I like every turn of this winter and think that all my constant remarks will tell well and if we have not the very best fisheries next Spring and Summer of any other these 20 years past I will forfeit my life and my wages, into the bargain, and I most sincerely wish that Mr. McFillin may be as lucky in the improvement of this Fishery as what I have been these 13 years past. God grant he may improve it altho' I doubt it much notwithstanding his loud bravado and if he improves the fishery I mistake him, but time will tell for him as it has done for me and 3 or 4 years will evidently shew his managements.

WATERKEEPERS FOR WINTER 1798 and SPRING '99.
    On the River Bann.

1.	Jno. Heyland, Gun & Bayt. to the Loughan &c.	Pd.	2. 5. 6
2.	Jno. Shannon 1st Load Salmon & remitts this.		
3.	Bryan Spallin on trial at Mullan, sworn.	Pd.	2. 5. 6
4.	John Dempsy at Portneill. sworn.	pd.	2. 5. 6
5.	James Crawford	pd.	2. 5. 6
6.	Will. Kane above and below Vow.	pd.	2. 5. 6
7.	John Boyd for the Rochan,	pd.	2. 5. 6

                                                               13. 13. 0

J. Shannon remits his wages for 2nd load.

8.	Jno. Stevens gun & Bayont. by L. H. Murray
9.	Thomas Dempsy
10.	Dickfell Dempsy } Notorious fishers.
11.	James Rowan for the Loughin – useless.
12.	Pat. Moony, 2nd load of fish or 5 Guins.
13.	Pat. Dougherty
14.	Ned Thorp. } Old offenders, now useless.

1798. On Bovagh River.

15.	Hu. McKeeman	a Gun from L. H. Murray		pd.	2. 5. 6
16.	Fred McGraw	a Gun from	do. sworn.	pd.	2. 5. 6
17.	Robt. Thompson	a Gun from	do. ,,	pd.	2. 5. 6

                                                     £6. 16. 6

For this river and the Bann.

1798. On Aughadowy River.

18.	Alex. Thompson at Ballinakelly, – sworn.	pd.	1. 14. 1½
19.	Pat. Quinn at Ballydavit Green. sworn.	pd.	1. 14. 1½

                                                     £3. 8. 3

                                 Carried forward   £23. 17. 9

		Brought forward	£23.	17.	9

Winter 1798.

On Garvagh River.

20.	Henry Mullan, first Keeper,	sworn in.	pd.	2.	5.	6
21.	Robt. Craig, a Gun from L. H. Murray, sworn.		pd.	2.	0.	0
22.	Neill Quigg, sworn into office.		pd.	1.	14.	1½
23.	John McCook do.		pd.	1.	14.	1½
				£7.	13.	9

1798. On Glenullar.

24.	Barny Mullan, sworn into office.	pd.	1.	14.	1½
25.	Dan. McClosky, Brockagh, sworn.	pd.	1.	14.	1½
			£3.	8.	3

1798. On Mettigan River.

26.	Mark Moony – sworn into office,	pd.	1.	14.	1½
27.	John McAllen do.	pd.	1.	14.	1½
			£3.	8.	3

1798. On Claudy River.

28.	An. McCann		pd.	2.	5.	6
29.	John Doorish		pd.	1.	10.	0
30.	Dan. Doorish.	Old Keepers all sworn in,	pd.	1.	10.	0
31.	Frank McShane.		pd.	1.	10.	0
32.	Par. Diamond, due Mr. Henderson money		pd.	2.	5.	6
33.	Fras. McLain a slippery blade, due do.		pd.	2.	5.	6
34.	Chas. Deehan by Mr. Galt, Mr. Brown orders him.		pd.	2.	5.	6
				£13.	12.	0

I had formerly in Deehan's place a man
for £1. 2. 9.

1798. On Coagh River.

35.	Mr. James Kane, in secret pay.		–	–	–
36	Wm. Carleton – looks doubtful.	pd.	2.	5.	6
37	Jno. Wright – looks rather better.	pd.	2.	5.	6
		Carried forward.	£4.	11.	0

Winter 1798.		Brought forwd.		£56. 11. 0

On the Black Water.

38.	Arthur Hobson first keeper,	sworn in	pd.	5. 13. 9
39.	John Hobson	sworn in	pd.	1. 14. 1½
40.	James Hughes	sworn in	pd.	1. 14. 1½
41.	Barny Hughes	sworn in	pd.	1. 14. 1½

£10. 16. 1½

1798. On Moyola and the Lough.

42.	William McCann, good for little without boat.	pd.	1. 14. 1½

1798. On Toom and Brackare Eel Wiers &c.

43.	Pat Neeson, Junr. – now Jno. Barry.	pd.	2. 5. 6
44.	Harry Gribbin knows this business well.	pd.	1. 14. 1½

£3. 19. 7½

Novr. 2nd. ordered Mr. Kane to get them attested.

1798. On the River Main.

45.	John Bates –	sworn in.	pd.	3. 8. 3
46.	William McCormick	do.	pd.	2. 5. 6
47.	Davidson Robinson	do.	pd.	2. 5. 6
48.	Oliver Neill.	do.	pd.	2. 5. 6

10. 4. 9

1798. On Kells River.

49.	Nath. Mathews, an old Veteran.	pd.	1. 14. 1½

1798. On Ballymena River.

50.	John McMullan, looks damnd suspicious.	pd.	1. 14. 1½
51.	Barny Gorman – looks best of the two.	pd.	1. 14. 1½

Both sworn in.

£3. 8. 3

	Carried over	£88. 8. 0

Winter 1798.		Brought over			£88.	8.	0
	On Gillgorm River.						
52.	John McElmon	sworn in.	pd.		1.	14.	1½
53.	James Mitchel,	sworn in.	pd.		1.	14.	1½
					£3.	8.	3
1798. On Ballymoney River.							
54.	Henry Mullaghan	active.	pd.		1.	14.	1½
55.	On Drumcroon Rivulet, Hunter.		pd.			11.	4½
	John Macky, Joint Inspectr.				£22.	15.	0
	Amt. of this season by this book,				£116.	16.	9
		McCasky river,			1.	14.	1½
	Together with Mr. Kane and 7 others on private pay.						
	Charges for Cotts seized on the Bann &c.				£118.	10.	1½

For ... Netts, some seized, old ones gathered,
Charges for Powder and Shott to the Keepers,
And Mr. McFillin's Sallary this season,

1799. April 30th. retained in part salary 5 Guins.			5.	13.	9
May 18th. retained for do. 6½ Guins.			7.	7.	10
27th. for myself 6 Guins. retained			6.	16.	16
Mr. Brown to settle and pay me this remn. of			2.	16.	10½
My former Winter Salary from L Hamilton			£22.	15.	0

This day Mr. Brown asked me in the Cranagh how the Watchmen are
or have usually been appointed at the Cutts, my answer to his
question was – That his first object should now be the choosing of fit
and proper persons for his Watchmen, that the Cutts was a place of
great trust and required men of sobriety and sound integrity, and
their place of residence remote from the Cutts, and if at the distance
of a mile or two so much the better, that they should not be men
confined to day labour but always at liberty to attend at their watches
by the time that the Loopers quit fishing in the evengs. and not to
depart from their duty till next morng. that the Loopers appeard at
the Cutts – that the watchman on the Antrim side of the river should
never depart his duty there from Saturday eveng. till Mondy. morng.

1799. Feby. 28. At the Cutts. On looking over a number of my former notes and remarks of the seasons these many years past, and by my remarks thro' the Winter to this day, and upon the whole I have excellent reason to think and to say we shall have a profitable fishery here this season if rightly managed, or managed even as formerly.

					£	s	d
	We have taken 3 salmon 34 lbs. at 3d.			is	£0.	8.	6
Sat. 9 March	4 do.	42 lbs. at 3d.				10.	6
Sat. 16 March	9 do. 3q.	12 lbs. at 3d.			£1.	5.	6

I already see Mr. Brown disregards my advice in the appointment of his watchman, but he will soon find his error as Mr. McFillin certainly observes it.

				£	s	d
Sat. 23rd March	4 Salmon 34 lbs. at 3d. –			£0.	8.	6

Surely Mr. McFillin knows and sees Alick Shannon's behaviour. I can already see that he watches none when on this side of the River.

		c.	q.	lb			
Sat. 30 March	20 fish	1	3	24 at 3d.–	£2.	18.	6

I see Ogie McCannfield every night regular on duty and 'tis strange how Shannon escapes Mr. McFillin's notice.

								£	s	d
Sat. 6 April	14 fish	Wt.	1c.	1q.	20lb at 3d. –	£2.	2.	6
Sat. 13 April	50 fish	Wt.	4c.	2q.	19lb. at 3d. –	£6.	19.	9
Sat. 20 April	173 do	Wt.	15c.	3q.	5lb. at 3d. –	£23.	13.	9

Not bad considering the ways of managemt. here and yet we shall do well this season.

						£	s	d
Sat. 27. April	441 fish	2.	5.	0.	3 at 3d.	£67.	10.	9

Upon my Soul I do not like Master Owiny Kelly for a Watchman here altho' so nearly related to the family.

I observe when Mr. Brown comes here he always takes Mr. McFillin to provide conference. I see he wishes to keep Mr. Moffet and me at a distance – No doubt they think their present managemt. surpasses all other before them – at some time I am of a very different opinion,

but if our Fishery be good (as I expect) I shall have all that my
employers wish for, and this satisfies me.

1799. Amount of Sales	No. 718	–	3.	10.	2.	13.	–	£105. 18.	3
Sat. 4 May	No. 759	–	3.	18.	0.	18.	at 3d.	£117. 4.	6½

Good Lord, is it possible that Mr. McFillin don't see his Watchmen,
one lodges in his own house and the other next door to him – can he
be insensible of the trust he holds under our employers.

Upon my word I see our Uncle Michael will be a thriving good
Carrier, he does not weigh his own fish and yet he is no way bashfull
at the scales and seems match enough for his Nephew Charley.

Sat. 11 May	1222	–	6.	4.	1.	7	at 30 –	£186. 9.	3
Sat. 18 May	1546	–	7.	17.	3.	21	at 30 –	£236. 17.	9

This is a grand week here and as Dougherty their shoreman at the
Cranagh is perfectly ignorant in the time and manner of drawing
home his shotts, I think our next week will exceed this one.

We are however losing fish from these Cutts every night – 'Tis
amazing that Mr. McFillin being so highly intrusted, cannot nor will
not see and reform these abuses. – I dare not report them.
Mr. Brown's continual distance tells me that I am not to intermeddle.
Mr. McFillin and his Watchman are too nearly connected for me to
say anything whatsoever about them. My life and money in this
lonely and defenceless appartment would acarcely attone for my
interference in the family now at this place.

Sat. 25 May	1676	–	8.	13.	1.	23	at 3d.	£260. 3.	3
At sold now is	5921	–	30.	4.	1.	22	at 3d	£906. 13.	0

I see I was perfectly right in my remark on last week, it exceeds the
former by £23. 5. 6 and is the best week of the season, because if the
Shoreman at the Cranagh has acquired any knowledge we must now
fall off here daily.

In some little converse this day with our Trustee I find my hints to
him are not acceptable, and therefore must take no farther notice of
his Watchman, or to things (as he remarks) not under my Inspection
lest I bring myself into a scrape and nevertheless I cannot avoid

wishing from my heart, that his present dwelling house and his Watchman Shannon's were both remov'd to the distance of 20 miles from the place – one of these houses has always been a pest and nuisance to this Fishery and the other house does not in its present situation seem to fit the purpose or design of our Employers.

Sat. 1st June	647	–	3.	8.	3.	29	at 30. –	£103 9.	9

Now here is a very sensible decrease, but if the water rises as it appears, we will certainly do better next week at this place.

Sat. 20 June	849	–	4.	9.	3.	17	at 30 –	134. 16.	9

Here I see my judgmt. was just right last week and this week counts better by £31. 7. 0

Sat. 15 June	502	–	3.	I.	I.	7	at 30 –	£61. 19.	3

Here is a great failure this week, but still we fish amazingly well considering the Trade carried on about these Cutts this season.

1799. June 15,   the amount of my Abstract this day is

	7919 Salmon	40.	4.	2.	16.	at 30 –	£1006. 18.	9
		t.	c	q.	lb.			
Sat. 22 June.	692 Fish	2	4	2	13	at 30. –	£66. 18.	3

This week counts better than I expected.

During the whole of my superintendancy at this place for 11 years past, no watchman was allowed any access to our Boat and I always took care to employ Watchmen from a residence as far distant from these Cutts as possible.

I now wish to know how they come on at the Cranagh, but still I can observe that Mr. Brown continues rigidly careful in withholding all sort of information as much as he can from me.

The great loss is that Mr. Brown or Sir George is very far mistaken in their opinion of some men here.

		t.	c.	q.	lbs				
Sat. 29 June	657 –	1	17	0	8	at 30 is	£55.	12	0

Here I find I am £11. 6. 3. short of last week, but still I am certain we shall have a profitable season.

		t.	c.	q.	lbs				
Sat. 6 July	895 –	2.	3.	1.	24	at 30 makes £65.		3.	6

Better than last week by £9. 11. 6 and by the state of the Water on the Rock and this evengs. run of fish, I think we shall do as much if not more next week.

		t.	c.	q.	lbs				
Sat. 13 July	1023 –	2.	3.	3.	5	at 30 is	£65.	13.	9

Mr. Brown should not lower our prices, or else he may salt all the Grawls .

		t.	c.	qr.	lb				
My Abst. Counts	No. 11186 –	48	13	2	5	at 30 –	£1460.	6	3

Monday 15th July 1799.

		t.	c.	q.	lb				
This day	612 fish –	1.	11.	3.	27	at 25 –	39.	19.	4

This is excellent and if the run of the water stands for us, we shall have a grand week.

		t.	c.	q.	lb.				
Sat. 20 July	1359 –	3.	11.	0.	9	at 25.	£88.	16	10½

I never can be persuaded to believe that men who are employed in hard labour all day can be serviceable in watching here at night. Must a Labouring Man never sleep.

		c.	q.	lb.				
Sat. 27 July	313 –	16.	3.	12	at 25 –	£21.	1.	3
Sat. 3 Aug.	79 –	4.	2.	24	at 25 –	5.	17.	0
Sat. 10 Aug.	488 –	1. 12.	1.	9	at 25 is	£40.	8.	1½

A rare good week at this season at this place.

Monday 12 Aug.   252 –   1.6.   3.   23 at 25 –   £33. 13.   7½

1799. August 13th, my abstract –

11186	Wt.	48.13.2.5 at 30 pr. Hund.	£1460.	6.	3
2491	Wt.	7.11.3.17 at 25 pr. Hund.	189.	17.	4½
13677	Fish	56.5.1.22 pr. Abstract	£1650.	3.	7½

Had our Watchman this Season been properly chosen and true to their Trust we would have had the most profitable fishery of any other since my commencement with Lady Hamilton in the year 1786, when I engaged and attended as a Clk. at the Cranagh along with Mr James Black a worthy honest companion our then Cashkeeper and I remember that on cloing our accts. of the season our Manager told us the fishery had for several years past been decreasing and losing but in that one the loss had amounted to £300 and he was therefore under the necessity of going and raising off her then Estate, cash to defray the expense of the Season.

13 Augt. 1787   L. Hamilton sent for me to her house where she made no scruple in telling over a number of her grievances and how she at same time suspected and blamed her late Inspector of the Rivers as being the sole Agent of of her failures and losses and therefore orderd me to set out that instant and try my fortune up the river and she hoped I would not deceive her – I thereupon set out by myself without a person to guide me or a Keeper's List to direct me as to wages or to point out the name or residence of my former Keeper. I walked up the Derry side of the river Bann and on my way happily met and engaged Keepers sufficient on that side and stopping at Portna I there put all Cotts of that Fishery under charge of Dan McKinny whom I there appointed as head keeper up the river.

14th   I crossed the Bann and on my way homeward agreed with and put in charge what keepers I thought sufficient on the Antrim side and all the way took notes of the Cotts at every place on or near the river and I then returned to L. Hamilton and produced her my List of Keepers, their wages and places of residence, upon her looking into my List she got into passion declaring she there saw that I had intended to deceive and ruin her by my not employing as many more men. I therefore had to reason with her so far as to make her sensible of my intentions and she thereupon returned to her former good humour. I then kept a strict eye to the Bann and never faild in traveling every week from the Cranagh to Portna and upwards on one side of the river and homewards on the other, always encouraging the Keepers to their Duty and by the 20 October had seized 5 pair of Cotts and levied and recovered the fines to the Keepers which I found my Predecessor had always retained to himself. By this means of fair treatment my Keepers exerted themselves and their Spirits were always aloft.

21 Octr I hired a horse and rode to L. Hamilton who orderd me to call with all such gentlemen as had annually gotten an early fish in present from her and to whom she ordered me to present her best respects and hoped they would favour her with a continuance of their former friendships to her and interest in the rivers of their neighbourhood. I did not fail in calling with those personages &c. and they at same time never faild inviting me to breakfast, dinner &c. which I always refused. They then requested my liberty to use a nett on their rivers as my predecessor had always done and my answer was, that I could not grant them a liberty which L. Hamilton could not take to herself. In this manner I got into the knowledge of all those netts in my passage thro' the Countys of Derry, Antrim, Tyrone and Armagh and noted them in my book with a strict order to the Keepers to bring me all these netts when they come for their wages. I neither eat drank or slept at any of their houses as Mr. McAnulty had done, nor did I set myself up for the fine gentleman in ruffles. I never ceased riding every day thro' these places as long as my money lasted and at length returned to the Cutts after a very troublesome passage of 16 days. I there produced my List and number of men in charge and Lady Hamilton then produced her last List from Mr. McAnulty and upon comparing found it exceeded mine by £37. 4. 1½. She seemd as if well enough pleas'd but feared I had not employd men enough. I told her she had Keepers sufficient and although less in number they were in my true opinion more judiciously appointed than formerly.

Thro' the whole Winter I kept walking up and down the rivers of McCasky, Aughadowy, Garvagh, Mettigan, Glenullar, Swatragh, Grillagh, Claudy, Portglenown, Ballymony, Bovagh, Mayochill and Agivy, always keeping the men to their duty and assisting them in levying fines and taking up all netts in the night time set on these rivers until the fish were all rooded and gone mostly by the middle of January and in this season I really became fully acquainted on these rivers and could count and tell the number of roods in every one of these rivers and fords and places, most frequented by the fish in those season, and by the knowledge I acquired in that winter I have ever since been directed and govern'd by remarking the different state of the water and weather in every month from the close of the fishery till the 25 March in every year since, and indeed the man who had the charge and management of the rivers and keepers ought to be a person of sobriety and integrity, calm and courageous without much noise or banter. His constitution sound durable and impregnable against strong drink. Our Spring fishery commenced and produced abundantly but that abundance I could not ascribe to anything of my labours until the Grawls appeared and that in such numbers as demonstrated to every part and purpose of my winter's management which made me so truly happy as to receive the thanks of my employer and every one concernd, and above all upon closing our acct. of sales, found we had fully clear'd off all former losses and a handsome remaindr of Cash upon hand. Lady Hamilton was a woman ever perceptive in her concerns and took some pains in getting into the acquaintance of her people and their general manner of conduct and on these grounds she formed her opinions, and on that account I was continued in my charge on the rivers these 13 years and always improving in every year since that season, and notwithstanding the insurrection of the Savage Shakers and the more recent depredations committed by them at a time when the civil power at Colerain ceased to act and Col. Warburton refusing us assistance to quell and disperse the armed assembly of robbers every night plundering and fishing in Dunboe, yet we still found the fishery producing a handsome net profit at closing our Sales.

Lady Hamilton never lost sight of all these occurrences nor did she fail in making me sensible of her then constant knowledge of my conduct and constant attention to her interests and she frequently gave me handsome presents exclusive of my salary of 40 Guins. Now Sir George Hill, Bart. God Bless him and may the Divine Favour attend him.

He has acted a most generous part in employing me at any rate. Having so many people of his own and they all so seemingly knowing in the business and conduct of this fishery and far more than I – dare or even pretend to be and I most heartily and truly wish the welfare of the fishery and the persons attending it. Because, if they are all so sincerely and firmly intent to the true interest of their Employer as what I am and shall be whilst in his employmt. I think that on these grounds his fisherys may and will flourish while the power of men can serve and prove useful. But I already know and can tell all these people, that men alone cannot (without the happy effect and concurrence of the Seasons) add anything to the yearly run of Fish.

But I don't offer this as a rule or reason that men should neglect their exertions at any time or in any place where their helps and exertions are in any shape necessary.

1799. Aug. 24   This day I have produced my Accts. of the fishery to Mr. Brown and he bids me revise and collect them into classes more brief and concise, he refuses paying me my former salary from Lady Hamilton and I suppose he is yet ignorant of Sir George Hill's promise to me before old Mr. Thomson on the 18th of August last.

I hope he does not mean reducing my salary by his advance to the Clarks at the Cranagh who serve there about 3 months and never had more than a guinea a week from L. Hamllton.

Mr. Brown says Sir G. Hill has orderd me a Hund. Wt. of Salt Salmon – This favour I shall gratefully rember as long as my name is J.M.

I find the now Oconomist at the Cranagh has sent me 24 Grawls and has served all other Clarks with Salmon. – Accursed be the man who muzleth the Ox that treadeth out the corn and I here say Amen.

1799   This day I have produced my revised state of the fishery Acts. of £1650. 3. 7½. Mr. Brown settles them making my salary £40 and refers me to Sir G. Hill for the remaing. £5. 10. 0, my usual salary from Lady Hamilton £45. 10. 0. I will not sign his Settlement.

Mr. Brown this day tells me I shall he thinks be continued on the rivers this winter, and I am ever obliged to my present Employers and also to Mr. Brown and I wish he had attended to my advice of the 23rd of Feby. last concerning the fixing of proper Watchmen at the Cutts, perhaps he forgot my advice and I can assure him our fishery suffer'd for that, insomuch that I shall (being alone here this day) look back a little into the appointment and conduct of the Watches employd here this season. Alex. Shannon and Ogie McCannfield both of Castleroe were the persons appointed and in my then opinion very injudiciously as being both living too nigh the Cutts and both on same side of the river. – Shannon nevertheless, was a person at that time highly in the favour of our Trustee, he kept a good stout dram and retaild Liquors in the very next house to himself. Ogie was our second Watchman and recommended as a very fit person being happily residing within a 3 minutes walk to the Cutts. Ogie always loved much whisky when it could be had on easy terms. He was strictly honest and regular upon duty when sober. Shannon was a man who liked a hearty glass in any hour thro' the day and especially from a good Customer in an evening and by this I soon got into the reason why he so seldom went out on duty no sooner than 10 or 11 and too frequently at 12 o'clock in the night, the Cutts unguarded and full of fish. These men watched week about on the Antrim side of the river, which I then noted and saw Ogie always regular, if he miss'd his passage by our boat, he then went round by Colerain and got to his duty commonly by the dark of the eveng. Shannon was always late, but still he could come at the keys of the fishery and take the boat at any hour in the night and pass and repass as matters suited. I saw and noted these and many other things which some, higher in office, never saw. If they did see things they passed them as unseen. I also noted, when Shannon watched on this side the river, he would sometimes in the dark of the evengs. and sometimes at late hour, bring his coal kindle his fire, leave his cabbin in smoke and return home to his house, and whether he was then drunk or sober I could not tell, but I still thought our Trustee had a full opportunity of seeing and knowing all these things, he was always officer of the 'watch' and closely frequented Shannon's by day and night which I never did. But whether our Trustee at length noticed, or that it was noticed to him by some friend who could use so much freedom (which I could not) he at length with Kack Heyland, set out to the old Cutts in the middle of the night and found Ogie asleep in his cabbin, and then with a Loop in the boat crossed the river and there looped a salmon unnoticed and unheard by Shannon who sat smoking in his cabbin. Nevertheless, Shannon was kept in his office and Ogie discharged and in my then opinion not so much in disgrace as in design to give place to a person no less than our Trustees own Nephew, and of course the real and fast friend of Sir G. Hill. He was but young, but yet he was exceedingly sharp, smart and active, fitted the place well and his name was Owiny Kelly. This master Owiny fitted his place so very remarkably and became so expert in Looping of Salmon, that in very short time, he opend. a Nocturnal Sale on the Antrim side of the river where his courteous deportment and kind treatment soon became conspicuous and customers thronged upon him, till at length the noise of his Trade reached the Custom House in Colerain where he was immediately taken and examined, and after going through the necessary forms of swearing he was nevertheless found guilty and thereupon dismissed and discharg'd he and his Colleague as Smugglers selling without Licence. Their places were then fill'd by Day Labourers sent here by Mr. Brown and I often wonder'd how that those' Day Labourers liv'd so long and so healthy without sleep.

Indeed our Managers and Trustees, both here and at the Cranagh have from the very moment of their commencements, been so wonderfully knowing in their several places and capacitys, that men of my now age and experience are become and are look'd upon as nothing but drones and blockheads.

The persons now in Office at these fisheries appear all very zealous in their attachments to Sir G. Hill, and I could with all my heart wish they were all sincere, it would certainly tend to his welfare in these fisherys, but upon my Soul he will in some time see and experienoe what i already see, and he will in some time wish he had collected some of his Trustees at some better market and I most heartily wish he be not late in his discoveries.

I have been most highly diverted here this season by Mrs. McFillin who is so strict in her friendship to Sir G. Hill, that she will not (in the absence of her husband) give the keys of the fishery to Mr. Moffet or to me without herself or some of her children coming along with us to see and tell the number and weight of what fish we sell in his or Shannon' s absence, and at same time I never could avoid thinking that if she and her children and house and that of A. Shannon were removed just 20 or 30 miles further off this fishery it would save more to our Employers than what she saves by all her present care and ceremony.

Monday 26th Augt.

Walked up the Bann to the Loughan and by the state of their Cotts I see they have been fishing, I have advised those people to bring and lodge their Cotts with Mr. McFillin or otherwise they may depend on it, he will seize their Cotts and perhaps themselves into the bargain. Returning from the Loughan I met with a gentleman friend of Sir G. Hill and my intimate friend and acquaintance these many years past. He tells me Mr. Brown and McFillin have it in contemplation (doubtless for the greater benefit of Sir G. Hill) when I have escorted Mr. McFillin a second time through his long Circuit on the rivers, they will then supersede me in that office as Inspector, but he makes no doubt of Sir. Geo. paying me my full salary. Before parting I have confessed to my friend how that I am now nearly worn out by a long and unremitting attention to the business of Waterkeeping these 14 years past and to his certain knowledge, that should I be removed I would still nevertheless wish their joint endeavours might truly tend to the interest of our present employers. That the yearly increase or decrease of the fishery would in some measure demonstrate for their course of action and judgment. That as to my Winter's salary of 20 Guineas it will appear very small in comparison to the annual decrease which they will in short time find advancing upon them and especially at the Cutt fishery where their loss will first and most evidently appear in future seasons, and to prove what I have now told him, I bid him remember that this year our price of fish did not exceed 4/3½. per pound, and these prices he has noted in his pocket book.

WATERKEEPERS FOR WINTER 1799

and SPRING 1800.

———

The following appointments and the behavr. and inspection of the Keepers for this season comes principally under the care and government of Mr. McFillin, and I am always to attend on him when calld upon.:–

1799. Keepers on the River Bann.

1.	John Heyland, a gun and bayt. pd. him per order			£2.	5.	6
2.	John Shanon first load of salmon and		pd.	2.	5.	6
3.	Pat Regan, a gun –	sworn in	,,	2.	5.	6
4.	Charles McDaid, a gun,	sworn.	pd.	2.	5.	6
5.	Peter McLain, at Portglenown,		pd.	2.	5.	6
6.	Pat Moony 2nd load of salmon,	sworn.				
7.	Jno. McDaid, 3rd load, a gun by McFillin, sworn.					
8.	Thos. Dempsy, on secret pay, pd. him per order 3 Guins.					
9.	Jno. Stephens on do.	a gun and Bayt. a useless man.				
10.	Dick feet Dempsy, sworn in a noted Villian.					
11.	Pat Dougherty, not sworn.					
12.	Ned Thorp, not sworn.	both useless in my opinion.				

		£11.	7.	6

1799. On Loughbeg.

13.	John Dowdle	will be found useless.	pd.	2.	5.	6
14.	Nich. Scullin.			2.	5.	6

		£4.	11.	0

1799. On Garvagh River.

15.	Harry Mullan, order'd this season 3 Guins,		pd.	3.	8.	3
16.	Robt. Craig, a Gun, ordered 5/6d. addition.		pd.	2.	5.	6
17.	Barny Mullan,	sworn in.	pd.	1.	14.	1½
18.	John Barber,	sworn in.	pd.	1.	14.	1½
19.	Arthur Henry,	sworn in.	pd.	1.	14.	1½

		£10.	16.	1½

1799. On Glenullar.

20.	Owin Boyd Mullan,	sworn into office.	pd.	1.	14.	1½
21.	George the man Mullan,	sworn in.	pd.	1.	14.	1½

		£3.	8.	3

1799. On Mettigan River.

22.	Mark Moony,	sworn into office.	pd.	1.	14.	1½
23.	John McAllen,	sworn in.	pd.	1.	14.	1½

		£3.	8.	3

		£33.	11.	1½

Winter 1799.		brought forwd.		£33.	11.	1½

On Claudy River.

24.	Frank McLain,	sworn into office.	pd.	£2.	5.	6
25.	Pat Diamond,	a worthless nobody.	pd.	2.	5.	6
26.	Art. McCann,	sworn in	pd.	2.	5.	6
27.	Andrew McCann,	sworn.	pd.	1.	10.	0
28.	Daniel Doorish,	sworn.	pd.	1.	10.	0
29.	Manus Kane,	sworn.	pd.	1.	10.	0
				£11.	6.	6

1800. July 2nd. Mr. Brown orders me to pay C. Deehan		2.	5.	6

Amount of Claudy River this year	£13.	12.	0

1799. On Coagh River.

30.	Mr. James Kane headkeeper and nett gatherer					
31.	John Donnelly an old Keeper –	sworn in	pd.	2.	5.	6
32.	Johnny Collum do.	sworn.	pd.	2.	5.	6
33.	Dan. Nelson, for Ardtray,	sworn.	pd.	2.	5.	6
				£6.	16.	6

1799. On Black Water.

34.	Arthur Hobson, first keeper,	sworn.	pd.	5.	13.	9
35.	John Hobson, an active fellow	do.	pd.	1.	14.	1½
36.	James Hughes, do.	do.	pd.	1.	14.	1½
37.	Henry Clarke, a notorious fisher	do.	pd.	1.	14.	1½
	Capt. Verner promises to appoint for the river foot }					
38.	a John Richy, and will be security for his behavr. }			4.	13.	9
				£16.	9.	10½

1799. On the Oona.

39.	John Clarke,	sworn in.	pd.	1.	14.	1½

Mr. Verner writes that he intends Art Doo Campbell as an Assistant to Jno. Richy, Campbell is a poor worthless Villian and a dear bargain at 11/4½d. the wages which I usually paid him.

Winter 1799.   Brought forward   £72. 5. 7½
                                                                            £72. 5. 7½

On Moyola River and the Lough.
40.   William McCann,   has no boat.   pd.   £1. 14. 1½

1799. On Toom Wiers &c.
41.   John Barry,   paid him in part   £1. 2. 9   1. 14. 1½
42.   James Barry,   paid him   £1. 2. 9   1. 14. 1½

                                                                           £3. 8. 3

1799. On the River Main.
43.   Mat Neill, yeoman (a stranger)   pd. him   £3. 8. 3   6. 16. 6
44.   John Bates, now Gribbin   3. 8. 3

                                                                           £10. 4. 9

I doubt our fish and wages both lost here.

1799. On Antrim River.
45.   John Small, yeoman, dead,   pd. his wife   £2. 16. 10½   6. 16. 6
46.   John Baird, yeoman and constable.   3. 8. 3

                                                                           £10. 4. 9

The Magistrates won't back them, – lost money.

1799. On Kells River.
47.   Nathanial Mathews,   1. 14. 1½
48.   William Allison,   relinquish'd.

                                                                           £1. 14. 1½

1799. On Ballymena River.
    Here I can find no fit men for Keepers, our late Keepers are
drunken, deceiptful scoundrels and I rather leave this river waste than
lose our money and fish.

1799. on Gillgorm River.
49.   John McElmon,   sworn into office.   pd.   1. 14. 1½
50.   James Mitchell,   sworn in.   pd.   1. 14. 1½

                                                                           £3. 8. 3

51.   On Ballymoney River, – Harry Mullaghan,   pd.   1. 14. 1½

                             Carried over   £104. 14. 0

Winter 1799..   brought forwd.   £104. 14. 0

On Drumcroon Rivulet.

52.   Mr. John Wilson's Watchman – Hunter   pd.   0. 11. 4½

1799. Aughadowy River.

53.   Pat. Quinn, at Ballydavit Green,   pd.   I. 14. 1½
54.   John Hagan, of Carnrallagh,   pd.   I. 14. 1½
55.   Bryan Mullan, Ringsend.   pd.   I. 14. 1½

                                                                £5. 2. 4½

1799. McCasky River.

No man of principle to keep this river, therefore J. Shannon,
J. Heyland and Aughadowy Keepers must attend it when fish are
running, and this next to nothing, because fishers will fish here every
Sat. night, especially if they see Mr. McFillin and the above Keepers in
Coleraine Market.

1799, On Bovagh River and the Bann.

56.   Hugh McKeeman, a gun,   sworn in.   pd.   2. 5. 6
57.   Fred McGraw, a gun,   sworn   pd.   2. 5. 6
58.   Robert Thompson, a gun,   sworn.   pd.   2. 5. 6

                                                                £6. 16. 6

1799. On Mayochill River.

59.   William McCay   sworn in   pd.   I. 14. 1½

Wm. Blair at Killure, in place of 30lb. of Grawls yearly
for his care at Mr. Gregg's mill dam,   pd.   10. 0
Paid Tom Dempsy on Mr. Brown's order   3. 8. 3
       And my Salary as Inspector.   22. 15. 0

                                                               £145. 11. 7½
Deduct from J. Smalls wages on Antrim river,   3. 19. 7½

       Amount of the Season   £141. 12. 0

I have paid Keepers £84. 1. 1½ ⎫   118. 17. 0   Keepers List.
Mr. Brown to pay   34. 15. 10½ ⎭   22. 15. 0   My Salary

       Whole amount   £141. 12. 0

Together with 6 Keepers on secret pay, and charges for Cotts seiz'd
and Netts gather'd &c.

I have this day been looking over all my remarks through the Winter and really I don't now like them so well as I did last month – Our Spring fish may not be so numerous as in last season, yet we may have Grawls in plenty to make good for such deficiency. However, to guard against failures it will be prudent in our Manager to rise in his price and continue it till he see the course of our Market else we shall (I fear) come considerably short of our last season's amount at this place and indeed I fear we shall come short at any rate.

Sat. 28th Feby. This week gives	5 fish	50 lb. @ 3½d.		14.	7½	
Sat. 29 March. This month gives	24 ,,	2. 1. 17. @ 3½d.	4.	3.	8½	
Sat. 5 April, This week gives	90 ,,	8. 2. 3. @ 3½d.	14.	18.	4½	

I never before knew that the Managers place here was so very lucrative, he will certainly keep a good larder and kitchen this Spring and I see he is very provident in that line.

1800. April 9th.	To Carriers 53 – 4.2.0. at 4d.	9.	0.	0
Sat. 12. April,	This week to Sundrys at 3½d.	19.	5.	7

I wonder that our Trustee don't fix a Watchman to Carrycam on Sundays, it is now full of fish and these Soldiers and Vagabonds do mischief there all day.

Sat. 19 April. Sundrs. this week at 3½d.	30.	4.	4			
To Carriers at 4d.	13.	0.	0	43.	4.	4
Sat.26. Sundry this week at 3½d. –	33.	18.	1½			
To Carriers at 4d. p.pound –	16.	0.	0			
To one Smack 170 Salmon 15c. at 5d. –	37.	10.	0	87.	8.	1½
Sat. 3 May. Sundrys this week at 3½d. –	33.	17.	3			
To Carriers at 4d. –	20.	0.	0			
To two Smakmen at 5 pence.-	78.	15.	0	132.	12.	3

I could wish my old plan was now practised here, we would certainly tell much better every Saturday Eveng.

1800 April 9th To carriers 53 — 4 : 2 : 0 a 4   9 : — : .

Sat 12 April, this Week to Sundrys at 3½ . . — 19 : 5 : 7

I wonder that our Trustee dont fix a Watchman to Carry cam on Sundays, it is now full of fish and these Soldiers and Vagabonds do mischief there all Day —

Sat 19 April, Sund.ᵗ this week a 3½ £30 : 4 : 4 ⎫
        To Carriers at 4 . . — 13 : — : — ⎭ 43 : 4 : 4

Sat 26 — Sundry this Week at 3½ . . 33 : 18 : 1½ ⎫
    — To Carriers at 4 ffpound 16 : — : — ⎬ 87 : 8 : 1½
To one Smack 170 Salmon 15 at 5 . 37 : 10 : — ⎭

Sat 3 May. Sundrys this week a 3½ . . 33 : 17 : 3 ⎫
      To Carriers at 4 pence . . 20 : — : — ⎬ 132 : 12 : 3
       To two Smakmen at 5 pence 78 : 15 : — ⎭

I could wish my old plan was now practis'd here, we would certainly tell much better every Saturday Eveng.

Sat. 10 May, Rec.ᵈ from Sundry a 3½ — 40 : 10 : 10 ⎫
       Rec.ᵈ from Carriers a 4 . — 04 : — : — ⎬ 224 : 10 : 10
        from 2 Smacks at 5 . . . 105 : — : — ⎭

Sat 17 May; this Week, Sundrys a 3½ — 47 : 7 : 7½ ⎫
      Rec.ᵈ from Carriers at 4 . . 68 : — : — ⎬ 220 : 7 : 7½
       sent off 2 Smacks at 15 . . 105 : — : — ⎭
better conduct would have produc'd just 10 more this Week

Sat. 24 May from Sundrys at 3½ . . 38 : 14 : 4½ ⎫
      rec.ᵈ from Carriers a 4 . 114 : — : — ⎬ 262 : 14 : 4½
      rec.ᵈ from 2 Smacks a 5 . 110 : — : — ⎭
Now, this is the only and best Week we shall have this Season —

Sat. 10. May. Recd. from Sundry at 3½d. –		40.	10.	10			
Recd. from Carriers at 4d. –		84.	0.	0			
From 2 Smacks at 5d. –		105.	0.	0	224.	10.	10

Sat. 17 May. This week Sundrys @ 3½d. –		47.	7.	7½			
Recd. from Carriers @ 4d. –		68.	0.	0			
Sent off 2 Smacks at 5d.		105.	0.	0	220.	7.	7½

Better conduct would have produc'd just £10 more this week

Sat. 24 May. From Sundrys at 3½d. —		38.	14.	4½			
Recd. from Carriers at 4d. —		114.	0.	0			
Recd. from 2 smacks at 5d. —–		110.	0.	0	262.	14.	4½

Now this is the only and best week we shall have this season.

Sat. 24 May 1800. Amount of Sales viz:							
To Sundries 1581 -- 7. 10. 2. 27		263.	15.	4½			
To Carriers 1743 – 8. 2. 0. 0		324.	0.	0			
To Smacks 1841 – 8. 12. 2. 0		431.	5.	0	1019.	0.	4½

Sat. 31 May. From Sundrys at 3½d. –		13.	8.	7½			
Recd. from Carriers at 4d.		58.	15.	0			
Recd. from Smacks at 5d.		100.	0.	0	172.	3.	7½

I see the Smackmen grumble at their treatment here.

Sat. 7th June. Sundrys at 3½d.		7.	17.	6			
Recd. from Carriers at 4d.		34.	11.	8			
Recd. from Smackmen at 5d.		82.	10.	0	124.	19.	2

I now perceive we must fall short of last Season.

Sat. 14 June. This week sundrys		3.	10.	0			
Recd. from Carriers @ 4d.		15.	19.	4			
Recd. from 2 Smacks @ 5d.		40.	0	0	59.	9.	4

I hope the Cranagh now gains on our failure here, the present price of Provisions much in our favr.

Sat. 21. June, Sundrys this week		6.	2.	6			
Recd. from Carriers this week.		13.	11.	4	19.	13.	10

Sat 24 May 1800 Amount of Sales Viz

To Sundries 1581 — 7.10.2.27 ... 263.15.4¼ ⎫
To Carriers . 1743 — 8.2.0.0 .. 324:—:— ⎬ 1019:0:4¼
To Smacks .. 1841 — 8.12.2.0 .. 431:5:— ⎭

Sat. 31 May from Sundrys at 3½ ... 13:0:7½ ⎫
Rec.ᵈ from Carriers at 4 pence 58:15:— ⎬ 172:3:7½
Received from Smacks at 5 100:—:— ⎭

I see, the Smackmen Grumble at their treatment here

Sat. 7th June, Sundrys at 3½ ... 7:17:6 ⎫
Received from Carriers at 4 .. 34:11:8 ⎬ 124:19:2
Received from Smackmen at 5 .. 82:10:— ⎭

I now perceive we must fall short of last Season

Sat. 14 June, this Week sundrys .. 3:10:— ⎫
Received from Carriers at 4 pence .. 15:19:4 ⎬ 59:9:4
Received from 2 Smacks a 5 pence 40:—:— ⎭

I hope the Cranagh now gains on our failure here
the present price of Provisions, much in our fav.ʳ

Sat 21 June, Sundrys this Week .. 6:2:6 ⎫
Rec.ᵈ from Carriers this Week .. 13:11:4 ⎬ 19:13:10

I observe 2 Great Oak Creels brought here from Bellaghy
for repairing the Cott walls, they are quite too large, and
our Uncle Rich.ᵈ tells me they cost 8:1½ at the Wood,
and he sincerely (damns his Soul but their Carriage
will be 2:8½ per piece and in that case each Creel
costs 10:10 Now I really think they will not answer
and in Colerain they might have got 7 old Crates at
the same money and our Boat bring them from Town
and we would then have 14 Crates in place of 2 Creels

I observe 2 great oak Creels brought here from Bellaghy for repairing the Cutt walls, they are quite too large and our Uncle Michl. tells me they cost 8/1½. at the Wood, and he sincerely damns his Soul but their carriage will be 2/8½. per piece and in that case each Creel costs 10/10d. Now I really think they will not answer and in Colerain they might have got 7 old crates at the same money and our boat bring them from town and we would then have 14 crates in place of 2 Creels

Sat. 28th June. This week at 3½d.			5.	12.	7		
Received this week at 4d. carriers.			19.	16.	8		
Recd. from 2 Smacks at 5 pence.			48.	15.	0	74. 4. 3

Our smack trade ends here this day.

Sat. 5 July. Sundrys at 3½d.			4.	13.	11		
This week's carriers at 4d. is			6.	19.	8	11. 13. 7

Amt. at 3½d.	2094	8. 14. 1. 6	305.	0.	6		
do. at 4d.	1823	11. 16. 3. 11	473.	13.	8		
do. at 5d	3127	14. 1. 0. 0	702.	10.	0	1481. 14. 2

I hope they rise at the Cranagh as we fall here.

Sat. 12 July. Sundrys this week at 3½d.			£4.	7.	6		
Recd. from Carriers this wk.			8.	14.	4	13. 1. 10

Sat. 19 July. Recd. this week at 4d. per pound.		17.	8
My whole amount this day is exactly —		£1495.	3. 8

By the crowds of workmen, or as I may more properly call them Idlers, bustling and running about these Cutts, day after day I find our fishery ceases and I already see our Projector a confirmed Blockhead tardily and awkwardly aiming at a few simple repairs in which he appears as ignorant as his Mother.

I have these several days past attended closely to this business and in my memory never saw so much Ignorance, Idleness and waste of money. The poor fellow is destitute of knowledge, void of information and a mere stranger to the business he is now engaged in. I sincerely wish Sir G. Hill would come here in time and stay in some secret place of view, he certainly and in one day's time would discover what I have remarked and he would instantly change all the present damn'd unmeaning, idle and ignorant measures.

This is Saturday. What will all these men do for their next week's provisions. It is 6 o'clock and is now 3 hours since this Projector and Mr. McFillin went to Colerain for Cash to pay them, and they have been idle ever since and numbers of them come teazing me for money, but I'm dam'd if they shall get the fishery money from me, and therefore I march this moment for Ballyaghran.

Sat. 26 July   No fish taken since Monday the 14th.

This Projector plagues me daily for advice and I have repeatedly advis'd him, he is daily wanting more men, and I daily advise him to discharge the half of his present number. He then runs to the next man he sees and he craves his advice.

Monday 28th July.   We can find no fish in the Cutts.

'Tis now 8 o'clock this morng. and I'm dam'd if I have yet heard the noise of a hammer, trowel or any other tool lifted here. I see them all crowded about their Projector, who is no doubt exhibiting some damn'd grand sketch of his late Loyalty in the little scuffle at Ballymena. I wish he was in any shape Loyal to his present Employer here.

Half-past 8, now they separate in the hurry of business, perhaps they will yet venture upon something before they go to breakfast and upon my Soul I am just sick and heartily tired in looking at them.

Tuesday 29th July.   Here, from the garden I see 8 and sometimes 10 men about the big band barrow with a stone upon it and by my watch it is exactly an hour and 27 minutes since they put it on the barrow and have at length got it to the new cutt wall. Now I'm damn'd if our 4 old Loopers would not carry the same stone the same length and to the same place without the least noise in the course of 10 minutes.

Here I see 6 or 8 men who by their aprons I take to be Masons, there are perhaps more than I now see, or by their works know them. No doubt these Masons have Wages from 2/8½ to 3/3d pr. day. I never can see more than 2 or 3 of them working at any one time. No, some are watching and gazing at the common crowd which all day encloses the Projector who stands in their centre consulting and advising and in this manner they shuffle alternately.

Here are Labourers in abundance and the half are most commonly idle – They have different wages from 13 pence to 2/2 and 2/6d per day and no doubt are intended for different purposes, but the purposes are in my now opinion not much heeded, because all this part of the day I see a great Grenadier soldier at 2/2d. or 2/6d. per day carrying a Barrow of small stones in partnership with poor little John Crilly a creature at 13d. per day and their burdens sometimes about 30 or 40 pounds and sometimes not so much.

I have frequently turned over all these matters in my mind and cannot refrain these remarks and what I have at sundry times suggested to this now Projector, who, if he was a man of solidity or in any shape perceptive in conversing on this business, he might (from the timely different hints given him) have so managed matters here, that with the sum now to be expended he might along with the intended repairs and by a very simple turn of ingenuity have made these Cutts the sole and Establish'd fishery on the River and the Cranagh left prostrate except in the last 2 or 3 weeks of the season when fish begin to lie, a boat and nett might be every day then employed in scouring the river from the Bar to the Cranagh.

He now has men and timber of all sorts, with creels, stones, ropes, sodds, stages, borers and blasters all on the spot and the season so favourable that every advantage might now be taken so as to make our employers ever hereafter easy in their common annual expense.

I already see he will render the New Cutt conspicuous in Botchwork, he is raising its walls 12 inches too high. He is not securing its underworks at the Cutt head and I could lay ten to one it will be carried away in the course of the winter or perhaps in spring when fish are runing. And its present bottom (if not taken in hand and floored by some judicious workmen) cannot be swept with a Loop so as to take all the fish. He has repaired some breaches above the waters present surface, but nothing in the least degree durable at the bottom, and all his works when ended, will never produce more fish than what we usually have taken. Alexanders Cutt Pier is dexterously botched.

Had Sir George Hill thought me an object worth notice, or had accidentally dropped into conversation so as to let me know his intention of these repairs, I would have produced him a man, who, with 4 masons, the 4 Loopers, 4 Labourers and a Carpenter, would have executed his orders and produced to him a thorough and complete repair of the Cutts, and other material improvements such as he or his present Projector never had in view or design.

Sat. 19th July.	Brought forward			£1495.	3.	8

Sat. 9th Aug.Sundrys @ 3½d	4.	0.	9½ ⎞			
This week from Carriers @ 4d.	I.	16.	8 ⎭	5.	17.	5½

Tuesday 12 Aug.Sundrys @ 3½.		I.	9			
Received from Sundrys @ 4d.		5.	8	7.	5	

2190 Fish. 8.19.00.19. at 3½d .	313.	10.	6½ ⎞			
2954 do. 12. 2. 2.14 ,, 4d.	485.	8.	–	1501.	8.	6½
3127 do. 14. 1.00.00. ,, 5d.	702.	10.	– ⎭			

The dearth of this Season has been favourable to our market at this place, and yet notwithstanding our advance in price, I see we come short of last years sales £148.15.1. I hope the Cranagh will make up for this deficiency. I am really grievd to see our only and best yawl this whole week lying full of freestone upon the rocks near the long cutt wall full of water and all its seams and timbers so strained that it never can be repaired and I am certain they never will purchase its equal for £25. There is no value upon the boats here or at the Cranagh now-a-days. I remember a time when great care and attention was had to them.

I see we have lost our old Cutt Boat and it is really a pity; it was most properly constructed for this place and am certain 5 or 6 shillings would have repaird it so as to serve at this place for 7 years to come.

Indeed I would this moment wager all the clothes on my back that in the course of another year we shall have no boat here.

1800. Receipts at Cutt Fishery. Dr.
Aug. 12. To Amt. of Sales as per Abstracts. £1501. 8. 6½

Mr. Brown tells me I shall get Sir George 's former allowance of Salt Fish this Season.

I am truly thankful to Sir George Hill for his kind treatment, and to Mr. Brown for his information.

Mr. Brown orderd me to call on Mr. Murphy for what dray salt I shall want to cure my winter's beef.

Mr. Murphy refuses giving me this salt when at same time I see my neighbours, Wm. Beeton and the Hunters carrying home burdens of this salt from the Cranagh.

1800. Sundrys by John Macky.	Cr.	
Aug. 12.By Deposits to Mr. Brown.	1268. 19. 9½	
By Mr. Hills fish A/c.	4. 18. 11	1273. 18. 8½
By Incidents paid.	37. 13. 0	
By Waterkeepers paid.	84. 1. 1½	
By Loopers & Watchmen pd.	37. 7. 10½	159. 1. 11½
By Ald. Heylands Bill for	1. 7. 8½	
By Loughridges fish pd. Mr. Brown	6. 0	
By Mr. Brown's fish A/C.	2. 4. 7½	
By. Mr. McFillins do.	4. 12. 4½	8. 10. 8½
By defect in my last years salary now charg'd here	5. 10. 0	
By my salary for this year	45. 10. 0	51. 0. 0
Ballance due the Fishery by Mr. Richardson		8. 17. 2
£		1501. 8. 6½

Sept. 1801. Settled with Mr. F. Brown and paid him the above balance of £8. 17. 2.

JOHN MACKY.

Mr. Murphy has given me this years complimt. of salt fish as ordered by Sir George Hill, Bart. Gave me ½ hund. Grawls and ½ hund. of salmon, one of them 18 lbs. rotten. I am really sorry on act. of the Fishery that this has so happened, because it is the first rotten fish from the Cranagh since my commencement in the Fishery.

Mr. Murphy has at length given me a little drag salt and says it is the half of his own share.

1800. Aug 13th — Ever since the 12th and 17th of last month I have observed the water lowerg. here daily, and the fish ascending the Leap, this day I see 3 large fish have passed the Rock. I have noticed this to our Inspector to proceed up the river without delay and by the 15th have all his Keepers in charge on both sides of the Bann as being his first chief object; he appears very easy.

Septr. 29th — In Colerain met with Patrick Moony with a hundred of Eels as a present to Mr. Brown and James Scullin a keeper from the Killens; they very sincerely damn their souls if they look to the Bann this year. Moony declared off on account of Mr. McFillin's not serving him with his Load of Fish in the time agreed on for his last winter's services.

Scullin declared off as having too little wages and that this season there are no Keepers on the Antrim side of the Bann from the Barr of Colerain to Portglenone only himself and Mooney who lives too far from him for any manner of assistance.

Christmas Saturday — in Coleraine met Gorman my old Keeper from Ballymena; he is damn'd if there are a salmon alive in that country because there are no Keepers fixed this season upon Kells, Ballymena or Gillgorm rivers. I am vexed that all these 3 rivers are so neglected, especially Kells and Gillgorm, as to Ballymena I never have found a Keeper to my liking at that place since the late Damn'd Rebellion and I doubt McCasky river will be left likewise unguarded.

1800 — Looking to the Bann every day during my last harvest I remarked that the Salmon were in no way so numerous as what I have seen alongside of my farm in years past. I wish I may be found wrong in my conjectures on this uncommon slack.

Janry. 20th. 1801 — I have all this day been turning over a number of old remarks and memorandums taken here at home and at the Fishery these 15 years past and now that I have compared them I cannot rest satisfied as to the course of the ensuing fishery. I must in the meantime suspend my doubts until latter part of April when all our matters will I hope shew to greater advantage.

If the Cranagh improves and continues so to the end, we may in that case make a happy and profitable conclusion upon the whole, and yet I nevertheless am in fear of a considerable failure at the Cutts, for as sure as God made Moses the new Cutt will give way, especially if it and the long Cutt be set too early and as I am now cast off from all manner of consultation or interferrence in the Fishery, I well know the present Managers will from their want of knowledge hurry and enclose these same Cutts too soon and perhaps to the loss of much fish.

There will, however, be much in our favour and what I at same time very much fear, and that many others will fear and feel the monstrous price of provisions which will enevitably be sufferd throughout the approaching summer, and therefore I think our Chief Manager may without incurring much illwill, open our market at the Cutts at prices superior to any former year back to Noah's flood, the current price of provisions will guide him thro the whole season and by this rule he must govern his proceedings to the end and if I durst presume to hold chatt with our present Employers or Managers I would openly and honestly tell them every sentence as here taken in these solitary and private remarks.

CUTT FISHERY 1801. a SHORT ABSTRACT

26 January, took 1 salmon	8 lbs. no price fixed.			
	C Q Lbs			
Sat. 7 Feby. this week 5 fish	0. 1. 20. at			
Sat. 14 Feby. this week 7 –	0. 2. 29 at 4½d.	1.	13.	4½

I see that McIlwaine will never be a Looper.

Sat. 21 Feb. – this week sold 5 –	0. 1. 26 at 4½d.	1.	1.	0
Sat. 28 Feb. Amt. this week 6 –	0. 1. 28 at 4½d.	1.	1.	9
Sat. 7 March, this week 43 –	4. 1. 13 at 4½d.	9.	16.	1½

I don't like our present watchmen nor the manner in which they attend, they are not men for the purpose, 'tis true, Dick feet lodges in Mr. McFillins, but why does he keep the boat and cross the river so often after night and by the dawn of the morngs. I see him too frequently coming down the Hill from the Steels old houses.

	No.	C.	Q.				
1801. Sat 14 March, this week only	39	3.	3.	@ 4½d. –	£8.	8.	9½

Upon my soul there is some foul play a going on at this Fishery, some damnd. knavery and missmanagmt. somewhere lurking and prevailing.

	No.	C.	Q.				
Sat. 21 March, this week mendg.	55	5.	0.24. –		11.	14.	0
Sat. 26 March, sales no more than	51	4.	3.25 –		11.	3.	1½

By the number of fish I observed every day in the Cutts I expected this would have doubled last week's money, but now I find myself 11s.1½d short of last week.

	No.	T.	C.	Q.	Lbs.			
My amt. of sales this day is	212.	1	0	2.	2. @ 4½ . –	46.	3.	3

Monday 30th. I see our Trustee intends well for his family this season. – Let me see

Last Monday Johnny Spallen brought him a Hund. Wt. of Meal which at the present price is	£2.	5.	6
and J. Bradley brought him 6 Bushs. Potatoes,	1.	2.	9
and next came McAlister and 6 Bushs. do. worth	1.	2.	9
this day C. Hany with his car and sack, he tells me he is taking his potatoes to Colerain, he goes.	1.	2.	9
the next I see is Pat. Mooney with horse and sack, damn him he is late and will be serv'd late	1.	2.	9
Last there is James Dempsy and his wife, their offering is wrapp'd up in an old Bagg and I may well suppose it is not worth less than		16.	3

Good friends, I wish you may all succeed in early load agreeable to your expectations and to these necessary and well timed offerings, I likewise see Charley O'Neill, damn his impudence, he sits on horse back and keeps jawing to Mrs. McFillin with his hat on, he shows her a bagg of meal and seems higgling about it and therefore I see he can have no great share in this spring's fishery.

Now there is not one of these (except Spallen) will take more than one load this season, When at same time here are Dom. Bradley, Barny Deehan, James Freele, Robert Warick, Hu. Dean and others all staunch, constant carriers to the close of every season these 15 years. Damn them they come here every day the whole month past, but they bring no offering, consequently can expect nothing.

No doubt but this ecconomist thinks he is doing as much for his Employers as for himself by engaging to give these men loads of 5 Hund. a piece for Belfast as soon as possible, but he does not consider that by his serving these men with these early loads he loses all these old carriers who would stick to us till Lammass and by his present managemt. I see we may salt some more than usual and altho' our salt comes cheap, yet many salt fish upon hand in any season is dangerous, especially if provisions fall in their price. During my 13 years management here, I never received 6 pence nor to the value of sixpence from any one, and my rule was to send only one load of 3 hund. Wt. weekly to Belfast untill the Cranagh Fishery opened and that I had first sent off all the smacks, they being still my first and chief in every season while upon hand.

1801. March 28th.		Brought forwd.			£46.	3.	3
Saty. 4 April.	this week	105 –	10.	2.	5¾ @ 4½d. –23.	14.	5½

Our Trustee ought to be now saving for the smacks and tis now time for the first of them to be sent off.

| Sat. 11th April, | amt. is | 133 – | 13. | 1. | 2 @ 4½d. –£29. | 17. | 0½ |

I find I must argue something in favr. of these Smakmen.

| Sat. 18 April, | this week gives | 143. – | 14. | 0. | 21⁶/₉ at 4½d. –31. | 18. | 1½ |

I think we may send off 2 smacks next week.

Sat. 25. By the Country	193 –	19. 1. 24⁶/₉ average 4½d. –			43.	15.	6
Received from 2 smacks	319 –	1½ tons at 55.			82.	10.	0
Amt. to the Country	786 –	3. 17. 3. 25⁵/₉	175.	8.	4		
from 2 Smacks for	319. –	1. 10. 0. 0.	82.	10.	0	257.	18.	4

	No.	C.	
Monday 27th April a Smack	162 –	15.	£41. 5. 0

I observe our Manager and the Trustee at present in close confab, they are (no doubt) exulting on their improved plans of management here and I think the Fishery will this season yield in abundance, and now at same time if I had 50 Guins. I would bett it in stake, that our fishery here this season will not equal our last by £250 and upwards. If it does I will from this moment be forever silent and nevermore pretend to know anything here.

	No.			
Sat. 2 May, Country,	90 –	8. 3. 16$^3/_9$ –	£19. 19. 10½	
From 2 smacks for	255 –	1. 3. 2. 0. –	64. 12. 6	84. 12. 4½

I must here stop a little, and look into the Phizz and complexion of this new Looper we have got. I suppose by his present garb and appearance he is a late Crier of Black Ball or else a prick at the Loopman and just eloped from some Jail in the County Tyrone and perhaps a former associate of our present Trustee But be what he may, by my soul he is a finishd villian. Good Heaven! Jack Heyland this moment tells me that this same young Lamb is a person in disguise and no less than the Nephew of Mrs. McFillin. – Lord forgive me. I might have known he was of some family in the County of Tyrone and so was our late Master Owiny Kelly.

Surely the Trustee will here now fix this mild youth in some place of trust and in some degree above that of a common Looper. Yes, I see him already invested with all the keys of the Fishery. He handles a Loop amazingly already and seems to delight in Looping. He keeps a sharp eye upon the old Clarks and seems and looks very knowing. Doubtless he will be always second in all trust and command over every one of us, and I'm told his name is Master Hu. McFillin and of course the second real friend of Sir George Hill, and so Master Hughey McFillin you are from this moment our Overseer, Day and Night in these Cutts.

Sat. 2 May –	Brought forward		342. 10. 8½
Sat. 9th. To the Country 489 –	2. 9. 2. 25$^7/_9$ –	£111. 17. 2	
Sent off one Smack with 189 –	18 Hund. at	49. 10. –	
			161. 7. 2

I wonder if our Managers can discover that in this week they have to the Country sold a ton too much and to the Smacks 22 Hund. Wt. too little. They are the only persons in trust at this place and yet they don't count this loss of £10.

By our present run of fish I plainly see we shall lose 2 tons of fish or perhaps more than £90 by the present breach in the new Cutt.

Damnation to these Loughridges older and younger they were always too self sufficient to be governd by reason or advice and this I discover'd early.

		Brought forward	£503. 17. 10½
Sat. 16 May To the Country at 45 – 535. – 2. 15. 1. 0²/₇			124. 6. 4
Recd. from 2 Smacks at 55 for 390 – 1. 18. 0. 0			104. 10. 0
		Amount this day	£732. 14. 2½

Now this is the best week we shall have here this season and by the present run of fish we ought to have more next week, but I see we have this season been lavish to the Country and too sparing to the Smacks so that their Trade will come far short of last year notwithstanding the advanced price of their fish.

Were I at liberty to intermeddle in any matters at this place as formerly, I think I could soon find out the Trade now carrying on at Steels old houses. Our Trustee will I hope bring all things to light as he and the Overseer are the only persons in trust or in any confidence hereabout.

Sat. 23 May. Country this week 482 – 2. 9. 2. 12⁸/₉ –			III. 12. 2½
To 2 Smackmen at 55 432 – 2. 2. 0. 0 –			II5. 10. 0
		Amount of sales this day	£959. 16. 5½

I hope the Cranagh will advance daily as we now fail and that they always take care and keep the Smacks in view and contribute to those still upon hand and not rashly glutt Belfast market to the hurt of ourselves and carriers.

Derry does nothing for us and the Smakmen are got sick of their treatment here, and none of these fellows who got early loads here will (except Gage and Spallen) call for a second this season unless for one trial of salt fish at the Cranagh where I fancy they will have a good store.

1801. Sat. 25 May		Brought over	£959. 16. 5

Good Lord! shall we never have any trusty men to guard these Cutts.

Sat. 30 May. To the Country	153 –	15. 3. $7^5/_9$ at 4½d. –		33. 6. 7
To one smack at 5½	160 –	15. 0. 0		41. 5. –
Sat 6 June, Smacks	162 –	14. 0. 20	38. 19. 2	
this week the country	71 –	5. 3. $14^1/_9$	13. 3. 5	52. 2. 7

My Abstract this day tells only			–	£1086. 10. 7

I wonder how all these Lampry are disposed of this season. I see our Overseer has outdone the Loopers in that line of business.

Upon my soul Mr. Overseer you are very handy and watchful and attentive in your present and quiet line of trade in and about these Cutts in all hours and I likewise observe Mrs. Kelly is your second upon all occasions and appears to be a handy and useful Agent, and is to all appearance a Godly Woman. She this morng. came and order'd me to leave the key of this room with her when ever the fishery ends, and that she intends it for a place of Devotion.

The family now living in Steels old house must certainly be sharers in the drink and in the plunder from these cutts, Boyd and young Heyland last week told me severally, a little of this matter, they seem shy and say they are afraid. I have reasond and pressed them to go and inform Mr. Brown; they say they would willingly do so, but that their Father being a Looper and the times at present so very hard, they fear Mr. McFillin would turn him off and perhaps would in his anger swear their lives away

1801.		Brought Forwd. –		£1086. 10. 7
Sat. 13 June, the last Smack No. 111 –		8. 0. 0 –	22. 0. 0	
To the Country this week	93 –	4. 1. $0^8/_9$ –	9. 11. 6½	

				31. 11. 6½

I frequently look into the Department of this our present Overseer, he is always on the spot and steady in his present and sundry employments, viz: Overseer, Looper, Watchman, Weighmaster and close Inspector of the Clarks; He is undoubtedly Sir G. Hill's steel anchor at this place and by the bye I see he has got considerably into cash.

Monday 15 June,

this morng. Mr. Brown has lowerd our prices here and by the quantity at present in the Cutts, the week's amount will I think, tell well.

Sat. 20 June, this week counts	138 –	6. 3. 7. at 4d.		£13. 12.	4
		Amount this day is		£1131. 14.	5½

The water is fallen so very low that all the strong fish will escape us, and I see them now daily passing.

Sat. 27 June, Sales of this week	63 –	2. 2. 11 @ 4d. –		£5. 3.	8

I hear that Sir G. Hill has rented the rock fishery of Mr. O'Neill, I wish he had rented the Capstan also. Now, who is the man to be entrusted in Superintending at this place, certainly old Macky is not the man to be put in trust so far from the eye of Sir G. Hill's Trustee or of the inspection of his overseer. William Thomson is not the man. Mr. Murphy is the sole key of the work at the Cranagh and I'm certain Mr. Patterson cannot remove, and therefore as the business has slackened here, Mr. McFillin is the only and VERY MAN for this very place, and upon my Soul Master Charley you will find that all your skill either in Logic, Physick and hard swearing will serve but very little among the Play Boys you'l find at this place. And, upon my word you will find yourself fairly flung and cheated and outcounted in mash fish on the drawing of every shott and by the time you have served but two weeks, you will wish you and the fishery were in Bottany Bay – I wish Sir G. Had let it lie over for this season in particular, he will find his Managers too long in setting out and ten to one the latter part of the Season will not answer.

	Brought forward	£1136. 18.1½

Sat. 4 July This week counts   14 –   0. 2. 14   1. 4. 8
I'm glad its no worse, 'Tis strange how in the evengs I can better see and tell fish in the Cutts than in the mornings.
Sat 11th July, Sales this week,   36 –   0. 3. 17 @ 4d.   1. 15. 8

	Our real amount this day is		£1139. 18.	5½

Mr. Brown will this evening wonder on seeing the poor amount of this week, and surely he would wonder far more upon seeing Wet Loops brought out of the Cutt house so frequent in mornings thro' the week. Monday 13th July, this morng. price lowered to 3d. p.pound.

Sat. 18th July, amount this week	146 –	8. 1. 14 –		£12. 11.	0

I see we improve this week and at the low price and the present fish in the river should add something to next week and perhaps double in fish and money if matters were conducted here as formerly. I am very much vexed and yet I dare not speak to any of these people who are over me. They are all Sir G. Hill's own people and he and they have always kept me at a great distance and am certain they take me as a person the very reverse of what I am, and of what I have been and ever shall be; but no matter their opinions shall never lessen my integrity towards my Employers who really should be acquainted with every occurrence here. Mr. McFillin has repeatedly told me never to mention anything to Sir G. Hill unless I can swear up to all I say, or else to produce sufficient evidence. I could and would declare truth to Sir George Hill or to any man or Magistrate or in a Court of Justice, and really at same time I am but a stranger in the late or common practice of swearg. I have never earnd a sixpence by swearing. I never was sworn up, nor sworn down, nor did I ever swear backwards and next forward. No, but I well remember 35 years ago I was elected as Mastr. in a Freemason Lodge No. 346, and on my Instalment was sworn in Allegiance to his Majesty King George, and that Oath I have always kept and will hold and keep sacred as long as I live.

Amount of Sales	Brought forward, –	£1152.	9.	5½
Sat. 25th July, week's amt. 134 –	8. 3. 10½ @ 3d.	13.	5.	1
My Abstract this day counts –		£1165.	14.	6½

and I see we have exceeded last week just by 14/1d. so that I find my remarks of last week were well founded. We have a good many fish yet in the Cutts, I wish we may find them all there by next monday morng. But why should I expect this, while Mr. Brown's Labourer in the 3 nights he watches, he is always 2 or 3 hours too late in the night and I am informed there is mischief too frequently committed before he comes on duty. I am this moment in the humour of thinking that if Mr. Brown could but trust me with the keys of the Fishery at nights we might (without either of these watchmen or overseer) take, at least, 10 Guineas by next Monday morng. I am still thinking and comparing the present and former methods and management at this fishery and I see all our old rules of conduct are here totally expelled and my first and only advice to Mr. Brown entirely rejected and unminded. I observe our Overseer has got a watch.

This day John Heyland went to Steels old house and on his going into a room where a Weaver was workg. he saw a quantity of salmon cut in pieces and newly salted in a crock and other vessels and he says the woman of the house got up hastily and stood between him and the fish.

Taken from my Day Book at difft. prices :–
Sat. 13 June. Amt. to the country and prices.

averagd at 4½d. pr. pound	2699 --	13. 6. 1. 11³/₉	599. 5. 5½
13 Smacks at 55 pc –	2018 –	9. 8. 2. 20	518. 16. 8
Sat. 11 July Amt. at 40.	251. –	10. 3. 19	21. 16. 4
Sat. 25 Amount at 30	280.	17. 0. 24½	
		24. 3. 0. 14²/₃	£1165. 14. 6½

Monday 27th July 1801. This morng. before day our Overseer came to my sleeping room and by his tone of voice seemed to be in very heavy trouble. I got out of bed and let him in; He then in much trouble and anguish began to recount the more than double care he had taken of the Cutts by day and night and of every thing belonging to Sir George Hill since the day of his commencement. That as he very well know Sir George Hill could not trust his affairs here to any other but himelf and his Uncle Mr. McFillin. He on that account had slaved himself by doing everything in his power to do, and he was certain he had done more than any other Looper in the Fishery. – That being just then on his duty in Cutts he perceived his Uncle's horse in Mrs Moffet's field and had hastily ran to remove him before Mrs. Moffet would rise, and that he unluckily forgot the key in the Cutt Gate and some malicious person did in his absence lock the Cutt gate and carried off his key, and he therefore had come to ask if I was the person who had taken so much freedom, and on my then declaring I was not the person he instantly withdrew, when shortly after John Heyland the younger came to this office and I being out of bed he requested me to go with him to his father's house and I went along with him and there he young Heyland told me how that last night being Sunday night he had gone to the Eel Wall below the old Cutt in search of Lampry and while lurking there he saw some persons in the Boat and crossing the river twice or thrice; that looking up to the old Cutt he saw two men fishing it with Loops and a third person which he then took to be Dick feet sitting in close by the Cutt house door. That having taken no Lampry he left the Eel wall and cautiously stepped to the outside of the Cutt Gate which was locked. That peeping through the hole in Cutt Gate he saw Hu. McFillin our Overseer and another whom he supposes to be Jno. McAlister both stooping and taking up some salmon they had killed. That on seeing them taking up 4 fish into each of their hands he hastily left the Cutt Gate and crept under the foot pace when the Cutt Gate was immediately opend and these 2 men and 4 fish in each of their hands passed over him where he stood and counted the tails of the fish hanging over each side of the foot pace as they passed it. That they went right forward to the street gate and there stopp'd short and peeped up and down street and then hastily ran into Mr. McFillin's house the door being then open, and when they went into the house the door was instantly shutt. That finding they had left the Cutt gate open he went in and saw the Loops lying by the Cutts and one grawl of 8 or 10 pounds lying dead on the ground, which Grawl he then took and locked the gate and carried the Grawl and key immediately to his father's house where he then and there shewd me the Grawl and key and asked me what he should do with them, and my direction was that he should carry both Grawl and key immediately to Mr. Brown and to tell him of all he had seen. Young Heyland objects against going to Mr. Brown by alleging – that Dick feet has made an information against him and Sam Boyd for fishing the far Cutt lately. That should he now go and inform Mr. Brown what would he and Mr. McFillin say, but that this is only a piece of fraud and spite and no more than a stroke revenge offerd against Dick feet for his late information.

His reasons for suspecting Jno McAlister to be the person concerned in this affair is, that late in the afternoon yesterday he met McAlister, our Overseer, and others of Mr. McFillins family all drinking together in Simon Hurleys.

I do now recollect that in coming from my own house to this place in yesterday eveng. late, I think I saw McAlister's horse feeding in the backlane at Summerset and then wonderd how he had come to that place. I likewise saw and spoke to Mr. McFillin as he was then coming out of Hurley's house, but I did not then see any other person.

8 o'clock. Here comes our Overseer with the key of the Cutt Gate Jack Heyland, Mr. Moffet with others wanting fish; the Loops are brought from the Cutt House wet and dirty, I see the old Cutt walls coverd with fresh scales and blood and our Overseer's gun stands near the watch Cabbin and daubd all over with fresh scales. After all that has happened I find we have – taken 65 fish, some of them very small. I have here just £5. 6. 0 – Damnation to these Villians, those 16 fish which they took last night, would have this day made my Book look more gracefully –

after all that has happen'd I find we have taken
65 fish some of them very small, I have here just £5:6
Damnation to these Villians, those 16 fish which they
took last night, would have this Day made my Book
look more Gracefully ———

Sat. 1 August. Weeks amt. is 102—5:2:4⅓ at 3 . . . 8:6:2
Amount brought forward - - - - - - - - - - 1165:14:6½
                          amount this day £1174:0:8½

———————————————————————————————————————

Perdition to the Man who first Plan'd this infernal
design in drafting all the old regular Loopers from this
place and in their Stead has left us a Wolf to Guard
these Folds ——— Had they left me even one old Looper
he and I would have every day fished these Cutts in
the former usual manner, the fish Women would have
bought all we took and our Employers got the Cash

    this even? I see some fish in the Cutts —
Query, Shall we find them there on Monday next
Certainly," "our Overseer will take all care of them ——

Sat. 8th Aug? this Week tells 21—1..00..26½ £1:16:7½

Damn this Labourer of Mr. Browns who in the 3 nights
of his Watching he never comes here till 9 or 10 at Night &
when I am in Bed —, Lord, is it not amazing how that
Mr. Mfillin, (ever loud in his attachments to Sir George
Hill and to his interest in this fishery, his Exploits and
Capture of two Cotts from the Temples &c &c) Notwithstand
all his Bombast, he never has yet challeng'd or noticed
a Wet Loop in any morn? of this season altho he assumes
the Character of the first Looper here and for which I have
this Day paid him 7:7, and yet when Jack Heyland and
                                            my self

	No.	c.	q.	lbs.			
Sat. 1 August Week's Amt. is	102 –	5.	2.	4⅔. at 3d. –	£8.	6.	2
					£1165.	14.	6½
				Amount this day –	£1174.	0.	8½

Perdition to the man who first plan's this infernal design in drafting all the old regular Loopers from this place and in their stead has left us a Wolf to Guard these Folds. Had they left me even one old Looper he and I would have every day fished these Cutts in the former and usual manner, the fish women would have bought all we took and our Employers got the cash. This eveng. I see some fish in the Cutts. Query, shall we find them there on Monday next. Certainly no our Overseer will take all care of them.

	No.	c.	q.	lbs.			
Sat. 8th Aug. This week tells	21 –	1.	00.	26½ –	£1.	16.	7½

Damn this Labourer of Mr. Brown's who in the 3 nights of his watching he never comes here till 9 or 10 at night and when I am in bed. Lord, is it not amazing how that Mr. McFillin (ever loud in his attachments to Sir George Hill and to his interest in this fishery, his exploits and capture of two cotts from the Semples &c.) Notwithstanding all his bombast he never has yet challeng'd or noticed a Wet Loop in any morng. of this season altho' he assumed the character of the first Looper here and for which I have this day paid him 7/7d. and yet when Jack Heyland and myself went to the Cutthouse last Monday morng. we there found a Loop as just lifted from the water.

This day I observe Dickfeet and the Overseer, they are lying now upwards of an hour in one posture on the broad walk in the garden, they front each other with their mouths close together – Damnation to them. I suppose they are now settling their Accts. as the fishery now ends. Their season's conduct has in great measure escaped my most minute attention. They lodge both in the same house with our Trustee and I often wonder he never notices their manner of conduct, indeed I fear he does not, and I now think he will not. So now my worthy Master Dicky and your colleague Master Hughey, have this whole season lodged with Sir George Hill's only and chief friend here. You have had his boat and the keys of his fishery at your commands by day and night and have done everything in your too common and constant power to do and your conduct and all your actions passed over with impunity.

During the 13 years of my management here under Lady Hamilton our Watchmen never resided nearer to this place than the Town of Colerain at least. They never changed their place of watching nor at any time permitted the freedom or privilege of the boat, no nor to converse together except for a few minutes on Saturdays here at this pay table.

Sat. 8 Augt. 1801. –	Brought forward	£1175.	17.	4
Aug. 12. Our last 3 days	28 – 2.00. 6 at 3d.		3.	0. 6
	My Abstract this day counts exactly	£1178.	17.	10

and is just £325. 11. 2½ short of last year's sales at this place.

I may here account for a part of the failure at this place this season in the manner following, viz: Our loss by the new Cutt I suppose from
90 to £100

By Dickfeet's drunkness and too
little attention from
10 to 15

By our Overseer's close and too
much attention from
10 to 15

Whole loss at the Cutts from
110 to 130

Besides the loss suffer'd last winter for want of Keepers on Kells, Ballymena, Gillgorm, and McCasky Rivers.

I am nevertheless in firm hope that the Cranagh will this season atone for the deficiencies here. The general run at the Cranagh has been good and the prices altogether well managed and therefore I conclude their amount of fresh and salt sales will come little short of £2,000. If it does then my skill in the Fishery is not worth the half of the time I have spent in Waterkeeping and in speculations these 16 years past.

'Tis true our salt comes I may say cheap, but I have never look'd on salt fish as a thing very profitable. N.B. In the night of the 12th inst. I and the Loopers, Bullin, Heyland and Jack Farren our Watchman and Hu. McFillin our Watchman and Overseer, about 2 o'clock counted the fish 53 or 54 in number, and after our Overseer had made the usual distribution to the Loopers, Clarks &c. and left the remr. in the Cutthouse the back door I myself bolted and asked the Overseer (who seemed fatigued) if he would trust these fish to my care or to the care of Farren till day light. He said he would not and theroupon locked Cutthouse door and the Cutt gate and went off with the Loopers &c. and I to my bed. In the morng. of the 13 going into Cutthouse with the Overseer, Mr. Moffet and others, found the backdoor open, the fish tossed and 8 of the largest taken away. I then sold some of the renr. to sundrys. On the 14th. Mr. McFillin had arrived from Derry Assizes, he brought 2 grawls and made some further distributs. and sent the remr. by Jack Heyland to the Cranagh – 19 in number.

I have recited the whole of this matter in my Day Book for Mr. Brown's perusal and farther enquiry

1801. SALES – AT CUTT FISHERY.				DR		
Aug 14. To Ballance due to the fishery by						
Mr. Richardson 12th Augt. 1800.				8.	17.	2
To amt. of this season per abstract viz:						
From 13 Smacks	2018 – 9. 8. 2. 28	at 55.		518.	16.	8
Carriers	1064 – 6. 18. 0. 10	at 50		345.	4.	2
To the country	1230 – 5.12.3.20	at 45		254.	1.	3
To the country	221 – 10.0.25	at 40		20.	8.	4
To do.	457 – 1.6.3.19½	at 30		40.	7.	5½
				1178.	17.	10½
				£1187.	15.	0½

Septr.   Agreeable to Mr. Brown's order I went to the Cranagh and Mr. Murphy has given me a Hundred weight of real good Salmon. He refuses to give me any old Netts without an order from Mr. Brown in writing. He has given me a little dray salt.

1801. SUNDRIES BY JOHN MACKY.   CR.

Aug. 14. By deposits with Mr. F. Brown,				921.	1.	4½
By Incidents, paid	24.	10.	3			
By Loopers & Watchmen	39.	10.	9½			
By Waterkeepers paid	110.	17.	1½	174.	18.	2
By Mr. Moffet's salary paid,				20.	0.	0
By Sundry pd. Mr. McFillin,	24.	0.	8½			
By his fish Act. due to the Fishery,	5.	12.	0	29.	12.	8½
By Mr. Hill's fish Acct. per books	3.	1.	6			
By Mr. Brown's do. per do.	4.	17.	5½	7.	18.	11½
By Mr. McCauslands order on Mr. Brown for				1.	1.	9
Septr. By Mr. Richardson's Ballce. now paid to						
Mr. Brown as charg'd me in this Acct.				8.	17.	2
By a part of the fishery money now paid him.					17.	3½
By my Salary as Agent at the Cutts.				22.	15.	0
				1187.	2.	5
Ballance due by sundrys and not yet collected;					12.	7½
Settled the day of 1801				£1187.	15.	0½

By Jno. Macky.

On settling with Mr. Brown I have this date left him a list of the
persons who owe the above Ballance, viz:

Jo, Sterling for pd.	1.	0
Andrew Kieth for	4.	1½
Neill McKillep for pd.	3.	9
Dennis Dempsy Drumale for	3.	9
	12.	7½

Septr. 18.   At the Cutts call'd to see Old Will Moffet and upon my soul he is a
quere old Wag, he has entertain'd me this hour in telling me of Mrs.
McFillin and her two daughters being on a late visit to the Cranagh
where Mrs. Murphy entertained them in a sumptuous and splendid
manner such as she nor her daughters had never seen nor partook of
before in their lifetime. He says he can easily discover how that Mrs.
McFillin and her daughters are ever since jealous of the happy
situation of Mrs. Murphy who they find to be in the favour and
notice of Sir George Hill, who has in every season since his
commencement to the Fishery presented Mrs Murphy with a new

gown and other wearables of much worth besides that of an umbrella and other lesser things as tokens of his good opinion of her and her husband. That Mrs. Murphy shew'd them the 3 fine muslin gowns, some brocaded others plain besides a very fine cloak &c. together with a piece of very fine holland for a dozen of shirts to Mr. Murphy and to be made in the same and exact form and fashion as Sir George Hill's shirts – That Mrs McFillin and the Miss McFillins are very much offended at Sir George Hill, and say that neither Murphy nor his wife ever merited anything equal to that of Mr. McFillin her husband either from Sir George or from Government. That Murphy was but a child in the late affairs of the country and never would be noticed by any Gentn. as her husband was both in Ireland and England where he did more in one day than poor Murphy could do in 7 years, a poor dog who had not a second rag of clothes but what was on his and his wife's bodies when they came to the Fishery. That this was not the case with her husband; when he came to the Fishery he was as well clothed as any other gentleman in Colerain, that when he went to London he there got all the clothes he had occasion for and he would have got twice as many had he been covetous.

Damnation to the poor low lif'd lousy breed of the Murphys; was ever any of them carried in a coach as Mr. McFillin was carried thro' England and attended all the way by some of the King's own messengers, who never parted from his company by day or night, and in Dublin they bought him a fine mare and all her riding furniture and gave him a fine watch in his pocket and an umbrella and sent him home to me not like Murphy or any poor vagabond, but like a gentleman with a party of the King's own horsemen who convey'd him all the way from Dublin to our own house. Damnation to Murphy and to McCleery his wife, Damnation to them, could they or any of their poor beggarly breed ever shew themselves in a fair or market in any shape equal to the McFillins'.

I observe old Moffet is highly tickled as he repeats this long story in high glee and flow of spirits, and he farther tells me that when Mr. McFillin got his tierce of salt fish from the Cranagh in the year 99 he sold them on same day to Johnny Spallin, but that ———— in the year 1800 Mrs. McFillin and the ladies sold all their salt-fish themselves and bought some very nice dresses for herself and her daughters, and that this season ever since our present overseer (who is Mrs, McFillin's nephew) came to the Fishery he carefully has kept the family in fresh salmon for the family's use and also as much to spare as to keep his Aunt and the ladies in Tea and sugar and other necessarys to the house, and as to the tierce of salt fish this season from the Cranagh they have already sold it all off and have purchased some very handsome dress for the mother and daughters, who attend to the play now twice a week in Colerain and think they are full as much noticed in the Play House as Mr. and Mrs Murphy.

I am at length cloy'd and tired of this long detail and I at same time can plainly see Mrs. Murphy's whole stretch of ingenuity display'd in her late interview with the McFillins whom she had blinded by her repetition of favours conferred on her and her husband by Sir George Hill. Mrs. Murphy is really a woman of ingenuity and ever since her commencement in the Fishery she has acted as prudently and managed her trade and deceptions more gracefully and with less noise than the generality of women are capable of doing. Indeed in the first season of Sir George's fishery, Murphy and his wife set out in trade rather too early and unguardedly and therefore soon noticed by carriers and others about the Cranagh, and I remember in that season how poor McDaid the Waterkeeper lost his place for attempting to shew and make known the facts he had seen, and he was wrong. Dan Branon was also discharged but the then Agents Nelly Houston and Matty Reed were and are still retain'd but not now employed in their former trade. Mrs. Murphy has ever since acted causiously and has made a very prudent choice in that of her present Manager who has since the hour of his commencement acted with the greatest secrecy and caution wth respect to his employer and himself. All that I know of the fellow is no more than, that this season he has either 6 or 7 cows upon fattening grass, and that 4 years ago he could not (without /borrowing) purchase one cow.

I know that old Moffet tells a dam'd lie respecting the piece of cloth which he mentions, for Mrs. Murphy made or got made herself the very piece of Linnen for her husband's shirts let them be made in what fashion she pleases.

Rogue watch Rogue catch; this I look upon as a very unsafe and uncertain proverb or maxim in the fixing of uncertain persons to places of high trust. Because, an honest man may be watched but he never will be catched and therefore moral honesty requires no watch.

Ever since I came home here from the Cutts I have been every day looking to the Bann at the foot of my farm and am really sorry to see so very few salmon which evidently tells me that Sir George Hills new managers (in order to make the most of it) rake and fish the river in all places from the Cranagh to the Bann much more than in former years and thereby have wasted the common stock of salmon which annually stop and lie there to take an early passage up the river to spawn.

This practice, if followed will reduce the fishery and I can perceive it has hurt it already, but why should I talk being an old fellow who knows nothing. No the present managers are the knowing gentlemen and so they are and shall remain so for me; nevertheless, if I had 1000 Guineas I would wager it with the most knowing of them that our next seasons fishery falls short of the last £500 and upwards, and at same time I am confident in my opinion that if the Cutts fishery be secured from depredators and prudently managed it will produce every shilling as much as last season and perhaps more. Now should our Managers see these my private Notes and remarks, surely they would first damn me to all intents and purposes and secondly report me to our employers as an old Villian inferior to them in every species of knowledge pertaining to the fishery. After all their cringing deceptions and all their grand managements are told over by the one and the other from the first man in office down to the lowest in employment, I am nevertheless certain that if the management of the Cutt fishery was given to me I would lay my life in stake to produce as much Cash at the Cutts fishery 1802 as that of 1801 –.

In order to effect this important matter I would on the 13th day of August last have discharged and forever banished our present overseer never more to come nigh the Cutts or to lodge another night in his uncle's house. Secondly I would in proper time appoint two watchmen such as I recommended to Mr. Brown on the 23rd February 1799 in the Custom House. Thirdly I would endeavour to stop the sale of all kind of Liquour at Castleroe, it is a nuisance and very hurtful to the fishery. Fourthly I would open Sales at the prices as ordered by my employers and would give no preference to particular carriers as of late, I would serve and send fish to Coleraine and Derry as early as possible, I would keep my eye carefully to the Smacks and send only 3 CWs weekly to Belfast and no more until the Smacks had first ceased or the Cranagh had began to sell, I would give over fishing every evening by 7 o'clock, secure the boat and lock up the oars in the Cutts House and keep all keys in my own keeping, my wife or children or servant should have no access to the Cutts by themselves to introduce any fellows there or to use any freedom whatsoever, and the Watchmen I would keep and order to my liking, I would go to my rest in due time and would rise so early as not to detain any neighbouring Gentleman or Linnen Drapers' servants by waiting from sunrise till 9 or 10 o'clock and this is the way by which the Cutt fishery may be improven and produce to our employers only and for them alone a sum equal and perhaps more than the amount of our last season especially if the latter part prove wet and Water high the Cranagh will not bring anything equal to their expense.

Our inspector is every year too late in securing the Bann the first great object which I every year had fully secured by the 14th of August from the Town of Coleraine to Portglenone and every week walked that ground till Christmas or that all the fish had taken to the lesser rivers when my attention was there necessary.

Septr. 10th. in Coleraine met two of my old trustys who tells me our inspector was up the river some days ago putting on the Keepers and that in Kilrea he has put on J. Smirl and others whom I know well and I look upon them as no security to the brood for the ensuing season. That on Antrim side there are but two men to guard that side from Coleraine to Portglenone and that in their memory they never knew of so much Cott fishing. Lord how I am inwardly grieved for this heavy loss and mismanagement.

Octr. 7th. in Coleraine met the Dalis's of Portglenone and J. McLain of Claudy and gave them a Dram for sake of information they solemnly declare they never knew of so much depredations committed on the River Bann in their lifetime and that Sir G. Hill's present inspector is a man so detestable to the people in that country and in the County of Antrim that they are watching him daily and are determined to do him and the fishery every hurt in their power and that he dare not appear publicly on any of the rivers there and for that reason there have no men been employed to keep the rivers. of B.mena. Kells or Gillgorm since I was superseded – .

What need I tell this to Mr. Brown he will only huff at me, get into passion and say as he has already said, that he will not be dictated to by any one.

Oct. 20 Every day this and last week have been watching the Bann but can see no fish playing and I already perceive our fishery will decrease.

Novr. 23rd met Tom Dempsy who tells me that he and Dickfeet have seized a pair of private Cotts and I wish they had seized all others of the same name and employment we would have saved some tons of our brooding fish – Now they have done this mighty fate and this is all they will do for this season. On Christmas Saturday I met a number of my old acquaintances from sundry places on the Bann and other Rivers, they all proclaim the vast havock committed on the brooding fish in their neighbourhood.

Jany. 27th. 1802 I plainly perceive that I am right in my remarks of the season, since the 12th of Aug. last I have paid my usual attention to the course of the season and the report of sundry persons in whom I have and can always confide – On the grand river Main I find there are but 3 keepers, and one of them I well know that he is not worth 6 pence as a Keeper and the other I do not know but am told he has been sickly throughout the Winter – I wish our new inspector had left Antrim river (as I from experience left waste) without cost, as money and fish are both lost at that place. There can be no other remedy for the failure of our fishery this season but that of a continued high price and a regular attention to the Smacks our fish should not be sent in such quantitys to Belfast but kept for the Smacks and indeed I have been too oft troubled these three years past seeing such quantities sent to Belfast whilst poor Smackmen were kept lying at Portrush for 6, 7, and 8 weeks unserved and this was and will ever be a loss to the proprietors while such misconduct continues – I shall wonder if Mr. Brown will continue our Overseer Mr. Hu. McFillin after his last seasons illicit practice through the whole & particularly for his inattention to the Cutt House in the night of the 12th. Augt. last which I inserted in my Day Book for Mr. Browns perusal 8 of our best salmon stolen & worth £3. 7. 6.

February 22nd. 1802 it the Cutts to	1 salmon 10 lb. @ 4½	3.	9
24th. As Do. took	1 Do. 8	3.	0
This week	2 salmon 18	6.	9
March 1st. & 4 at the Cutts took	3 Do. 28	10.	6
These two weeks	5 ......1: 16	17.	3
March 8th & 11th. at Do. took	4 ...... 1: 6	13.	6
These 3 weeks	9 0: 2: 22	1. 10.	9
March 20th taken this week	13 1: 1: 8	2. 19.	3
amt. of these 4 week	22 2: 0: 0	4. 10.	0
Saturday 27th. amt. taken this week	28 2: 3: 5	6. 5.	7
Sold these 5 weeks	50 4: 3: 5	10. 15.	7

I perceive how that the old Cutt produces no fish this year and I think the reason is because our Overseer has the Keys of the Fishery at his command and I observe on sundry mornings one of our Loops wet and the others dry and I all the last summer noticed this and found it never noticed or challenged by any other but the Loopers and myself – If the Trustee noticed it he never once challenged it.

There are always some persons of Castleroe on foot in the night and I think I shall soon find my suspicions fully cleared up – on Sat. the 27th in Colerain I see John McAlister who I imagine will certainly make his Lodgings good in Mr. McFillin's for this night.

In the eveng. of Sunday 28 the overseer came into this office and told me that being suspicious of some one fishing the old Cutt he had been watching on Saturday night and that on his opening Cutt gate something had been put to the door in the inside so that the Door would not open, till he ran against it with all his force, and that he searched all the Cutts and places about but could see no person, that he went and awoke his Uncle Mr. McFillin and the family and young Mr. Heyland who came all to his assistance but could find no person and that after all these assistants were departed from the place he went to the old Cutt and there found a Loop left wet as if fishing but could find no man.

Monday 29th

I find myself perfectly right in my conjectures for I find by Jack Heylands children James Deehan and others who were looking at the Overseer & McAlister fishing the old Cutt and afterwards going to the Alds. Boal and croping the Bann that it being then so dark these people could not observe what they done on the far side, but that upon their seeing these persons all looking at them they on their return went again to the Old Cutt where McAlister disappeared and the overseer then raised the hue and cry.

	S.	£.	s.	d.
1802 March 27 Bro. Fowd. 5 last weeks	50 – 4: 3: 5 –	10.	15.	7½
April 3d this weeks sales	22 – 1: 3: 27 –	4.	8.	10½
amt. these 6 weeks	72 – 6: 3: 2 –	15.	14.	6
April 10th. this week sold	55 – 5: 1: 28 –	12.	6.	9
amt. for these 7 weeks	127 – 12: 1: 0 –	27.	11.	3

I see our Trustee has at length set a Watchman on the Antrim side and the old Cutt left to the tender mercies of our Overseer this all for the saving but I fear, not for the benefit of our employers.

		£. s. d.
April 17 Sold this week	37 – 3: 1: 29 –	7. 17. 1½
amt. of 8 weeks sales	164 – 15: 2: 29 –	35. 8. 4½
April 24 Sold this week	56 – 5: 2: 5 –	12. 9. 4½
amt. these 9 weeks	220 – 1: 1: 1: 4 –	47. 17. 9
May 1st. Sales this week	137 – 13: 0: 20 –	29. 12. 6
amt. of 10 weeks sales	357 – 1: 14: 1: 24 –	77: 10: 3
Recd. from 1 Smack 19th April		17. 17. 6
From another the 26th. Do.		33. 0. 0
The whole amt these 10 weeks		128. 7. 9

	£ s.	
May 3rd recd. from 1 Smack	27. 10 ⎫	
„ 7th from another	33. 0 ⎬	
		60. 10. 0
Amt. this week to the Country	154 – 14: 2: 8	32. 15. 6
Whole amt. these 11 weeks		221. 13. 3

By my hand Book I see, on the 28th April sold P. Dougherty 49 fish
4:2:0 at £10. 2. 6 and the 5 May to Hu. Gage 46 – 4:2:0 at £10.2.6. The
fish in my opinion should have gone to the smacks rather than to
Belfast – Perhaps Mr. Brown has his private reasons for serving these
men, but I think he should keep his eye to our employer – 3 Hund.
per piece to these men was enough for Belfast so early and would
have kept the price better in that market, but I see it is no matter and
we only by this method of ecconomy lose £4.10.0.

May 10 and 14 recd. from 2 Smacks.		93. 10. 0
15 this Week from the country for	259 – 1: 4: 0: 17	54. 6. 4½
1802. May 15 whole amt. of 12 Weeks sales		369. 9. 7½

I also observe in this last week is sent to Belfast by John Shannon 53 –
4:2, to Derry by Thos. Smyth 33 – 3 Hund. by John McAlister for
Belfast 33 fish 3 Hund. to Johnny Spallin 44 fish 4 Hund. and to Hu.
Dean 50 fish 4:2, the whole is 211 fish weight, 19 Hund. makes £42.15. 0
– a lesser quantity might have served for Belfast and all the rest
should have gone to the Smacks but our Managers know all things
best and I must consent myself, only I see on this Weeks sales we
might have saved to our employer £9. 10s.

Again on May 10th to Johnny Spallin and partner 4 Hundwt.

          19th to Pat Moony   4   Do.

now I really think 8 Hundwt. of fish to Belfast in any week whilst Smacks are waiting or till the Cranagh fishery begins is a quantity too much for that market as it must lower the price too long before the Cranagh begins. in all the time of my managemt. here I never sent more than 3 Hundwt. weekly to Belfast untill the smack trade had first ceased or that the Cranagh had began and by this method I kept up the price in Belfast untill Carriers were served at the Cronagh where they must and ought to sell rather than salt – however I see that by the last 2 loads we lost £4.

		£ s.	£.	s.	d
May 17 recd. from one Smack		46. 15 }	96.	5.	0
21 recd. from another		49. 10 }			
22 amt. this Week from the Country		227 – 1: 0: 3: 17 –	47.	0.	1½
			512.	14.	9
		£. s			
May 24 Recd. from one Smack		41. 5 }	85.	5.	0
28 from another Do.		44. – }			
29 the Country this week		187 – 17: 2: .8	39.	10.	6
whole amt. these 14 Weeks			£637.	10.	3

I observe that the 24 April I pd. a Keeper on this side the river for 5 nights watching I wish they had employed him from the 1st of March it would have saved us some fish – Hang the man who has no shift, and Him who has too many – on the 5th of May inst. I see my knowing Jocky Mr. Brown fairly taken in. Our Trustee and Overseer have in conjunction told Mr. Brown how that last night they patrolld the Cutt fishery and that they found Mr. Browns own favourite Labourer John Campbell who watches on the Antrim side fast asleep on his Duty and my worthy Manager by their advice has yielded so far to their insinuations not to turn him off but to appoint our overseer an assistant watchman and for his assistance I have paid Our Trustee 3s. 3d. for 3 nights this Week ending the 8th. inst. I dare say he will be continued for several Weeks to come and upon my soul Mr. McFillin (Sir G. Hills Trustee) this is a most grand scheme to put – 13s.6½d. into your own pocket Viz. 6s. 6d.to our Overseer as Looper and 7s.0½d.to Do. as Watchman. I have questiond Campbell concerning this and his answer was, That having Mr. McFillins Dog with him when on Duty, the Dog knew his Master and the overseer and that when he himself found who they were he was so simple as not to walk out of his Cabbin to Challenge them. O Campbell you are in my eye as great a Vilian as the Divil wants.

		£	s.	d.
Note I have now from Smacks recd.		386.	12.	6
and from the Country recd.		251.	2.	9
My Amt. these 14 Weeks is just		637.	15.	3
May 31st. Recd. from Jn. Davison Smackman		37.	2.	6
June 5th. Recd. this week from the Country:	65 – 5: 2: 25	12.	16.	10½
Amt. taken these 15 weeks		£687.	14.	7½
June 7 Recd. from one Smack;		34.	7.	6
11 From another Do.		13.	15.	0
12 Amt. of sales this week to the Country :	55 – 4: 2: 14	10.	7.	9
Amount recd. for 16 Weeks		£746.	4.	10½
June 18 Recd. from the last Smackman		28.	17.	6
19 this week recd. from the Country:	131 – 9: 1: 4	20.	17.	9
Whole amount these 17 Weeks		£796.	0.	1½

	No.	T. c.		£	s.	d.
1802 Recd. from Smacks this season for 1995 –	9: 2:	@ 5½d	500.	10.	0
Recd. from the Country this Week for					
281 fish	15: 2: 6:	34.	19.	9
Whole recd. from the Country to the 19th. 1435 –	6: 11: 0: 27:	295.	5.	1½
June 26th. amt. for 18 weeks this day		£830.	14.	10½
Note our sale to Smacks last year was		£518.	16.	8
our amount from Do. this year is		500.	10 .	0
Deficient for want of attention		£18.	6.	8

I observe on 5th June our assistant Watchman is pd off for 4 Weeks and 3 Days £1. 11. 5 I really could wish he had advantaged the fishery one single 6 pence in the time.

Tis really amazing that Mr. Brown who is seemingly active (or would at least wish to be thought so) would suffer himself or rather Sir G. Hill to be so imposed upon by any Man, especiallv by Sir Gs. Trustee who hires a servant to work his own work, then sets him out as a Looper and Overseer of the Fishery at 6s. 6d. per Week, Mr. McFillin Loops in his place perhaps one hour in the day if reckoned except on particular days when Mr. Brown comes here Whilst at all other business of the fishery the 3 other Loopers are left to do it and the 4th Looper working to his master who indulges him with the keys of the fishery where he has free access at all times by day and night and his behaviour in conjunction and colusion last season.with the Watchman Dick feet was so very conspicuous that I shall now pass it over in silence only I cannot forget his ingenuity in the night of Sunday the 26th. July 1801.

Should this Diary fall into the hands of a person unacquaint with my real Character he would in all probability suspect and Damn me as an officious old insinuating rascal reflecting upon others in order to ingraciate himself: Here he mistakes me, Because my present place in the fishery is the only and very place which suits my present age and ability of Body, my Constitution is much worn by more than common fatigue and exertions on the Bann and other rivers in a course of 14 Cold winters, the last of which was the easiest and the reason for this was my Coadjutant boastingly told me he could do everything so effactually that I took especial care not to hinder him – I never was a Boaster or Bragger but a strict attendant to my duty.

In the year 85 or 6 I commenced as Inspector of the Rivers and at a Time when these fisherys were unable to defray the Expenses untill Lady Hamiltons manager collected off her then Estate a sum of £300 to pay off the then deficiency, however I acted in my place these fisheries bore Testimony and an annual increase was the consequent of my exertions and the fisheries of 1799 allowd to be the most profitable of any other upon record – In Winter 1800 our Manager not in his own judgement but by advice and for the benefit of our employers superseded me in the Office of inspector and saved me the trouble of resigning a place in which such a change of measures and managements shewd me my credit must sink if I continued in place and under the controll of strangers in practice and scornful to advice – Had the fishery increased yearly since the time of my discharge the

persons in office had merited the thanks of our employers – Happy I
am in that of my right times discharge and also at the great distance
in which I am kept at all times since my commencement.

		£.	s.	d
Brought forward		830.	14.	10½
July 3 Sales this week is 253 –	12: 1: 19	27.	18.	4½
Our sales for 19 weeks is		£858.	13.	3

Notwithstanding the distance which I am kept by Sir G. Hills
Managers here I am nevertheless oft times vexed when I see matters
misconducted & losses sustained by my employers. For instance last
Summer Sir Georges Trustee bought from Dick Bullin 3 Thrave of
Straw and for which I paid him 9s. 9d., the Straw was intended to
thatch the Watch House but instead of thatching the Cabbin it was
left in the Cutt House and in the Course of Ten Days it was every
grain taken by the Carriers to pack their fish. In Spring when our
Loopers were setting the Cutts, the Trustee then bought off Wm.
Balmer 55 Thrave of Straw to thatch the Cutt House, I then thought
he intended the refuse of this Straw for the Cuttheads, but, to my
surprise I found he fed his Horse and Cow therewith and bought
from Jack Shannon the refuse of his Cattles fodder which was taken
from their heads every morning and afterwards compicted to be 17
thrave at 13d. and for which I paid him 10s. 5d. per order of the
Trustee and in reallity I was much vexed on paying it. He afterwards
bought for thatching Cutthouse a quantity of straw by bulk and
unfortunately it turned (when brought here) to be nothing other than
the refuse straw taken from before the mans cattle every morning
and thrown together in a lump and then sold, I upbraided the parties
when I was paying the Money for it as ordered, but to my inward
vexation I could not redress it.

Good Lord would it not vex the heart of any person of feeling to
stand and observe at a distance the thatcher obliged to come from his
Ladder at sundry times and on sundry days and draw straw and make
scollips while our Trustee, his overseer, and the three Loopers are
sitting all contentedly drinking. Damnation to this Tippling house, it
was ever a nuisance to this place and this fishery and ever will be so
while sufferd to retail liquours and as to our Trustees house I most
earnestly wish it was placed at some greater distance from this
fishery and our present overseer removed along with it, this story is
long enough.

I am certain the trustee wishes well to the interest of his employer, but alas, he is unsteady and altogether a stranger to the ways and means whereby to improve and secure that interest –

			£.	s.	d
	Brought Forward		858.	13.	3
July 10 this week at 4½d	52 –	4: 2: 8	10.	15.	6
Do. Grawls at 3½	556 –	22: 3:14	40.	0.	4
Amount these 20 weeks			£908.	19.	1

As the rains are at present so very constant and the Water so high all this day I am certain the Netts will not lie on the bottom so as to take fish therefore we will I hope have a great store in these Cutts by Monday next.

It vexes me to see such quantity of straw left to rot under these rains, had it been put dry into some one of these Houses we then would have sufficient for the Setting of the Cutts these two years to come, or had our Trustee thought right he might have had this room and Stable thatched with the present straw on hand and with the little which he took to the Cranagh.

July 13th

I am really and at present much afflicted on seeing our Overseer upon sundry days past and this day Cutting and carrying to his Masters House so many good Cuttstakes and there burning them, I dare not question or forbid him lest Mr. Brown turns me out of place. Good Heaven don't Mr. McFillin know that these stakes Costs our employers 8d. per piece when brought here, so that every dozen stands as 8 shillings these two or three years past. I wonder at McFillin to see this done, but indeed he is seldom in his own House or in the way to see many things else, we can all see and tell when he rises every day, but where is the person can tell what time he goes to Bed. –

			£	s.	d.
	Brought Forward		908.	19.	1
July 17th.					
Grawls sold this Week at 3½d. –	568 –	1: 2: 3: 4	39.	17.	5
salmon sold at 4½ –	28 –	2: 2: 15	5.	18.	1½
Amount of Sales for 21 Weeks			£954.	14.	7½

Monday 19th.

I observe some Carriers here who have lost by their last Weeks sales notwithstanding the handsome allowance given them by Mr. McFillin and certainly they had their Grawls at 3d. and their salmon at 4d. per pound, Mr. Brown should have ordered here and at the Cranagh a stone of such additional weight to carriers alone as would bring their grawls near 3d. and salmon near 4d., and this would have kept up their courage on seeing all others from town and Country paying us the present price of 3½d. and 4½d. I dare not presume to mention this to Mr. Brown no no he is above advice especially from me, I wish he may not fall under the Censure of his employers, I see these Carriers are all going away without fish, and I see we can easily keep all the fish we have in the Cutts, but if there be any run, they must salt at the Cranagh and that will not be found so beneficial as the scheme above hinted.

			£	s.	d
July 24 Sales this Week @ 4½d.	5 –	0: 2: 13	1.	7.	4½
Do. Grawls @ 3½d.	302 –	13: 2: 6	23.	14.	3
Brought Forward			954.	14.	7½
Amount these 22 Weeks			£979.	16.	3

Monday 26th. July 1802.

I am truly glad to find our Trustee has got information against Mr. Browns favourite Watchman and Labourer, Damn the Vilian, he is the very Vilian I ever took him to be and I have along suspected him of Colusion with Wallaces family in manner and Villiany as that of Dickfeet Dempsy thro the course of last season – I am glad to find they have got Wallace into Jail and hope he will not depart until he has paid the uttermost Farthing – I wish he may be persuaded to become approver against our Damd. Watchman as being a sharer of the fish taken and that he may be fined and confined in proportion to his viliany but when I look a little back into the arrangements and managements and course of matters as they occurrd, I shall forfeit my Ears if Campbell suffers any fine or infliction whatsoever, because, if he suffers, he will be spurrd to tell and declare things disagreeable and perhaps very hurtful to some persons of the family who preside over us at these fisherys – There had not been a fit Watch on these Cutts (except old Miller) since Sir G. Hills commencement a heavy loss.

	Amt. brought forward		979. 16. 3	

Sat. 31st July

Grawls this week @ 3½d –	508 – 1:2:3:15 –	40. 0. 7½ }	
Salmon @ 4½ –	18 – 2:0:20 –	5. 5. 0 }	45. 5. 7½

Amount these 23 Weeks.   £1025. 1. 10½

Aug. 1st.

This morning it is said here that our employer intends salting all salmon to be taken here untill the quantity salted shall amt. to his purpose – Why do they sell these fish? If the Bann rises (as I am certain it will) I think we may take half a Ton and upwards during the continuance of the fresh, they say Sir George will send salt here for this purpose and indeed I can see no purpose it will answer except Mr. McFillins purpose, and I shall forfeit my Ears if half the fish will be salted when taken and the Salmon will fail with the Flood and gradually fall off together, here I shall wait the issu.

I observe that last week we sold		18 –	2. 0. 20	
Monday 2nd Augt.:sold to Jack Bradley		8 –	1. 0. 0	
	To sunmerseat House	13 –	1. 2. 0	
	Mr. Orr of Lanmore	1 –	19	
	To Johnny Spallin	10 –	1. 0. 28	
Tuesday 3rd.	To Mr. Hyland by I. Shannon	10 –	1. 2. 0	
Wednesday 4th	To Josiah Bryans	4 –	2. 0	
	To Mr. Hill of Colerain	6 –	1. 0. 0	
Thursday 5th	To Mr. Hyland by I. Shannon	12 –	1. 2. 0	
	To Josiah Bryans	4 –	0. 2. 0	
	Mr. McFillin for himself or some friend by the name of Grawls salted here and 5s.lost }	5 –	0. 2. 0	
	Sold since the flood commenced and salted for Sir George Hill only }	91 – 7 –	11. 2. 7 1. 0. 0	
Saturday 7th.	Sold to sundrys	3 –	0. 1. 9	
	Salted for Sir George Hill	8 –	1. 0. 0	
	Amt. taken this Week	91 –	11. 2. 26	

I see they have lost the method of taking fish at the Cranagh and they don't know how to recover it, I would willingly go down and put them on the only and true way of fishing but am certain Mr. Brown would never forgive me such offence but my comfort is, if they miss at the Cranagh we take at the Cutts which I look upon as one and the same for our employers. We should had a happy fishery this season had they not fishd. at the Cranagh longer than the 25th July except with the Trout nett in the last fortnight of the fishery – We would have saved Money –

			£	s.	d.
Amount of sales Brought forward			1025.	1.	10½
Augt. 7th. Grawls this week	451 –	1. 0. 2. 3. @ 3½d	35.	18.	4½
Salmon @ 4½d.	71 –	9. 0. 26	20.	14.	9
Amount these 24 weeks			£1081.	15.	0
Augt.12th. This Weeks salmon on	30 –	3. 3. 52	8.	17.	0
Grawls @ 3½d	205 –	9. 1. 15	16.	8.	1½
Amount at this place 1801			£1178.	17.	10
Amount of Cutts 1800			1501.	8.	6½
Cutts 1799			1650.	3.	7½
This year			1107.	0.	1½
Worse than the year 1799		By	£543.	3.	6

I here see how Managemt. can shew for itself and here I am much vexed on seeing our Overseer carrying such armfuls of our Cutts. stakes to burn in his Uncles House, but who is the person who dare forbid him. I wish the Keys of the fishery were lodged elsewhere Turff are scarce and very dear, Stakes and Boards will go.

Augt. 18	another grand Burden, the Uncle this day gone to Kilrea to fix Keepers, gave him 5s. 5d.
1802 Aug. 19 and 20	I shall here mention an occurrence of the 26th May last Viz. Mr. Brown sent his tenant Thos. Sixsmith with written order to serve the bearer with a load of fish for Belfast, the order was instantly attended to and the fish got and as soon as weighed and paid for this worthy Tenant that instant at the Cutt Gate sold these same fish to a carrier for Belfast at £13:11:0 which was just 4 Guins. profit — I could not help grieving at this piece of managmt. knowing how much the Smackmen wanted at same time.

these heavy rains and floods are the very worst Hurt to our fishery, I know it well, the present floods carry our fish from the grand Nursery into the smaller rivers 2 or 3 Months too soon, consequently they are all killd. before Keepers are set to guard them. I am daily telling the inspector of this and urging him to go and fix his Men on All the rivers as the present floods evidently call for every effort in his power, he says he has no Money to carry him, I offer him money for this purpose but he says Mr. Brown will not allow him a Shilling – This is vexation and ruin – find Mr. McFillin has never yet surveyed or inspected the Registered Cotts and Boats on the Bann since his commencement. I suppose our employers think themselves secured by that statute, and I think otherwise I look upon the requisite inspection of these Cotts as vastly more troublesome than the inspection of the rivers and Keepers – during my time of inspecting under Sir G. H. I made one survey from the Bar of Toom to the Barr of Colerain and in my way found 30 all registered and letterd and I think that without a very frequent inspection the use of registry not worth 6 pence to the fishery but rather hurtful as the Keepers do not Challenge or notice them as formerly and I am of opinion that our inspector (unless he makes a survey this year) knows nothing as to their number or owners and their securitys nor the places whereto they belong.

| 1802 | SALES AT THE CUTT, FISHERY. Dr. | | | | | | | | £ : s : d |

		s.	t.	c.	q.	lb.	£	s	d	
	To balance due on last years acct.									12. 7½
Aug. 13.	Smacks at 55 –		9	2	0	0	500.	10.	0	
	Country @ 45 –		9	2	1	26	410.	11.	0	
									1107. 0. 1½	
	Grawls at 35 –		5	11	3	27	195.	19.	1½	
										£1107 12. 9

1802	SUNDRIES BY JOHN MACKY Cr.			£ : s : d
Augt. 13	By Deposits with Mr. Brown			780. 4. 3
	By Incidents pd.	31.	3. 2½	
	By Loopers & Watchmen pd.	43.	0. 1	
	By Waterkeepers paid part	83.	0 . 10	157. 4. 1½
	By Mr. Hills fish acct.	8. 0.	1½	
	By Mr. Browns Do.	2.	8. 10½	
	By Mr. McFillins Do. 8:2:9			
	By his Cash act. for 18:6:8½,	26.	9. 5½	36 . 18. 5½
	By Mr. Moffets salary pd.	20.	0. 0	
	By Agents salary at the Cutts pd.	22.	15. 0	42 15. 0
Augt. 31	By Cash now pd. Mr. Brown	77.	5. 2	
	By Ald. Hyland order on C. House	1.	18. 3	
	By Ballce. retained per order of Sir G.H.	11.	7 6	90. 10. 11
				£1107. 12. 9

1802 Cash paid Mr. McFillin Weekly at the Cutt Fishery.

					£	s.	d
March	27	Paid him as a Looper from 11th Jany. till this day			I.	II.	8
April	3	Week ending this date				5.	5
	10	for this Week	paid him			4.	4
	17	for this Week				3.	3
	24	for this Week				3.	3
May	1	For this Week :				6.	6
	8	As Looper and Watchman	this Week			9.	9
	15	As Looper and Watchman	this Week			13.	6½
	22	As Do. and Do.	this Week			13.	6½
	29	As Do. and Do	this Week			13.	6½
June	5	As Do. and Do.	this Week			13.	6½
	12	As Do. and Do.	this Week			13.	6½
	19	As Do. and Do.	this Week			13.	6½
	26	As Do. and Do.	this Week			13.	6½
July	3	As a Looper only	this Week			6.	6
	10	As Do.	this Week			6.	6
	17	As Do.	this Week			6.	6
	24	As Do.	this Week			6.	6
	31	As Looper and Watchman	this Week			13.	6½
Augt.	7	As Do. and Do.	this Week			13.	6½
	14	As Do. and Do.	this Week			13.	6½

Amt. paid him for Looping and Watching   £11. 5. 7

Sunday 10th Octr.	at the Cutts with Mr. Moffet and from his room I observe our Overseers Brother (who is at present under the Overseers tuition,) walk into the Cutts with a Handsaw, then lock Cutt Gate & walk into Cutt house & in the space of ½ an hour return to his Uncles with his burden of Cuttstakes sawn in pieces for the fire.
Octr. 25th 1802. –	At the foot of my farm I see an amazing Tide of salmon in the Bann and all playing upwards I wish Mr. McFillin may have the river well found with Keepers and all the lesser rivers near the Bann for in Case of a fresh the whole Country will turn out with Rods and flies and prey upon them like Sharks – the McCanns Cotts and others will take every advantage of such a grand run of fish, indeed by all accounts they have done pretty well in their trade since Lammass 1800 – Is it possible that Tom Ogue & Dickfeet don't know this –

Novr. 7	Met 2 of my old Keepers from the Vow who tells me that about the latter part of last Month they saw more Salmon in one day than they had seen these two years past and that they never in their lifetime saw so many Rod fishers, and that the McCanns & Dickfeets son had made a very fine fishing with their Cotts almost every night since Lammass and that some other Cotts had fished also, but they were not certain of their owners –
Novr. 15th. 1802 –	waited on Sir George Hill Bart. with a letter from Mr. Thompson he conversed some time with me in a friendly manner which I shall gratefully remember.
Novr. 18th	Met Wm. Beeton who tells me that on his return from Scotland with Sir G. Hills Sheep he called at Kilrea and there dined on fresh salmon.
Novr. 20th.	At the Cutts where Mr. Moffet declares he never saw in his time such a trade of carrying & Burning of Cuttstakes –
Decr. 28th. 1802 –	this day I have been looking through all my remarks of this Season since Lammass last and really I see nothing promising to an early brisk fishery and I am inwardly grieved at the accounts I have had from the River Main, Antrim, Kells, Ballymena and Gilgorm, I could most heartily wish that Sir G. Hill could spare some little time to visit these Rivers himself and get into the acquaintance of the Gentlemen, Magistrates & Linnen Drapers residing on and near these Rivers for indeed I am almost certain that our inspector has few friends in these parts of that Country –What a mighty matter That Tom Ogue & Dickfeet have taken the McCanns Cotts after fishing these two seasons past, and now when they have killed all they could their Cotts are seized – I remember a matter similar to this in last Winter 1801, Drumale Cotts were seized by these men just when they had nearly given over fishing
January 1st. 1803	this day I have been consulting my old Almanack Viz. the Sea, the Bar and the Bann, and I see no great encouragemt. for early fish, and I could wish our managers to keep patience and not to set any of our Cutts untill the Waters are turning clear and the Bar less noisy, by this piece of patience they wd. save expense –
Jany. 13th	on going to Cutts I saw Sir George Hill in Town he bade me send him a salmon for Dinner, on my arrival at the Leap I found the Loopers preparing to sett the old Cutthead and had it not been for fear of giving offence I would have advised them not to trouble themselves in such business until the Month of March when perhaps the Waters might be clearing off the mud. Experience will tell which of us are right – I never looked upon an odd Wandering Salmon as a suitable

atonement for the expence attending the taking it in a course of 6 or
7 Weeks fishing. I find Mastr. Owiny Kelly has resided with Uncle
here through the Winter and that he will remove immediately to
make way for our Overseer who is expected to return to his former
employments by the time fishing commences.

March 3rd.
1803

at the Cutts and to which I have travelled every Monday and
Thursday since the 13th. Jany. without seeing a Salmon taken, I could
wish the Cutts had remand. unset till this day; it would have saved a
needless expence to our employers and saved me one pair of shoes

March.7th

at the Cutts I find the Loopers have this day found a salmon in the old
Cutt which they have left in the Cutt till Sir G. Hill comes to Colerain
this I have told to Mr. Brown p. order of Mr. McFillin. query, will this
salmon be found again? No, upon my soul it never will

March 17

this day we have taken a salmon of 12 lbs. I wish these Cutts were
found with two fit persons to watch them – The old Cutt was so
carefully attended to last year as to produce nothing for our
employers till old Miller took it in charge and then it produced as in
former years – I have spoke to Mr. Brown about this matter, but I see
it is but foolish in me to give advice to a Man who shuns me, Charley
will I hope keep him right, and therefore I have done and as sure as
God made Moses, Hughey will be the Man and the produce of the
old Cutt will evidence for me whether I speak truth or lies – I see I
must get my bed to the Cutts tomorrow as I find myself done out
with walking.

21st

This day we have taken 8 salmon on the Antrim side where there is
no watchman, and the old Cutt produces nothing no, nor will it
produce, until some person of integrity is put in Charge – I could
wish they would employ nobody on this side of the river and that
Charles would keep the Keys of the Cutt and Cutt house in his own
pocket but what need I talk of Keys, for last year I observed that one
Key was laid aside and the Key of the Cutt Gate adapted to the
opening of the Cutt House and so I see it is continued; and now what
is the reason for this? Why my opinion is, that he who watches the
old Cutt has at the same time free access to the Loops in the House
and the Loopers (as well as myself) often noticed this and saw always
either one or two wet Loops every morning but poor Charlie never
observed this. And before the Key of the Cutt Gate was adapted to
the opening of the house I observed the stones pulld. out of the Wall
opposite the Lock of the Cutt house door and which I supposed was
done for the purpose of shooting the Lock, and even this very season
I observe that one of the front Windows of the Cutt house has been

pulled out and thrust in again and I have wondered that Charley did not get it some way replaced and repaired before it would be much observed indeed one of the Coach House Windows was pulld. out the same way the year before last when Charleys sister Mrs. Kelly was Hugheys Carrier and it was never heeded since. I wonder what has become of all the Dealboards that were left in the Cutt House on finishing the repairs of the Cutts in the year 1800 I am certain there were between 30 and 40 of them and I never saw one of them put to public use since that time only 11 or 12 which Mr. McFillin got wrought into a Desk for his own use –

April 2nd

this day I have paid the Loopers and Watchman and now see Mastr. Hughey is to act in the capacity of Looper and Watchmen, I could heartily wish this scheme would answer our employers as well as it does Charley and his Man, Charley will receive just 13. 6½p. week for his man and the Man will trust himself to Gods mercy and the produce of the old Cutt for his own private Wages – Now I am told Sir George intends building this Season on his own Ground – If this Building is intended for his own use it is well, but if for Mr. McFillin, I would wish it to be built at a vast greater distance from the Cutts. Where now is all the Boreing and building utensils which were collected into the Cutt house on finishing the repairs in 1800 – Where are all the Crows Jumpers Needles and ramers, Where are our Handbarrows & Wheelbarrovs Our Sledge and Hamers, Mortar Boxes and Our Sledge and Hamers, Mortar Boxes and Hods for carrying Mortar – Where is the 5 full Bars of Iron which were applied to the head of the new Cutt in the year before last – I wish they be all ready to produce at a Call, and where is now the great Iron Crane which was removed from the old salt house into the Cutt house shortly after Sir George Hill got the fishery, yes, I see it yet in Cutt house, and as to Dealboards for scaffolding etc. I doubt they are gone hence. The old Beam of New Cutt head is still I see in the same spot where it was first carried to altho I often ordered it to the Cutt house where it might be dry and ready for cutting up for certain uses – I sincerely wish that Sir George Hill would throw down the old Salt House, Build up the Doorway from thence to the Cutt house and likewise build up the Backdoor of Cutt house & all the Back windows thereof all with Stone & Lime this would considerably tend to his Advantage and at same time publish a Statute to prohibit the sale of all manner of Liquors at Castleroe:

1803 April 30   this day Mr. McFillin tells me that he intends putting Jack Shannon to Watch the Old Cutt and middle Cutts. I am sorry he did not do so a Month ago, he says he farther intends sending Hu. McFillin as an assistant Watchman to the Antrim side of the river. What is the use of this? Why really I don't know any purpose it tends to, except to put 7s.0½d. into Charleys pocket every Sat. morning.

I am heartily glad that Shannon watches the old Cutt it has not produced 3 Guins. to us this year nor last year untill old Miller took it in charge – Now by God I will forfeit my Ears if this Cutt will not produce 3 Guins. a day if fished out clean, and the produce will evidence how far I am right or wrong – indeed the season for the old Cutt is now nearly at an end so that we have lost by it every day since the fishery began and every Looper knows that it was always the most early in taking fish till within these two or three Seasons last past.

May 1st   The old Cutt was watched by H. McFillin and on Monday the 2nd. it produced £1: 19 : 2, Shannon watched on the night of the 2nd. and Tuesday produced upward of 1 Hundwt. for the Smack beside what was sold to the Country amounting to £3:9:7.

Wed 4th   we sold from the old Cutt 12 Salmon Wt. 1c. 0qr. 25lbs, – £3: 0: 5 and this eveng being

May 5th   I find we sold from the old Cutt this day 29 salmon Wt. 2:3: 5 which brought me in cash £6: 19: 7 and there are a number still in the Cutt so that I plainly see how much and how far our managers keep their employers interest in view – I could most heartily wish that Sir George would call on Mr. Brown to produce John Mackys Leger for the Cutt fishery 1801, Sir George would see on the last written leaf of that Book the manner in which the fish were kept by Hu. McFillin in the night of August 12th. and yet after all, he was continued in same trust last year and this year – perhaps Mr. Brown does not wish to interfere between Sir George Hill and the McFillins and I have often thought this, and I declare I am in fear of these Men myself – I live here in a very lonely manner without a friend or Weapon of any kind allowd. me since the day I commenced to the rect. of the Cash – indeed I now recollect that Mr. Brown about this time 2 years asked

me here one day if I had any sort of Arms and on telling him I had
none, he went immediately to Mr. McFillin and they together
brought me a Gun without a flint or ramrod and without any sort of
Amunition whatsoever so that it continued with me in that state till
12th of August when I was obliged to return it safe as I had got it and
I have not troubled any of them for the like security since that time.

				£	s.	d
Sat. 7th. May Sales to Country	363 –		1. 15. 1. 22	88.	11.	8
To Smacks	588 –		2. 16. 0. 00	166.	0.	0
amount	951 –		4. 11. 1. 22	256.	11.	8

Monday 9th May

last Sat. night Gregory Reny of this Town died and has appointed C.
McFillin and John Shannon Execrs. in his Will. These 2 men were sent
for in the night, J. Shannon being Watchman left his Br.in.law Barny
Dougherty in charge & when these Excers. were gone off to Renys
H. McFillin got in to Dougherty and told him he had just seen 2 men
at the far Cutt and insisted that Dougherty should go over the Water
with him and stay there for some time, on which Dougherty went
and before he and Hu. McFillin returnd, the accomplices of H.
McFillin had pulld. out a Windw. of Cutt house and took out Loops
and fished the old Cutt and afterwards put up the Loops and thrust
the Windw. Case home into its place – I now do well remember that
on Sat. last I saw Hu. McFillins Bror. in the Cutts and it inwardly
struck me that something was to be done, and indeed I am fully
persuaded that no other person but this Br. and Sam Boyd of
Castleroe who is now and all this Spring the real and intimate friend
in connextion with Hu.McFillin. I wish he was banished from this
place.

May 17th

This day I am told the Hu. McFillin has taken his departure from the
Cutts, I pray he may never return – I think he robbd. my press
yesterday morning – Lord. Is it possible or impossible that his Uncle
should or did not know the Trade practised and carried on here ever
since his commencemt. which was in May 1801 – and he or his Br.
have hurt me much – I observed his actions in some measure all that
season and by the night of the 12th. August. I noted in my then
Ledger to Mr. Brown and for his perusal wrote down the transactions
of the day and night which was (as I thought) sufficient to discharge
him that inst. Had our managers got such information against me a
Gaol would have been my portion for the deed & a trial by Jury
would have determined my fate.

	No.		£	s.	d
Week ending 15 Amt. of sales is	498 –	2. 8. 0. 13	120.	5.	5
Smacks and Carriers	1001 –	4. 15. 0. 15	285.	7.	6
Whole amount is			405.	12.	11

What will poor Charley do now for his 13s. 6½d. every Saturday will
he now rate himself as a Looper at 6s. 6d. per week – What is the use
of 2 Watchmen on the Antrim side – one honest Watchman on that
side is sufficient – But if both men are roguish it must require more
stealth for 2 than for one – unluckily for the fishery Samuel Boyd still
remains in Castleroe and will be our most steady attendant at all
hours for an opportunity of stealth, he was the constant companion
of Hu. McFillin and his House the common recepticle for all the
Women of Castleroe and the Summerseat Servants who revell there
at all hours and the Whisky House of Castleroe is and ever was
Hurtful to the fishery as any other thing within my knowledge I wish
it was burnd.

			£	s.	d
Sunday 29 May Amt. to the Country	745 –	3. 10. 3. 24	177.	7.	6
Smacks and Carriers	2468 –	11. 7. 0. 22	681.	11.	0
Amt. is			£858.	18.	6

I observe the long ladder is at last broke into pieces, in last April it
was used in thatching Mr. Moffets House and was then left by the
Garden Wall, I bade Mr. McFillin at sundry times to put it in the Cutt
house where I always kept it dry for 13 years, he never minded my
advice so now we have no Ladder, perhaps he thinks there is no
necessity for a Ladder here. I observe there is not a board of the 40
which was left in the Cutt house when the Cutts was repaired –

30th   I see clearly that it will be a good season at the Cutts the continued
high price is our grand mark and the state of the water at the Cutts
will save the heavy expence of the Cranagh for some time yet to
come and if grawls run as I wish them to do, the fishery at the
Cranagh will bring a profit but otherwise the loss will be felt by the
Cranagh.

			£	s.	d
Sunday 5th June Country @ 5d –	828 –	3. 18. 0. 22	195.	9.	2
Smack Trade @ 6 –	3261 –	14. 18. 0. 22	894.	11.	0
Amt. sold			£1090.	0.	2
Sat. 11th. Sales to Country @ 5d –	1332 –	5. 19. 2. 18	299.	2.	6
To Smacks @ 6 –	3751 –	17. 2. 0. 22	1026.	11.	0
Amt. this evening			£1325.	13.	6

18

The Smackman says he calld. yesterday at the Cranh. and orderd. that the salmon might be saved for him till this morng. and that he deposited there 7 Guins. to secure the fish till today, and that when he called there this morng. they told what they had taken were sold to Carriers. Good Lord what managemt!

Here we have fish and the poor Man cannot take them –

Sales here @ 5d.	1537 –	6. 9. 3. 23	324.	17.	1
Smack Trade	4126 –	18.14. 2. 22	1124.	1.	0
			1448.	18.	1

I really think Mr. Brown should lower the present price of the fish else he will Salt too soon to the loss of our employers.

June 20th   Mr. McFillin tells me he has orders to lower the price, I am glad it is so, it will renew a spirit in the Carriers for 2 or 3 Weeks longer.

June 25 to the Country @ 4½d –	196 –	17. 0. 23	38.	13.	7½
Grawls @ 4 –	517 –	19. 2. 21	39.	7.	0
Now I see this season will do			78.	0.	7½
Brought Fowd.			1448.	18.	1
Lord we will I see, come up as I wish		£1526. 18. 8½			

July 2nd. for Salmon @ 4½d Viz.	86 –	7. 0. 20	16.	2.	6
For Grawls @ 4d.	477 –	17. 2. 8	35.	2.	8
This will do			£51.	5.	2

4th		upon my soul my Dear Charley you should have fished the 2 far Cutts or your fish will be all spoild, I wonder what he is keeping them for ever since I bade him fish them out.	

4th upon my soul my Dear Charley you should have fished the 2 far Cutts or your fish will be all spoild, I wonder what he is keeping them for ever since I bade him fish them out.

5th at 4 o'clock this eveng. recd. orders to lower the Grawls ½pr. lb. therefore these 2 days at 4d. produces :

	£25. 4. 0 ⎫	
4 days at 3½d gives	30. 15. 1½ ⎬	55. 19. 1½
9th. Salmon this week		8. 2. 9

the 2 far Cutts are still full of fish after taking   £64. 1. 10½

11th on going to fish the 2 far Cutts this morng. found a Stake taken out of the land Cutt head and all the fish (except 2 Grawls) gone through the opening. upon my word I am sorry for this loss of 5 or 6 Guins. at the lowest computation. Will Mr. McFillin make this loss known to Sir G. Hill I think he will not – I have oft advised him to continue his Watchman on that side without leaving the spot from Sat. eveng. till Monday morng. at 7 o'clock, it would hinder Soldiers and other Vagabonds from abusing the fish and the Cutts every sunday from morng. to night. The Watchman for 14 years under my care, never left the far side from Sat. eveng till Monday morng. and during that time I never lost a Cuttstake nor a fish, I vex that it is not so ever since Sir George got the fishery and my advice rejected always by Brown and McFillin.

Augt. 12th. 1803   Amount of Sales as follows Viz :

4126 Weight 18 : 14 : 2 : 22 @ 6d pr. lb.		1124. 1. 0
1537 ,, 6 : 9 : 3 : 23 @ 5d. ,, ,,	324. 17. 1	
1342 ,, 2 : 9 : 3 : 11 @ 4d. ,, ,,		99. 13. 8
401 ,, 1 : 16 : 3 : 4 @ 4½d ,, ,,		82. 15. 3
1248 ,, 2 : 5 : 1 : 24 @ 3½d ,, ,,		79. 10. 9
1492 ,, 2 : 17 : 3 : 2 @ 3d ,, ,,		86. 13. 0
10146 Weight 34 : 14 . 1 : 26 Amount		£1797. 10. 9

Here I now see the above amount is very pleasing but when I consider the vast failure in the quantity I cannot help grieving at the vast loss of fish since the year 1799: I remember in that year we reckoned at these Cutts 13677 fish Wt. 56 t. 2c. 3q. 13lb. which we sold at 4d, 3d, and 2½d per pound and the amt. of our Cash was £1650. 3. 7½ and was the most profitable season in my memory notwithstanding the depredations comitted both before and in the time of our late damnd.

Rebellion, but why should I grieve for although we had 3531 fish that year more than we have this year, yet we count better in Cash this year by £147.7.1½ but the Cranagh is vastly deficient this year and far short of its amt. in the year 1799. upon the whole I see we are failing.

1803	SALES AT THE CUTT FISHERY	DR.		£	s.	d
Augt. 12. To Ballance last years acct. 10 Gs..				11.	7.	6

	To amt. at 6d.	No.	T. c. qr. lb.			
		4126 –	18.14. 2. 22 –	1124.	1.	0
	at 5d.	1537 –	6. 9. 3. 23 –	324.	17.	1
	at 4½	401 –	1. 16. 3. 4 –	82.	15.	3
	at 4d.	1342 –	2. 9. 3. 11 –	99.	13.	8
	at 3½	1248 –	2. 5. 1. 24 –	79.	10.	9
	at 3d.	1492 –	2. 17. 3. 2 –	86.	13.	0
		10146 –	34. 13. 1. 26 –			
				1797.	10.	9
				£1808.	18.	3

1803	SUNDRIES BY JOHN MACKY	CR.		£.	s.	d
Augt. 12.By Deposits to Mr. Brown				1510.	12.	0
By Incidents paid			26. 3. 1½			
By Loopers and Watchmen pd.			47. 4. 5			
By Waterkeepers pd.			88. 17. 7½	162.	5.	2

		£. s. d				
By C. McFillins fish act.		7. 7. 2				
By Cash pd. him		33. 10. 9	40. 17. 11			
By Mr. Moffets salary pd,			20. 0. 0			
By my years Salary pd.			22. 15. 0	83.	12.	11
By a yrs. rent of C.McFillins house pd.			3. 8. 3			
By Ald. Heyland on the C.house for			3. 3. 9	6.	12.	0
By Mr. Hills fish act.			6. 10. 2½			
By Mr. Browns 1.7.6						
Miss Crafords 7. 10			1. 15. 4			
By Pat Doughertys due see June 6			7. 14. 8½	16.	0.	3
By Mr. Murphy returnd. here due					16.	3
Ballance due by me this Settlemt.		£28. 19. 8		1779.	18.	7

Total £1808.18.3.

Here I see that there is a very heavy Ballance against me and no wonder as I have an Office so ill provided with Locks and Keys, this I told Mr. Brown on my first entrance in rect. of the Cash. Hu. McFillin or his Br. I suspect for my loss of Cash this year. Now to explain this affair, I am afraid to speak it to any one, all I have done on that head is no more than a memorandum in my Hand Book of the time and manner in which my Room and Cupboard Doors were both opend. and room Door locked again and either 10 or 11 Guins. 2 Seven Shillg. pieces and some few shillings taken while I was in the Cutts in the morng.

Novr. 4th | Since the close of the fishery I have been looking to the Sea and the Bann and other objects which I have noted these 17 years past and really I don't see any material good tokens but rather bad ones, and I think our Winter will be unfavourable by too much rain and swelling floods too great and rapid I wish I may be mistaken.

Oct. 7th | We have now had a long time of Dry weather but I see it will soon change. I hope Mr. McFillin has fixed all Keepers before the first flood arises.

1804 Jany. 7th | I have been since Novr. last noting the Weather and am afraid the state of the rivers are by no means promising for certainly there are a number of the Roods buried and many carried away. I wish our managers may be so prudent as to set no more than one Cutt till the 1st of March for indeed if they set any more they will most certainly be carried away, therefore, I could rather 2 or 3 Salmon should ascend the Rock than to hazard the loss of a Cutt.

Feby. 20th. 1804 | Went to the Cutts where I found the Beams of the old Cutt head started and the Wings stakes and tongue all carried away but some of them found again. This accident I feared seeing they had set the Cutts too soon, but no matter, experience will teach them what my advice cannot.

27th | went to the Cutts and found the 3 Loopers setting and repairing the old Cutt.

March 5th | went to the Cutts and found the old Cutt in fishing order. The Loopers say they taken taken 11 or 12 fish. Mr. Murphy tells me that Sir George Hill has let the Salmon (all but a fourth part) to some Scotchmen for 15 years at 6d. per pound (Except for Grawls) I am sorry that Sir George has not the proper idea of his fishery as he ought else he would not be so easily taken in. Would he but only consider the failure of his fisheries since 1799 and that he cannot mend the failure but by raising his prices, which if the fish keeps decreasing in number as they have done Salmon will, before 3 years are expired sell on the street of Colerain for a Shilling per pound and Bushmill fish will this very season sell in Belfast for a Shilling per pound.

1804. March 19th.

at the Cutts.

I have several grand reasons to think we shall have a handsome fishery here this Season, I have very strong hopes that the river will not fall soon and in that case our Spring fishery will turn out well but really I do not expect this season will give as many Grawl as it ought because the Winter was unfavourable, therefore, we must depend on the Sea principally for this seasons fish and that of a continued high price.

May 22nd

I plainly perceive we shall have a great fishery here this season and principally Salmon and I see they are beginning to die in the Cutts for want of being fished early enough every morng. but all I can say is of no avail with our manager here. Damnation to this Whisky shop it seems to be our present chiefest hurt, it is now 9 o'clock and not a weak or dying fish lifted, so that by the time they are lifted they must be sold at ½ price besides the loss sustained by the weak fish falling backward thro the Tong and appearing on the surface of the water below the rock, neighbours will get them.

1804 May 25

I have over and over advised that all these weak fish which lie in the Wings should be lifted every morning early and such as cannot be sold even at ½ price, they ought to be salted, because I think it would be better to salt than to let such vast numbers die and glide thro the Tongues and the Country carry them away for nothing, I do not like salting, but in our present situation we ought to salt rather than lose them entirely. I sincerely wish Sir George Hill would come here were it but for one Day, or even a few Hours, I dare not write to him, no, it is dangerous and therefore to my inward vexation I must be silent. I shall stop any farther notice to my superiors in Trust, lest I should be deemd. what I am not. Viz a Tatler I remember I once slightly hinted to Sir George Hill that the selling of whisky in Castleroe was hurtful to his fishery, and he told me if the present licensd. retailers were stopped it woud. only encourage private selling, here he was entirely mistaken in the matter and therefore he now suffers what he was not aware of.

March 13. To my draft Bill on Mr. Alexander Murdoch
             Writer in Ayer for the amt, of my legacy of
             Lady Hamilton for principal and Interest
             amountg. to   128.   4.   3

         To drawback on the above the writers Bill on costs
             amounting to   8. 16.   4

                                                                                119.   7. 11

   ,,   30 Drawn my bill on Mr Murdoch for the Ballance
             in his hands after deducting the shillings and
             pence so that my Draft for Mr. Blacks comes to   119.   0.   0

1807 CONTRA   CRS   £.   s.   d

March 13. By Cash to pay Stamp for Bill   3.   4
          By Do. to pay postage   2.   6.   16
   ,,   16. By 2 lb. Sugar 22d. & 8 oz. Tea 4s.5. 10
   ,,   21. By a Banknote 34s. 1½d. Cash 11/4½.   2.   5.   6
   ,,   28. By Jhn. Black to pay County Sess   1.   2.   9
   ,,   30. By Cash to pay fishery Sess   1.   14.   1½
April   2. By Cash for Cha. McFillin   2.   5.   6
                                                                        7. 19   6½

1791 Augt. 13   Memorandum of C. Stakes :

Far C,. Head	69	}		Waste	19		
Wings of Do	81	} 150		Long Cutt	67	}	
				Wings of do.	79	}	46
Alexanders	60	}		Murphy	48	}	
Wings of Do.	61	} 121		Wings	61	}	109
N. Cutt	67	}		o Cutt	65	}	
Wings of Do.	72	} 139		Wings	89	}	154

132 D. Boards for Cuttheads   111 Do. for Wings –

3½ Hund. 5 Nails for Heads & Tongue posts and 3¾ Hund. 40d. Nails for Wings – a Board gives 3 for the Head and 4 for the Wings.

2 before 1 and 3 before 5, first 2 and then 2 and 4 came belive first 1 and then 1 and 3 at a cast, Nicholas and twist 2 and Jack at the last, these are to be counted by Tens.

IIOIIIOOOOOIIOOIIIIOIOOOIOOIIO

From numbers aid and Art, Never will Fame depart.

OOOOIIIIIOOIOOOIOIIOOIIIOIIOOI

these are to be counted by Nines.

a e i o u

1 2 3 4 5

– FOR DEAFNESS –

Take oil of bitter Almonds ¼ oz. Castor 1½ Drahams Chymical oil of Rosemary, Cloves and Cummin seeds of each 2 Drops – Drop 3 drops into the Ear going to Bed puting in some Black Wool: Warm the Spoon when you put the oil in it and – shake the Bottle before you use it –

approvd. CHAS. HAMILTON.

———————

FOR THE RHEUMATISM BY THE LATE DOCTR. SMYTH of DAWSONS STREET DUBLIN.

Six Drachms of Dwarfllder, made into one pint of Tea, Rose Water, and Mindererus's Spirit, of each half an Ounce; Salpollycrist three Dratrams, Huxams Antimonial Wine two Drachms Syrup of Orange Peel, Half an Ounce –

DIRECTIONS –

Mix these Ingredients together and take a small Teacupfull three times a day when the Stomach is most empty –

Another, take 4 oz. Mustard seed ground or pounded, 4 oz. Horse Raddish scraped put these into a Gallon of oldest strong Beer and after 48 Hours half a pint of it may be taken before Meals – the same quantitys may be repeated.

10th April 1809	was the last day My Husband took a pen in his hand, he departed this life the 24th May.

POSTSCRIPT

John Macky was buried in Agherton Old Graveyard, near Portstewart.
The headstone to his grave was recorded by Mr Sam Henry FRSA,
of Sandelford, Coleraine in July 1938.

The headstone to his grave reads

HERE LIETH THE REMAINS OF

JOHN MACKY

OF THE CUTTS FISHERY, COLERAINE

WHO DEPARTED THIS LIFE

20TH MAY 1809

AGED 70 YEARS

To the right hand side of the headstone, and next to it,
another bears the inscription

SACRED TO THE MEMORY OF

ROBERT MACKY, AGED 15 YEARS

AND

JANE MACKY, AGED 16 YEARS

CHILDREN OF JOHN AND SUSANNA MACKY

No date was given on this latter stone but it is almost certain that the John
Macky mentioned was one and the same person. Mr Henry made further
inquiries and found that a family named Macky lived at Carnalbanagh but none
were left, the last of them going to Australia.

APPENDIX

Narrative of the FISHERY CAUSE lately depending between the
Society and the Marquis of Donegal, and statement of the Society's
title to their fishings.

By

DAVID BABINGTON, Esq. Law Agent to the Society

SIR,

I HAVE had the honour of receiving a letter from you as Secretary to the Honourable the Irish Society, mentioning their wish that I should furnish them with a statement of the case, and of the proceedings that have been had, and the steps that have been taken from time to time to protect their rights in the fishery of the river Bann, against the different attacks made upon them by the family of Lord Donegal, as the owners of another fishery in the same river, and in Loughneagh; a task which I undertake with very great pleasure indeed, for although the prospect was frequently gloomy, the business has at length been brought to a state so gratifying and pleasant to my feelings, that I am happy in an opportunity of doing what they require of me.

Loughneagh, which is one of the largest fresh-water lakes in Europe, is situate in the province of Ulster in Ireland, and is bounded by the counties of Antrim, Armagh, Downe, Tyrone, and Londonderry, and it empties itself into the sea about three miles below the town of Coleraine in the county of Londonderry; the river by which it so empties itself is called the Bann, which in many parts is very deep and navigable, in others shallow and rocky, particularly near Coleraine, where the rocks are known by the name of the Fall, or Salmon Leap. The whole distance from the lake to the sea is about twenty-five Irish, and something more than thirty-one English miles.

Various grants appear to have been made at different periods, of certain fishings in different parts of the lake and river but I do not deem it necessary at present to go back above two centuries, as no prior grant has been acted upon or accompanied with possession, and of course no question will be likely to arise hereafter on any grant not followed by possession, or acted upon within that period; and although it might be most methodic to state the grants which I shall mention as they run in order according to their dates, yet, with a view to be more clear and satisfactory, I shall state those on which the society and lord Donegal found their respective rights separately, and begin with those relating to the society.

On the 20th of July, in the year 1605, a grant appears to have been made by patent to James Hamilton, esq. of one free fishing in the river Bann, every Monday next after Saint John Baptist's day; on which day all fish taken in the river belonged to the dissolved priory of Coleraine; and a salmon every day yearly from every fisherman fishing in that river during the season; being part of the possessions of said priory.

In the same month and year another grant was made to Mr. Hamilton, of the entire fishing of the lough and the Bann, to the rock and the salmon leap, with some old eel weirs upon the Bann near Castle Toome, and all the islands of the lough and river.

On the 2d of March, 1605, a grant was made to John Wakeman, of Beckford in the county of Gloucester, esquire, of the entire river; from the salmon leap to the sea, and the fishings thereof, with the salmon leap.

On the 3d of March, in the same year; Wakeman conveyed all that had been granted to him, to Hamilton; so Hamilton being then possessed under his own grants of the lough and river to the salmon leap, and under his purchase from Wakeman, of the salmon leap and river to the sea, he in fact had the entire of the lough and river, with the soils thereof and every thing appertaining thereto, down to the main sea.

On the 10th of April, 1606, Hamilton sold to Sir Arthur Chichester the fishing of the river between the lough and the salmon leap that had been granted to him in the month of July, 1605.

On the 14th of May, 1606, Hamilton sold to Chichester one moiety of the fishery from the rock to the sea.

On the 3d of April, 1611, Chichester sold and surrendered all his interest to King James the First, and his majesty made compensation to Hamilton, and got a surrender from him also and then the entire of the lough, river, and salmon leap became vested again in the crown.

On the 29th of May, 1613, the same king, by his letters patent under the *great seal of England,* constituted and created a certain number of citizens of London a corporation, by the name of the Governor and Assistants London of the near plantation in Ulster in Ireland; which corporation has been since commonly styled the London Society, when spoken of or treated upon in Ireland, and is generally styled the Irish Society when spoken of in England.

By the said letters patent a large track of country, comprising numerous denominations of land, to be thenceforward called the city and county of London-derry, and the fishery of the river Bann, from the sea to Loughneagh and the soil thereof, and the rock or salmon leap in the said river, were amongst a great variety of other things granted to the said society.

The parts of the grant that relate to said fishery are extremely full, and give as extensive power of taking fish in every way possible as could be expressed by the Latin language, in which the grant was written.

These letters patent were duly enrolled in the proper offices in England and Ireland, and from their date until the present time the society and their successors, and those deriving under them, have uniformly possessed and enjoyed the rock or salmon leap, and that part of the river which lies between the rock and the sea; but it does not appear from any research I have been able to make, that they ever availed themselves of the grant of that part of the river which lies between the rock and the lough, or ever were in possession thereof, and the reason why they did not will fully appear hereafter.

Some years previous to the breaking out of the Irish rebellion of 1641, King Charles the First, among many acts of a similar kind, as the history of that day fully tells us, caused informations to be filed by his attorney-general against the mayor, commons, and citizens of London, and against the Society of the Governor and Assistants of the new plantation in Ulster, complaining, amongst other charges, of irregularity and misrepresentation in the manner of obtaining the letters patent of the 29th of March, 1613, alledging that King James was deceived therein.

Upon hearing these informations in the Star-chamber; about the tenth year of the reign of the same King Charles, the mayor, society, &c. were sentenced to pay a fine of 70,000l.; and a *scire facias* issued in pursuance of said sentence to repeal the grant and charter, on which judgment was had in the court of Chancery of England, and a decree pronounced, whereby the letters patent and the enrollment thereof were declared void and ordered to be cancelled, and possession was ordered to be taken from the society and companies of London; and the enrollment of the said letters patent in England was vacated accordingly: but the enrollment in Ireland never was vacated, nor does it clearly appear that the possession was changed; on the contrary I believe it was not, but that the society was mulcted in a sum of money under the name of composition; a practice very familiar at that time.

The city of London, conceiving the proceedings in the Star-chamber and Chancery grievous, petitioned the House of Commons, and on the 26th of August, 1641, it was voted and resolved, that the sentence and order of the Star-chamber were unlawful, as well against the mayor and commonalty of the city of London as against the Society of the Governor and Assistants London of the new plantation of Ulster in Ireland:

That the king was not deceived in the grant, or in creating the corporation called the Society of the Governor and Assistants London of the new plantation of Ulster in Ireland, and that the king had not granted more lands by said patent than he intended to grant thereby. The house then proceeded to assign reasons, and amongst others gave the following:

"That breach of covenant (if any such had been) is not sufficient cause to forfeit lands; breach of covenant being no crime, but tryable in ordinary courts of justice.

That the Star-chamber had no power to examine freehold, or determine breach of covenants or trusts.

That the sentence against the two corporations aggregate, no particular person being guilty, was contrary to law, and every other article was in like manner illegal.

That the sentence of the Star-chamber was unlawful and unjust; and the composition with the city made on such terms, in time of extremity, ought not to bind it.

That when the king repaid the monies received on the composition, and such rents as he received by colour of the sentence, that then he should be restored to the same state he was in, and the patent surrendered.

That the citizens of London, and all against whom the judgement in *scire facias* was given, should be discharged of that judgement.

And that the citizens of London, those of the new plantation, all their under tenants, and all those put out of possession by the sequestration, or king's commissioners, should be restored to the same state they were in before the sentence in the Star-chamber."

In the fourteenth year of the reign of the same king a special patent passed under the *great seal of England*, whereby, after reciting the proceedings aforesaid, his majesty pardoned, forgave, and exonerated and released the said mayor, &c. and their successors, from the said fine of 70,000*l*.

On the 24th of March, 1656, the Society of the Governor and Assistants were restored to the said river, salmon leap, &c. by letters patent, dated at Westminster; but it does not appear that the society ever availed themselves of this grant, owing, most probably, to the circumstance of its having been made by Cromwell, their being previously in quiet possession, and the restoration following soon after.

On the 10th of April, 1662, by letters patent under *the great seal of England*, after reciting the patent of 1613, and that the society, by virtue of a licence under *the same seal*, dated the 30th of September, in the thirteenth year of the reign of the late king, had granted to the twelve companies of London several parcels of the estates that had been granted to the said society, who had retained other parts not properly deviseable in their own hands; and also reciting that the said letters patent had been repealed in the court of Chancery, and that King Charles the First had agreed to restore the premises to the said society, which intention was prevented by the troubles (but without taking any notice whatever of the patent of the 24th of March, 1656), King Charles the Second reincorporated the said society by their former name, and granted and confirmed to them and their successors all that had been given to them by the former grant of 1613; and amongst the rest the river Bann, *from the sea* to Loughneagh, and the rock or salmon leap, and the whole fishing and taking of fishes, as well salmon and eels as all other kind of fishes whatever, within the said *river and salmon leap*, as well with nets of what kind so ever, as otherwise howsoever, excepting only thereout the piscary belonging to the bishop of Derry, found by inquisition bearing date the 30th of August, 1609.

These letters were enrolled in the proper offices, both in England and Ireland; but it appears to me that the society and their successors rather considered them as a confirmation of the former grant than as a new grant, and I think I am fortified in this opinion by the following circumstances: The then bishop of Derry having claimed several parts of the fishery, and having brought ejectments for the recovery of them in the year 1670, the society took defence thereto and nonsuited the said bishop, founding their title *solely upon the patent of* 1613; the society apprehending further trouble from the bishops of Derry, afterwards, on the 22d of April, 1684, filed a bill for perpetuating the testimony of their witnesses, in which bill they made title under the charter of 1613 as the original foundation, and charge the grant by Charles the Second to have been in confirmation of it.

By this bill they claimed all the fishery from the sea to the lough; although, as I have already observed, it does not appear that they ever possessed more than from the sea to the rock or salmon leap inclusive.

Witnesses were examined in this cause, and a compromise was afterwards made between the society and Dr. King, then bishop of Derry, whereby a yearly sum was agreed to be paid by the society to the bishop and his successors, and the agreement was afterwards ratified by act of parliament.

Thus stands the title of the society, brought down to the latest period that any grant appears to have been made to or to have been accepted of by them from the crown: and I shall now proceed to state the title under which the marquis of Donegal claims the right of fishing in Loughneagh, and the part of the River Bann which lies between it and the rock: but it is right to premise that in doing so some little inconsistency will appear, that part of the river that lies between the rock and the lough having been granted both to the society and the Donegal family at many different periods, several of them not very remote from each other.

On the 20th of November, 1621, a grant was made by patent to Sir Arthur lord Chichester, ancestor of the marquis of Donegal, of Loughneagh, the soil and fishing thereof, the eel weirs and eel fishings about Toome, and in the river Bann, as far as the rock called the salmon leap.

On the 1st of July, 1640, Edward viscount Chichester, the descendant of Arthur, and Arthur the son of Edward, surrendered the premises comprised in the patent of the 20th of November, 1621, to King Charles the First, in pursuance of an order of composition made on the 19th of September, 1639, between them and the commissioners, for the remedy of defective titles; and it was then agreed that his lordship and son should have a sufficient estate granted to them of all the premises granted by a former order of composition bearing date the 7th of December, 1638, and a patent accordingly passed on the 22d of September, 1640, granting to them all the estates, except the lough and river so surrendered, which were specifically excluded and left out of the said last-mentioned grant.

On the 14th of August, 1656, a lease was made of said surrendered premises by Oliver Cromwell to Sir Arthur John Clotworthy, knight, afterwards viscount Massareen, for ninety-nine years, from the 13th of May, 1656, at a small rent.

This lease comprised the lough and Toome, with the fishings and soil thereof, the islands and the river Bann, as far as the salmon leap.

On the 15th of November, 1660, King Charles the Second confirmed the lease to the Massareen family.

On the 3d of July, 1661, the same king, by letters patent *under the great seal of Ireland,* granted and confirmed to Arthur Chichester then earl Donegal, and his heirs, all the fishings in Loughneagh and the river Bann, from the lough to the rock or fall called the salmon leap, to hold the same as they had been granted by King James the First, on the 20th of November, 1621; and also the rents reserved upon any lease or leases, the premises comprised therein to go to the said earl of Donegal and his heirs; and under this grant it is that the Donegal family have since enjoyed, and still continue to enjoy, the premises comprised therein; and amongst the rest the lake and river; from the lake to the rock or salmon leap.

Having now gone entirely through the matter of title, I next come to that which has given cause to so long and expensive litigation; but before I enter upon it I beg shortly to observe a little upon salmon and eel-fisheries generally. The time for taking salmon as regulated by law, and that in which they are in best season and fittest for use, is immediately on their leaving the sea, and making their way into the fresh-water rivers, for the purpose, as is generally supposed, of depositing their spawn.

The spawn is generally lodged in shallow streams, or creeks in small rivers, in the harvest season; is lightly covered with gravel by the mother-fish, as they are called, and continue there until the months of March, April, and May following, when it vivifies sooner or later; according to the heat or coolness of the season, and to the quantity of covering that may have been upon it, and which is frequently increased or diminished by the winter floods. And almost as soon as they are able to swim the young brood begin to make their way to their sea, where their growth is so wonderfully rapid, that although when they pass to the sea they may not weigh more than one or two ounces, they are found to return in July and August into the fresh water, grown to the enormous weight of from four to ten pounds; and it is equally remarkable of this species of fish that it always endeavours to return into the same river it was spawned in, which facts of growth and propensity to return to their native rivers are ascertained beyond doubt by a practice that I have frequently assisted in, of taking up the fry on its passage to the sea, in different rivers remote from each other, weighing and marking them by the introduction of threads of silk into the fins, cutting the fins in different ways, and the like, and entering down the respective weights and particular marks of each in a book made for the purpose, and afterwards catching and weighing them on their return; and no instance was ever found of the fry taken up and marked in one river being caught in another.

The eel tribe perform their functions in the very contrary way, and their history is not so perfectly well understood.

They spawn in the sea; and the fry, when not more than from an eighth to one-fourth of an inch long, nor thicker than the hair of a horse's mane, make their way into the fresh waters in the summer months, and return to the sea full grown the following year, from whence it is conceived they never come back.

Salmon are uniformly taken in their passage from the sea to the fresh water, and eels on their passage from the fresh water to the sea, and of course whenever there are two salmon-fisheries on the same river that next the sea must have the benefit of preception, and *vice versa* with respect to eel-fisheries.

To resume, or rather proceed, in the matter of controversy, it appears to me, from the best information I have been able to collect, that before the time of the grant to the society, in 1613, those who were entitled to the fishery of the rock, and of the river from the rock to the sea, caught all the salmon they could with nets in a particular part of the river between the rock and the sea, called the Cranagh, which happened to be best adapted to net fishing; but as fish were then comparatively extremely plentiful (which, with the causes of its diminution, will be more fully explained hereafter), and as many fish escaped the industry of the net-fishers, men were employed to stand upon the rocks at the salmon leap, who were called loopers, and they used to catch some fish, especially when the river was not in a favourable state for the net fishing; still the number taken in this way was comparatively small, and it was at best precarious, as may well be conceived when described to have been performed by watching the fish in the water until they attempted to ascend the rock, and, while in the act of leaping, catching or receiving them in a small net fixed to the end of a pole; and so few were skilled and expert in this art that the expense nearly equalled the gain, fish being then very cheap.

The river at the salmon leap is between three and four hundred feet wide; and the rock, which is about four hundred and fifty feet in length, extended in breadth entirely across the river, and rendered it so shallow and rapid as to preclude all possibility of navigation while it continued in that state; wherefore the society, shortly after the passing of the patent in 1613, as tradition informs me, made a cut through the rock, almost close to the shore, on the west or Derry side of the river, for the purpose of conveying timber down the river to build their town of Coleraine; but it is certain that the passage was converted into a trap for the taking of fish very many years ago, and has been uniformly employed in that way, if not before, at least since the year 1620; and it is material to observe, as bearing very much on the case in controversy between the parties, that it was and is constructed of wood, lime, and stones, and built in a most permanent manner.

From the time their rights first accrued, the society, by their under-tenants, uniformly fished on the rock and in the river from thence to the sea, with nets and loops in the ways already described, and also used the cut or trap from the time it was converted into an engine for the taking of fish, without molestation, hindrance, or even claim by the Donegal family, or those deriving under them; and in like manner, the Donegal family and their tenants fished without interruption in the lake, and in the river Bann, from the lake to the rock. But it is an important fact, that the sole profit of the society's fishery consisted in the taking of salmon, and that of the Donegal family, principally if not entirely, in taking eel, as more fully mentioned hereafter; and that the society's tenants uniformly defrayed all expenses attending the preservation of the salmon spawn and fly in the breeding rivers, as did the tenants of the Donegal family that which attended the preservation of the eel fry on their passage from the sea up the river, that being the only part of the eel-fishery that required attention.

The society from time to time were in the habit of making leases of their fishery; and amongst others, one was made to a gentleman of the name of Williams, who first thought of the practicability of erecting traps upon the rock, instead of incurring the excessive expense of cutting the rock in the manner hereinbefore described with respect to the old cut, as it is called; and he caused a second trap to be erected in this way on the surface in the year 1744; and finding it useful, he erected another in the year 1745.

In the year 1755, a third was added. In 1756, a fourth.

And the last in 1759 or 1760, by the late Sir Henry Hamilton then tenant to the society; and no objection whatever was made to the erecting of any of those works at the times they were going forward, nor for eleven years after the erection of the last of them, although the tenants of the Donegal family were eye-witnesses of their progress, being themselves daily employed in fishing in that part of the river that lies immediately above and adjoining to the rock. And all those works were composed of materials similar to those of which the cut made in or before the year 1620 was constructed, and bear complete resemblance to it in form and mechanism.

At length however, but not until the year 1771, it occurred to Arthur, then earl of Donegal, to contest the right of employing the traps I have mentioned, and to make the experiment of an action at law for the purpose of contesting that right; and he accordingly brought an action in the court of Exchequer against Sir Henry Hamilton for erecting a certain work on the rock or salmon leap and for the recovery of damages for the injury his fishery was alledged to have suffered in consequence thereof; and he laid his venue in the county of Armagh, but on application to the court, and a statement by affidavit that questions of title were likely to arise that would require the production of various patents, a trial at bar was granted.

In this action he did not complain of any of the cuts or traps specially, but of the whole, as if they had been of a single compact work and had formed one general obstruction to the passage of fish across the entire course of the stream; and he claimed to be seized in fee of the soil of a free passage over the rock, although the whole soil thereof, as already mentioned, had been granted and belonged to the society and possession had followed the grant from the year 1613 (or at least from 1662) uniformly down to the present time.

A trial of this action was had at the bar of the court of Exchequer in the year 1771, and a very long special verdict was found, embracing an immense variety of matter, which was set down for argument in the court of Exchequer.

In this stage of the business when the cause was in the courtlist for argument on the special verdict, I entered upon my apprenticeship with the late Messrs. Kane and King, who were then, and had been for above half a century before, the law-agents of the society; and as I chanced to have been born within less than a mile of the river Bann, about half way between the lough and the sea, and had a tolerably good notion of the nature of the fisheries, my attention was more particularly directed to the subject in dispute than it might otherwise have been; and from thence until now the case has had my best consideration, especially for the last twenty years, during which time, or rather as much of it as he lived, I was in partnership with Mr. King, who survived Mr. Kane, and since his death I have had the honour of being myself concerned for the society in the defence of the cause, and such other general business as they have had in Ireland.

The special verdict having continued in the list for a considerable time, was found, by those concerned for the plaintiff, to be so confused and informal as to be utterly untenable; and being at last called on, immediately on opening the cause, the counsel for the plaintiff admitted its insufficiency, and the first of its many imperfections was decisive; namely, that it did not find that the plaintiff in the action was the heir at law of the original grantee, and the court was pleased to order *a venire facias de novo* to issue; but Lord Donegal, or those concerned for him, did not think fit to issue the *venire*, nor was any other step ever taken by them afterwards either to revive or proceed in that cause, or to commence a new one during the remainder of the life of Sir Henry Hamilton; and he and his people continued to fish exactly in the ways they had theretofore done.

The interest that Sir Henry Hamilton then had in the premises was for a residue of a term of years; and he, being so possessed, on the 16th of January, 1775, made his will, and thereby bequeathed his lease of the fishery to his wife Marianne.

On the 12th of November, 1778, he obtained a new lease of the fishery from the society for the life of his wife the said Marianne, and for twenty-four years, being the number of years then to come of his original lease, and thereby acquired a freehold interest in the premises; and he afterwards died on the 26th of June 1782, without republishing the former, or making any new will.

Shortly before the death of Sir Henry, heads of a bill were laid before the Privy Council, which was the practice then in Ireland, the object of which bill was to oblige the proprietors of salmon fisheries, where permanent works were made of wood, lime, and stones for the taking of fish, to leave the traps open from Saturday Night until Monday morning, in every week of the fishing season; but as I well knew that the complying with such a statute would be ruinous to the society's works, as from the rapidity of the stream, and other causes, it would be morally impossible to re-erect the traps in the rest of the week, and that of course they might as well be left open altogether, I attended with counsel on the part of the society at the Privy Council chamber, and showed so clearly by my own testimony and that of others, that at Coleraine there was at all times a large portion of the river quite free and open for fish to pass, that I had this fishery exempted from the operation of the act; and from thence forward the act, instead of a mischief, has been a great benefit to the society; for it fully, and in terms, recognizes cuts and traps as legitimate modes of taking fish.

In the year 1783 the same earl of Donegal, or those concerned for him, brought a new action against Lady Hamilton, not as the former brought against Sir Henry in 1771, for erecting a certain work generally, as already stated, but for maintaining and continuing the four last made cuts only; and gave up entirely the claim of a seizin in fee of the soil of any part of the rock: and the venue as before was laid in the county Armagh.

In this case also a trial at bar was granted, and the cause was heard in the year 1784; when, as before, a special verdict was found, and in like manner it fell to the ground without determining any thing whatever on the question of right between the parties, as from the way the plaintiff made up the verdict it appeared on the face of it, and such indeed was the fact, that the last lease to Sir Henry was executed after the publishing his will, and of course the freehold descended to his heir at law, and Lady Hamilton, the defendant, appeared to have no interest therein.

After judgment was given by the court on this special verdict, report was propagated with much industry, that Lord Donegal had finally succeeded in totally defeating the London Society and their tenant, Lady Hamilton, in the great fishery cause, which greatly alarmed Lady Hamilton (who had then got a conveyance from the heir at law of Sir Henry, conformably to his intentions); and for her satisfaction a case was laid before Mr. Boyd, then recorder of Londonderry, and afterwards second justice of the court of King's Bench, stating the circumstances exactly as they occurred on the trial; and he gave an opinion on the 17th of April, 1787, "That the question of law between the parties was one that never had been decided; that he ever was, and then was of opinion, that Lord Donegal ought not to have judgment on any action that might tend to prostrate the works; and that he knew the prostration of them would totally destroy the society's fishery in the river Bann."

Down to this period, then, I may truly say that all the attempts made on the part of Lord Donegal were a mere nullity; indeed this is so unequivocally admitted in the subsequent proceedings as to preclude him from ever resorting to, or making use of, them in any way to the prejudice of the society hereafter.

While the actions already mentioned, founded on the alledged illegality of the works on the salmon leap, were in progress, it may surprise the society to be informed, yet it is not the less true, that Lord Donegal and his tenants began themselves to erect, and actually completed a work on the river, a few miles above the salmon leap, at a place called Movanagher, composed of materials exactly similar to those of which the traps on the salmon leap are constructed, for the express purpose of taking salmon.

And what is still more extraordinary after all this, his lordship, with the same spirit of litigation, determined on trying another action, grounded on the very same allegations of illegality; and accordingly, in the year 1787, he brought a new action against Lady Hamilton in the same court, the language of which also differed from that of 1777; and to it, under the opinion of council of the first eminence in Ireland, assisted by the advice of others resorted to by the society in England, the general issue, not guilty, was pleaded, and a trial at bar applied for, which however was refused; and in the month of March, 1788, the cause was tried by *Nisi prius* in the county of Armagh (where, as before, the venue was laid).

For this trial every preparation was made by both parties, who thought, from the light thrown on the subject in the former stages, that they perfectly saw their way to the real merits, as well on the questions of law as the matters of fact; but I am free to confess that for one I was mistaken, and that scarcely half an hour had passed in the course of the trial, which lasted from eight in the morning until ten at night, that something new did not occur; and then it was that I had the full advantage of the abilities of Mr. Attorney-general Fitzgibbon (very soon afterwards appointed lord chancellor), who knowing me to be at that time under the severest weight of family affliction, and that the trial at that assizes was pressed most painfully upon me at short notice, the right of doing so resting solely with the plaintiff, broke through a rule he had laid down against going specially to any assizes, and not only attended the trial at Armagh, but took the entire burden, responsibility, and management of it upon himself, scarcely sitting down from the beginning to the end of the business; and that too on the same fee that any other gentleman of the bar would have thought himself only compensated by.

On the trial many points of nonsuit were made, and several bills of exceptions taken and tendered on both sides, especially one on our side, grounded on the act called the Act of Settlement in Ireland, taken by Mr. Attorney-general Fitzgibbon, and an exception of an apparently serious nature by Mr. Solicitor-general (Wolf) for the plaintiff, that the grants to the society in 1613 and 1682 were both under the great seal of England, instead of being, as they should have been, under the great seal of Ireland; but at last it was agreed to turn the whole into a special verdict, as that would come more immediately to a final decision, and be of course much less expensive to the parties; and a dominical of a special verdict was prepared accordingly, in which Mr. Fitzgibbon contrived to have included as much as he thought necessary to ensure the defendant ultimate success, and the matters of fact were given to and found by the jury on separate issues.

The special verdict was afterwards made up from the dominical under the direction of Mr. Fitzgibbon.

The case was afterwards set down for argument in the usual way in the court of Exchequer; and was argued accordingly for several days; and the principal or almost only ground taken by the plaintiff's counsel was, the unconscionable use defendant made of the cuts, which, as they expressed it, wrought night and day: and on the 28th of November, 1792, the court gave judgment, in which two of the judges, Lord Avonmore and Mr. Baron Hamilton, were in favour of the plaintiff, and one, Mr. Baron Power, in favour of the defendant; the fourth judge, who had been conducting counsel for the defendant when at the bar, was indisposed and unable to attend the court, and Mr. Baron Power took that opportunity of declaring in his place, as being then the only one of the judges that composed the bench when the first trial was had in 1771, that it was the unanimous opinion of the court at that time, and their determination to pronounce judgment in favour of the defendant if they could have done so, which they were prevented from doing by the circumstance of the plaintiff having made up his special verdict in such way as to put it out of their power to do so, although they were perfectly satisfied of the law and the merits being both with the defendant. And he was pleased to add, by way of observation, that Mr. Baron Hamilton was shortly after made a judge of that court; and in conversation appeared to hold a different opinion from the information he had got, as having been conducting counsel for Lord Donegal.

In the course of giving this judgment, the lord chief baron said he was glad it was not necessary for him to give any opinion whether a grant under the seal of England would pass lands in Ireland, — that it was a weighty question; and that if he was obliged to give such an opinion, it would be that such a grant would not pass lands in Ireland: which appeared to me to be a most important subject of consideration for the society, and all those deriving under them, the whole county of Londonderry and its dependencies resting upon it.

I may safely say that this judgment had not the general approbation of the bar; I mean of those not employed on either side; and therefore, and under the sanction of the gentlemen concerned for the defendant, and knowing as I did what the opinion of Mr. Attorney-general Fitzgibbon (then earl of Clare and lord chancellor) always had been on the subject, I conceived it to be my due to the society to endeavour to reverse the judgment of the court, and for that end brought a writ of error returnable into the Exchequer Chamber which at that time was composed, as in England, of the lord chancellor, assisted by the two chief justices.

In the Exchequer Chamber the case was most ably argued on the part of Lady Hamilton, especially by Mr. Chamberlain, afterwards a judge of the King's Bench (for it was always my study to retain men of the first abilities, and of the greatest professional weight and character, and that I succeeded in doing so only requires the mention of the names of those I from time to time employed); and such was the effect of his argument alone, and so thoroughly did he establish that, in point of law, Lady Hamilton had a right, as tenant to the society, to intercept every fish that came from the sea while floating in her fishery, provided such interruption was for the purpose of, and ended in, the taking of the fish, that coupled with questions put, and observations made, by Lord Clare from time to time in the course of the argument, the counsel of Lord Donegal were obliged to abandon totally the line of argument they had pursued in the inferior court, and to take entire new ground, as if the action sought only to be reprised in damages for the loss incurred by interrupting and turning back fish not taken at all by her ladyship: which must be admitted to have been a poor subterfuge, no way justified by the fact, or by the original intention and object of the suit, but which must ever be decisive for the society as long as the law stands as then laid down and acquiesced in by the plaintiff's counsel, "That the society had a right to take all they could, but not to intercept those not taken."

When the argument closed on both sides, the cause stood over for judgment, a day was appointed, and when it arrived such was the opinion of the gentlemen concerned for Lord Donegal, from what they observed in the course of the cause, and so completely had they given up every idea of succeeding, that they actually decided coming into court, imagining that we only wished to exult in their defeat. Yet most unexpectedly, indeed, the two assessors gave their advice to the lord chancellor to decide in favour of Lord Donegal; and on the 31st of January, 1794, his lordship pronounced his judgment, in which, although he directed the judgment of the court below to be affirmed, knowing that the case would receive the ultimate decision of the final tribunal, he went so fully into the merits, and to the entire conviction of the bystanders, that in justice to that great man, and in order to give a more complete view of the case, I beg leave to annex a copy of the note I took of the judgment at the time it was pronounced, and only add an observation, that there seemed to be but one opinion upon the law as laid down by his lordship in pronouncing judgment; and that it was then admitted on all hands that the society and their tenantry had a clear and legal right to take all the fish they could while in their fishery, provided that in doing so they did not interrupt, turn back, or prevent those they did not take from going into Lord

Donegal's fishery: and that a single fish is not so turned back or interrupted, except those taken, nor has any been so turned back in the last century, is a fact as generally believed as that the lake empties itself into the sea, through the medium of the river Bann.

About this time a bill was proposed in parliament, and I had the satisfaction of assisting and carrying it into a law, whereby it was enacted, that it should not be lawful for any person to take salmon in the sea, at the mouth of any river; or within one mile thereof, during the seasons that the taking of salmon was forbidden in such rivers, under certain penalties mentioned in the act: which was most materially serviceable to the Bann fishery, the fishery at the mouth of the river belonging to another person not friendly to the society.

It is scarcely necessary to say, after what was thrown out by Lord Clare in giving judgment, that I proceeded to bring the matter before the house of lords, and the case was removed and argued there accordingly, where I thought his lordship's name and influence would have insured a majority of votes; but being matter of law, the peers at large declined taking any part in the question, and of course the judgment was affirmed, the only persons who voted being, in fact, the two justices and the chief baron, who had been of opinion with the plaintiff in the court below, they being peers of parliament. This affirmation took place on the 2nd day of March, 1795; and Lord Clare, notwithstanding the reasoning of the other law lords, continued to be still of his former opinion, and gave his reasons at large, nearly in the same language and quite to the same effect of that which he had done in the Exchequer Chamber.

Here again the circumstance of the grants to the society being under the great seal of England only was greatly talked of, and revived the alarm already mentioned; and being much impressed with the importance of the matter to the society, and having then a seat in the house of commons, I had the satisfaction of contributing to the passing of an act of parliament, whereby all grants under the great seal of England, of lands in Ireland, were enacted to be equally valid with those under the great seal of Ireland. This act will be found in the Irish statutes of the 35th Geo. III., cap. 3, vol. 17, p. 640.

On the 16th of June, 1795, a notice was served on Lady Hamilton by Lord Donegal, requiring her forthwith to abate and remove four of the cuts; to wit, those called Williams's, Alexander's, Murphy's and Moffet's cuts, on or before the first day of July then next; and that in case of refusal further proceedings at law or in equity would be taken for removing them, and for obtaining full redress and satisfaction.

On receiving this notice a copy thereof, with a statement of the case as it then stood, was laid before Sir John Stewart, afterwards attorney-general, Mr. Plunkett, now solicitor-general of Ireland, both retained as counsel for the society, Mr Serjeant Duquery, and Others most eminent of the counsel formerly employed, for their advice and opinion; and they desired that no answer should be given to the notice, and gave an opinion that as the law then stood there was quite sufficient to defend and protect the society and their tenants against any new attack that might be made.

On the 12th of September, 1795, Lord Donegal filed a bill in the equity side of the court of Exchequer against Lady Hamilton *only*, in which he stated the titles of the parties pretty much in the same way they are herein mentioned, the judgment at law and the notice to remove the cuts, and he prayed that four of the cuts *only* might be demolished.

On the 29th day of February, 1796, Lady Hamilton put in an answer to the said bill, and I risk nothing in saying that a fairer or fuller answer never was given in to a court of justice.

In this answer, amongst other things, she says that no fish were obstructed from coming into the plaintiff's fishery but those that were taken by her in engines known to and recognized by the law of the land, one of which had stood since the year 1620, and that all the rest, constructed of similar materials, were made before the year 1760;

That plaintiff made considerably more by his fishing now than he had before the erection of the four cuts complained of;

That she did no more than she had a right to do, in taking in the cheapest manner the greatest quantity she could in her own fishery; that the traps were not prohibited by law, and that the fish were taken by legal means;

That plaintiff's fishery was of great value, and the most valuable part consisted in the taking of eels in their passage towards the sea; that her's was a salmon fishery, and the salmon taken in their passage from the sea;

That plaintiff, by late improvements in weirs and other engines, had stopped more eels from coming down the river than were accustomed to come, and thereby rendered his profit more considerable, and her's less;

That she had done the like, and that by additional diligence and increased expense as many salmon could be taken with nets and other engines as were taken by the traps; that each party had taken the natural advantage of their respective situations with respect to the species of fish that must pass through their fisheries; that she expended considerable sums merely for the protection of the salmon; and that plaintiff did the like in protecting the eel, each taking care of that from which their profit was principally derived; and that at all times plaintiff's fishery was principally considered an eel and her's a salmon fishery;

That the decrease of salmon in plaintiff's fishery was in a great measure owing to the increase of the machinery, for carrying on the linen manufacture;

That the decision in 1792 was in part influenced by a finding, that by the continuing the traps the current was so increased as to prevent as many fish as formerly used to pass; and that the declaration not being pointed to any such mode of obstruction she was not prepared; nor could she be called upon, or expected, to produce evidence relative thereto, which she otherwise would have been easily able to have done;

That plaintiff himself varied his case in his different declarations; that it could not be said that the only judgment plaintiff had was founded upon such clear grounds as to close for ever all questions between the parties; that by his declaration in 1771, he only complained of one cut, erected in 1762, which probably was the last erected cut, and thereby acquiesced in the other three; and that it did not and could not appear, if one cut was removed, whether the jury would have considered the rapidity of the stream to have been so increased by the remaining three as to warrant them in finding, even upon the *ex parte* evidence already mentioned, that fish were stopped;

That plaintiff was not warranted to come into a court of equity to procure an order to prostrate the four cuts for catching fish, having remedy, if any, at common law;

That so far from the cuts being an illegal mode of fishing, the twelve judges had said they were not; and if her right to maintain them should ever again be questioned, she was advised that she could show that the law was clearly with her;

That in other parts of the river the rapidity of the stream had ever been much greater than where the traps were erected; that they opposed little or no obstruction, the parts which crossed the river being constructed of thin and slender rails of wood; whereas on the verdict they appeared as solid obstructions, and were so erroneously supposed to be by the jury; that no fish were obstructed but what were taken, and the only loss to plaintiff arose from her diligence, and that he, by the very same means he complained of, greatly increased his own fishery; that the first cut, built of the same materials with those complained of, was used as a mode of fishing before any of the grants the plaintiff claimed under, so that at the time of the grants fishing by traps was a known and practised mode of fishing; and that on the rock there were free passages, amounting in all to one hundred and thirty feet;

That by the common law she had a right to fish with traps constructed as the four complained of were, and that the statute-law acted as a confirmation of that right requiring only a passage of twenty-one feet, even in navigable rivers, where traps so constructed were erected; and that by the express grant, under which the London Society derived title, she, as their lessee, was entitled to fish upon the rock, and from thence to the sea, by all means in her power; and of course by means of such traps as were used before and at the time of the grant.

She disclaimed all intention of harassing plaintiff by a variety of suits, or of availing herself of the circumstance charged in the bill of the fishery claimed by plaintiff lying in five different counties; and she offered to leave plaintiff at full liberty to conduct himself in ascertaining his rights as if the whole fishery lay in a single county, her sincere desire being to have the question brought to a solemn and deliberate decision, and that she was ready to have the matters in controversy settled by the trial of an issue to be directed by the court; and she relied on the justice of the court, that in a case, new and complicated, her rights might not be concluded by a single verdict in a species of action where, as the declaration was framed, the judgment of the court could not ascertain the limits of right between the parties with a satisfactory precision; and the more especially as the plaintiff had put on record, by his last declaration, a case differing materially from the one he attempted by his declaration in the year 1771. In this equity cause issue was joined, commissions issued, and a great variety of witnesses were examined by both parties in different parts of the kingdom; and I had the satisfaction of fully proving, in the clearest manner, by numerous and respectable witnesses, every particular of the honest case that had been put on record by her ladyship's answer.

Amongst a great variety of other matter, I proved, and in many instances corroborated by the cross examination of the plaintiff's own witnesses, that the plaintiff's fishery was always considered by the whole country as being an eel and the defendant's a salmon fishery, and that the plaintiff's was by much the more valuable and productive; that he had no less than twenty-eight weirs for the taking of eels on different parts of the river between the lake and the rock, in one of which only, and not the best, but with respect to which I was best able to procure proof, the enormous quantity of eighty thousand eels were caught in one single night, and which were worth 5l a thousand; that besides covering the river completely in three different places from side to side with these eel traps, the plaintiff himself, during the very tendency of his first action of 1771, which complained of the illegality of the works on the rock, but which afterwards fell to the ground as before mentioned, erected a work entirely across the river at Movanagher, a few miles above the salmon leap, constructed of the very same materials of these complained of, for the taking of salmon, as will appear by reference to maps of these works now in the society's possession in London, and worth their turning to; that more fish could be taken by the tenants of the society with nets than by the traps, but at greater expense; that none were ever obstructed except those taken; on the contrary, that they had a free passage up the river;

That fish passed with ease at Ballyshannon and other places (from whence I brought witnesses), where the ascent was twice as great as at Coleraine, and that the true cause of plaintiff's taking fewer fish than formerly was the rapid increase of the linen manufacture in the breeding rivers, and the recent improvement in the agriculture of the country, the former (to wit, the linen manufacture) having multiplied to such a degree that there were forty mills for every one there had been forty years ago, every one of which produced an obstruction to the passage of the mother-fish up the breeding rivers, and the certain destruction of the fry, which were dashed to pieces on the mill-wheels and other mechanism, on their endeavouring to get to the sea, and by the steeping of flak in the small rivers, which rendered these waters so noxious as to kill the fry directly; and the latter, agriculture, having so opened the drains in the mountain and swampy countries, that after every heavy rain the floods came down in such torrents, and carried with them so much gravel and earth, as to smother the fry, or cover them so deeply that they never could extricate themselves.

I also proved that there were not near the number of fish taken that used to be taken before the erection of the cuts and of the bleaching-mills, and that the plaintiff then took as many in proportion to the number that came into the river as he used to do before the cuts were erected, it having been very common formerly to take forty hundred-weight of salmon in one draught of one net, in that part of the river called the Cranagh; but that then it would be a rarity to take one-hundredweight at a draught, that all the cuts are similar in their construction to that which was made in

1620; and that they were all left entirely open from the 12th of August in every year, for the purpose of letting the breeding-fish pass freely up the river, &c. &c. &c.: in fine, there never was a cause that the counsel for the defendant looked upon with more certainty of success, if proofs could be applied to and in support of the defence set up by the answer; and I am proud to say, there never was a case more completely proved in every point that counsel thought in the slightest degree necessary, as indeed appeared by certificate under their hands, when they advised the appeal hereafter mentioned.

When the examination of witnesses closed on both sides, publication of the depositions of the witnesses, as it is called, passed, and the cause was set down to be heard on pleadings and proofs; and it may well be supplied, from the encouragement given me by the counsel and the fulness and extent of our proofs, that I had formed pretty sanguine hopes of the result; but to our mutual astonishment, when the cause came on to be heard, the court at once decided that they would not go into my case, or hear any evidence, however strong, that might tend to contradict or militate against the verdict at common law, and at once refused to grant a new trial; although we offered, by counsel at the bar, to take an issue or issues to try whether a single fish was ever obstructed, save those taken, or any other issue or issues the court thought fit to be framed or directed by themselves, and that too at the peril of full costs in case of a verdict against us, and not to seek any costs if the verdict should be found for us; and on the 22d of November, 1798, the court decreed "That an injunction should issue, directed to the sheriffs of Derry, requiring them to prostrate, demolish, and remove four of the cuts; and that the defendant, Lady Hamilton, should be restrained from rebuilding them or any of them; and that the defendant should pay the plaintiff the costs expended by him in the prosecution of the cause; and that the plaintiff might make up and enroll a decree accordingly against the defendant, with costs". Knowing as I did the consequences that would follow to the Society if this degree should be carried into effect, and as it had struck my own judgment so powerfully many years ago, that the society, as the inheritors and owners of the soil, should not either in law or conscience be bound by decisions to which they were not parties, as to induce me to leave the idea in writing sealed up amongst the papers in the cause, lest any accident should befall me before it was fit to bring it into action, the same thought never having occurred to any one else concerned for the society, I resolved to prevent or retard the operation of the decree by every possible means; and the inducements for doing so were strengthened by the decree being merely personal against Lady Hamilton, then in so bad health that there was a reasonable prospect of the lease granted to Sir Henry, and which depended on her life, soon falling in, and the moment it did so the entire effect and operation of the decree would fall to the ground and become perfectly inoperative, being personal against her ladyship, as already mentioned; and the cuts, if not destroyed, would give us the advantage of their being ancient erections, the most modern having been erected forty-five years ago: whereas, if pulled down in Lady Hamilton's lifetime, the society might find difficulty in rebuilding them, from the opposition to be expected from

Lord Donegal's tenants; and even if not opposed they would still be but recent erections, instead of ancient ones; and I accordingly turned my ideas into a case for counsel, and laid it before the most eminent of the gentlemen then retained in the cause; and they were unanimously of opinion that the decree of the court of Exchequer was erroneous and ought to be reversed: that it was a fit subject of appeal, and that they were perfectly willing and ready to sign a petition of appeal for the purpose, and had little doubt that the decree would be reversed *in toto*; but that in all events it would be, so far as related to granting a new issue, to try whether fish were obstructed in their passage in any way, save by taking while in the society's own fishery. The result of which issue may easily be gathered from what has already been said and proved on that subject; and with respect to that part of the case which related to the society's never having been made a party to any suit whatever, either in law or equity, from the beginning, and that it appeared unjust and unlawful to do any act which would so materially affect the inheritance, behind the backs of the inheritors, and without calling upon them in a legal manner to defend themselves, they were clearly, distinctly, and unanimously of opinion that a bill should be immediately filed in the court of Chancery, in the name of the society, stating that their property was about to be injured by a decision hastily obtained in a cause to which they, as the inheritors, were not even parties, and praying an injunction to restrain Lord Donegal from demolishing the works &c.; and were pleased to add, that the proofs in the Exchequer cause had been so carefully collected, and were so full and satisfactory, that they presumed they could easily be made again in the society's cause, if Lord Donegal's agent should object to consenting to have these already made read upon the hearing.

Under the sanction of these opinions I prepared a petition of appeal to the House of Lords of Ireland, in the name of Lady Hamilton, praying a reversal of the decree of the court of Exchequer, or such other order as their lordships might think fit to make, which was afterwards perused and signed by the counsel in the cause, and lodged with the clerk of the parliament when the cause abated by the death of the plaintiff, Lord Donegal; and as delay was with us a most desirable thing, on account of the declining state of health, of Lady Hamilton, the advantage to result from her death having been already stated, I of course rested and lay by until the cause was revived by his son, the present marquis.

On the 25th day of November, 1799, the present marquis filed a bill of revivor, praying that all the proceedings had in the life-time of his father should be revived and stand in the same plight and condition they were at the death of his father, and that he might have the full benefit of the former decree, and that it might be carried into execution. As in this interval the decision was very much talked of and frequently quoted as an authority in other cases somewhat similar; and as often denied to be any authority as not having been yet ultimately decided, I deemed it prudent again to consult not only the gentlemen formerly resorted to, but to take in others of those that had been employed in the cause, to be advised whether any defence could be made against reviving; and they in consultation thought that a bill of revivor was almost matter of course after a decree pronounced, and that no defence could consistently be made in that particular stage of the business; but that after the further decree on the bill of revivor, the directions formerly given should be followed; and that both causes, to wit, the appeal cause, and that directed to be commenced in Chancery, would most probably receive favourable determinations, as they saw no reason for changing the opinions formerly given by them respecting them.

The revived cause was afterwards set down for hearing as of course, and on the 17th day of July 1800 it was heard, and the former decree ordered to be carried into effect.

Immediately on the pronouncing of this decree I prepared and lodged a new petition of appeal to the lords in the new cause of the present marquis against Lady Hamilton, and also prepared and filed a bill in the name of the society, stating such parts of the matter aforesaid as were thought material; and in addition, that if the decree in the court of Exchequer; in which they, though the owners of the inheritance, were not parties, should be carried into effect in the way it then stood, that others of their cuts and traps never even complained of must be demolished, for that those complained of and those not complained of were erected on the same party walls, a thing I always prepared to bring forward when occasion required, and praying an injunction to restrain Lord Donegal from abating the works until some opportunity should be given to the society of defending their rights. It turned out a most fortunate circumstance, that I filed this bill and raised the injunction upon it, for want of an answer, as on account of some defect in the Union Act, or for want of some explanation respecting it, the appeals sent from Ireland were not sufficient, and new petitions addressed to the united parliament were ordered to be prepared; and before that could be completed the cuts would most inevitably have been pulled down under the Exchequer decree; but I afterwards prepared a new petition of appeal to the united parliament, and it of course operated as a further injunction against the demolition of the works.

Pending this appeal (which, as we were in possession and full enjoyment, and for the other reasons already assigned respecting Lady Hamilton's state of health, I did not press to an early hearing) Lord Donegal put in what was called a demurrer to the bill, filed in the name of the society, in Chancery, the event of which, if he had succeeded in it, would have been a total end to the suit and all its objects; and after a hearing of many days (and the case was argued by nearly twenty lawyers) I had the mortification to see the demurrer allowed by the master of the rolls, on the following grounds: that if he should overrule the demurrer, retain the cause, and grant an injunction, it would operate as a contradiction or suspension of the decree of the court of Exchequer; and that he thought it wrong to set up the orders of one court against those of another court of equal jurisdiction. Discouraging and unexpected as this determination was, I resolved to follow the matter up, from the thorough conviction I felt that what was then allowed on all hands to be the real merits had never been fairly discussed in any stage of the business; and accordingly I preferred a petition to the lord chancellor, praying that the cause might be reheard by himself, which was granted; and in less than half an hour's hearing I had the unspeakable satisfaction of obtaining his lordship's decision in our favour, with costs, and that, too, to the thorough conviction, as it should appear, of Lord Donegal's own counsel; the chancellor having offered to indulge them in as much time to prepare for a reply as they pleased to ask for, if they thought they could offer any new argument, or could find any authorities of cases where demurrers were ever allowed under such circumstances, which they declined availing themselves of, and admitted that they had already on the cause being set down for re-hearing made every research in their power without effect. It was on the 12th day of November, 1801, that this demurrer was overruled by his lordship; and the injunction I had before obtained, until Lord Donegal should answer the allegations in the bill, was continued; and from thence, until the present time, he never has attempted to give in any answer, nor is there any great probability of his speedily doing so, as when he does he must admit the matter aforesaid, and the necessity he was under of making such admissions, if he had answered, was his inducement to put in the demurrer; and thereby preclude all further enquiry into the merits: neither has he paid one shilling of the costs awarded by the lord chancellor against him.

Shortly after this demurrer was overruled, the other occurrence which I had looked to as material took place in the death of Lady Hamilton, on whose demise the lease granted by the society to Sir Henry Hamilton determined, and thereby the decree of the court of Exchequer became totally inoperative, as much as if it never had existed; and as the costs awarded by the decree were like the decree itself, completely personal as against Lady Hamilton, I had the additional satisfaction of saving all these costs by the appeal which suspended the operation of the decree until her death: and when that event took place the whole fell to the ground, so that at this day I have the comfort, and I hope I may add the credit, of having so wound up the matter, that things stand now as between the society and Lord Donegal exactly as if there never had been any litigation whatever, with this additional advantage to the society, that, if any new attempt should ever be made by the Donegal family hereafter, the antiquity of the cuts can with every propriety be urged, the latest of them having now stood above forty-five years.

And as the law has been so settled as not to bear new argument, as to the right of taking all the fish that come into the society's fishery if thereby no obstruction be given to the passage of those not taken, and as the fact is so universally known, and of course so perfectly capable of proof, that no fish are obstructed by the works except those that are taken, I may fairly say that nothing but the extreme of stupidity or the grossest neglect in those that may have the honour of conducting the affairs of the society hereafter, can subject them to a defeat in any action that may hereafter be brought against them, if any such should ever be brought; which, under all the circumstances, I deem highly improbable.

I regret that this report has run to such a length; but I thought it better to trespass a little on the patience of the society than to omit any thing at all material, my object being to give such a view of the subject as should serve not only to convey the information the society seems to wish for at present, but also as a key by which all documents, from the beginning of the title down to this present time, can easily be discovered, and resorted to as occasion may hereafter require. And if I have been so fortunate as to accomplish these ends I shall not regret the labour it has cost me.

I am, sir, your most obedient humble servant,
DAVID BABINGTON.
Rutland square, Dublin, Dec. 11th, 1804.

TO ROBERT SLADE, esq.
Secretary to the Hon. Irish Society, London.

Extracted from *"A Concise View of the Origin, Constitution and Proceedings of the Honourable Society of the Governors and Assistants of London of the New Plantation in Ulster, within the Realm of Ireland, commonly called The Irish Society"*

INDEX OF NAMES

Publishers Note: In this index surnames only are given. The reader is directed to refer to diary entries for the few occasions where first names are noted by John Macky. Minor variants of names were noted which could be assumed to be a spelling/written error on John Macky's part. Where some spellings of a possibly identical or similar name occur, these are standardised to one name entry. In all other cases names are as recorded in John Macky's diary.

INDEX OF WATERKEEPERS

Bann

Boyd	John	1792
Bradley	John	1797, 1798
Cassidy	John	1796
Craford	James	1791-99
Crawford	Hugh	1791, 1794
Dempsey	Bryan	1791-94
Dempsey	Dickfeet	1798
Dempsey	James	1793
Dempsey	John Sr	1791, 1792
Dempsey	John Jr	1791-99
Dempsey	Pat	1795
Dempsey	Thomas	1798
Heyland	John	1791-99
Kane	Will	1791-99
McAlister	John	1797, 1798
McCann	Ned	1792-96
McCarrell	Robert	1795, 1796
McCarter	John	1792-94
McClern	Pat	1793, 1794
McCoy	Pat	1795
McDaid	Jon.	1794-98
McGarrel	John	1796
McGonagle	Dan	1791-93
McKeag	Pat	1791
McKinny	Dan	1791-95
Mitchell	Ben	1791
Mooney	Pat	1797, 1798
Rowan	James	1798
Shannon	Jon.	1797-99
Spallin	Bryan	1799
Stephens	Jon.	1798

Antrim river

Baird	John	1799
Small	John	1799

Aughadowy

Garvin	Dan	1793
Hagan	John	1799
Henry	John	1793
Kane	James	1791, 1792, 1795
Kane	Manus	1794
McAllen	Neill	1793
McFawl	Will	1791-93
McFetrish	John	1795-97
McGraw	Fred	1791, 1792, 1794-98
McGraw	John	1791, 1792
McKeeman	Hugh	1796-98
McWilkin	Neill	1798
Mullan	Bryan	1799
Quinn	Pat	1793, 1794, 1798, 1799
Thompson	Alex	1793-95, 1798
Thompson	Robert	1794-98
Wright	Joseph	1795

Ballymena

Gorman	Barny	1794-98
McMullan	John	1794-98
Turner	Oliver	1791-93

Ballymoney

Boyd	William	1791
Mullaghan	Henry	1793-99

Blackwater

Clark	Henry	1799
Clark	William	1791-94
Hobson	Arthur	1791-99
Hobson	John	1795-99
Hughes	Barny	1798
Hughes	James	1791-99

Neill	James	1792-94
Quinn	Eneas	1791, 1795-97
(also noted as Jackson's Watchman)		
Richy	John	1799
Trotter	J	1791-95

Bovagh and Mayochill

McClern	Hugh	1791, 1794, 1795
McFetrish	Jack	1791-94
McGraw	Fred	1798, 1799
McKeeman	Hugh	1791-95, 1798, 1799
McWilkin	Neill	1795-98
Mullan	Ed,	1791, 1793, 1794
Quinn	Pat	1792
Thompson	Robert	1798, 1799

Claudy

Deehan	Chas	1798
Diamond	Pat	1798, 1799
Doorish	Dan	1791-99
Doorish	John	1791-98
Kane	Manus	1799
McCann	Andrew	1799
McCann	Arthur	1791-99
McClain	Barny	1791-97
McClain	Frank	1794, 1795, 1798, 1799
McClain	James	1791-97
McClain	Pat	1792, 1793
McShane	Frank	1791-98
Mulholland	Neil	1793-97

Coagh and Ballinderry

Buck	William	1791
Carleton	William	1798
Collum	John	1793, 1799

Donnelly	John	1791, 1794, 1799
Dunbar	Robert	1793-97
Kane	James	1798, 1799
Mallon	John	1792
McAuly	Hugh	1794
McKinny	Alex	1792
Mullon	Hugh	1791, 1795
Nelson	Dan	1799
Taylor	Ambrose	1791-93, 1795-97
Wilkinson	James	1796, 1797
Wright	Jon.	1798

Drumcroon Rivulet

Hunter	1792-98
(Mr Wilson's watchman)	

Garvagh

Barber	John	1799
Craig	Robert	1793-99
Gilmore	Sam	1792, 1793
Henry	Arthur	1797, 1799
Hill	Hugh	1791-96
McCook	John	1798
McWilkin	Neill	1791-94
Moony	Mark	1793-97
Mullan	Barny	1794-97, 1799
Mullan	Harry	1791-99
Quigg	Neill	1798
Wilson	John	1791, 1792
Wilson	Matthew	1791-93

Gillgorm

Anderson	William	1793
Armstrong	William	1791, 1792, 1794
McElmon	John	1795-99

Mitchell	James	1798, 1799
Mitchell	Thomas	1791-97

Glenullar

McClosky	Dan	1798
Mullan	Barny	1798
Mullan	Bryan the man	1791-95
Mullan	George the man	1799
Mullan	Owin Boyd	1799
Mullan	Paddy the man	1791-95

Kells

Allison	William	1799
Mathews	Nathaniel	1791-99

Lough Beg

Dowdle	John	1799
Scullin	James	1791
Scullin	Nicholas	1799
Scullin	Peter	1791

Main

Bates	John	1794-99
Black	Thomas	1791-95
Coshnaghan	Pat	1795
McCann	Hugh	1791, 1792
McCormick	James	1797
McCormick	William	1796, 1798
Moffet	Thomas	1794
Neill	Mat	1799
Neill	Oliver	1798
O'Neill	Frank	1795
O'Neill	Tatty (Clotworthy)	1791-95
Robinson	Davidson	1798
Shales	James	1796, 1797

Moyola and Lough Neagh

McCann	William	1798, 1799
McLornan	Pat	1791-93
Walls	Pat	1794-97

McCasky

McAlister	Andrew	1791-93, 1795

Mettigan

McAllen	John	1791-95, 1798, 1799
Moony	Mark	1798, 1799

Oona

Clarke	John	1799

Toome Weirs

Barry	James	1799
Barry	Jon.	1798, 1799
Campbell	John	1795-97
Gribbin	Henry	1793, 1794, 1798
Magee	Edward	1791, 1792, 1795-97
Neeson	Owen	1791
Neeson	Patroe	1791, 1793, 1794, 1798
Toal	Barney	1792-94